THE TAFT RANCH: *A Texas Principality*

NUMBER 5 THE M. K. BROWN RANGE LIFE SERIES

THE TAFT RANCH

A Texas Principality

By A. RAY STEPHENS

With Introduction by Joe B. Frantz

UNIVERSITY OF TEXAS PRESS  AUSTIN

Library of Congress Catalog Card No. 64–10314

Printed in the United States of America
by the University of Texas Printing Division

INTRODUCTION

I do not know that anyone has yet counted the number of ranches in the trans-Mississippi country, though I suppose that armed with a calculator and a census return I would discover that the chore requires no great effort. The greater difficulty would probably lie in defining what constitutes a ranch. Sometimes, however, it seems that such a head counting might be fruitful, if for no other reason than to forecast the number of ranch histories still destined to spout from the ink faucets of the various presses of the United States. These manifold studies, tributaries to the main stream of ranch scholarship, combine to follow the same course, with only a date here and a name there and a detail somewhere else changed to justify the latest accounting.

Here, though, Ray Stephens has written a ranch history that can't be dismissed as "just another ranch history." Tom Lea plus a small legion of transient journalists told the lively tale of the mammoth King Ranch, which sprawls along the Gulf littoral; Chris Emmett wrote an excellent but highly personalized account of Shanghai Pierce's experiences as a cattleman not too far outside Houston; and that is about it, insofar as ranching below San Antonio is concerned. The remaining myriad of such accounts describe the development of ranches that sprawl over the western portion of Texas all the way across the Rockies or up onto the grassy defiles of Montana, the Dakotas, and even the Western Canadian provinces. But, except for the King and the Pierce empires, the story of ranching in the Gulf Coast vicinity has failed to attract much attention.

Perhaps geography is at fault. After all, since water is less of a problem, the country seems more nearly Southern than Western. In reality it belongs to the same broad Mississippi-Gulf basin as, say, the flat parts of Mississippi and Alabama. Although the terrain is unbroken and the horizons are distant, the air dances thicker and that special Western spaciousness is missing.

And yet this country is the seedbed of the North American cattle industry. In this country the range-cattle industry and its successor began and first flourished. This is range country, ranch country, even if it is not emotionally what J. W. Williams would call "Big Ranch Country."

But, though it is ranch country, its problems differ from those of traditional ranch country. Like the Chicago owners of the vast XIT of the Texas Panhandle, the Cincinnati proprietors of the Taft Ranch of the Texas Gulf Coast never fought the onrush of settlement, but did everything possible to encourage population pressures. Environment was kinder to the Taft Ranch, since its location was ideal for settlement and favorable for diversified farming.

So this ranch history not only analyzes the growth of a cattle kingdom, but delineates the unfolding of an area into the modern, relatively urban region it has become in the 1960's. This is a story of conscious town building, of establishing the varied industries which can make payrolls and can bring profits of entrepreneurship, of social experimentation and of social progress, of conflict of racial cultures, of the uses of water, and of the big citizens and the anonymous little people who invariably combine to create a regional civilization.

The story is told by a relatively young man who trains the critical eye of the scholar on a unique facet of Southern-Western ranching, but who also never lets that critical eye get crossed with his enthusiastic eye. Ray Stephens has raised a cow or two in his earlier years, knows how to make it to the end of a furrow without meandering all over the cotton patch, comes natural by crop and cow talk, can teach a hound to jump a fence or tree a 'possum, and appropriately enough professes at a university whose graduates talk ticks, grow grass, and win more than a few national agricultural awards. What he writes here, he writes from natural strength, and the result promises to be a book unlike any other.

In the pages ahead lies the history of the Taft Ranch. The reader will soon discern that, as already said, it is not just another ranch history.

JOE B. FRANTZ
Austin, Texas

PREFACE

The story of the influence of a big western ranch upon its surrounding region is to a large degree the history of the Great Plains during the half century following the Civil War. Although some of the extensive cattle spreads resisted the change from an open-range operation to livestock farming and still later to cultivation of crops, other ranches fostered the growth of agriculture and related industries. This narrative is the story of a corporation that belonged to the second group and that led the Texas Coastal Bend to unprecedented prosperity through progressive techniques, maintenance of soil fertility, and aggressive leadership—a formula for success that required all three elements. The soil was already there, and the other integral parts were provided by executives in the company. George Ware Fulton, Sr., was the dominant figure in the Coleman-Fulton Pasture Company from its organization in 1880 until his death in 1893. Realizing that the range-cattle industry of the 1880's must give way to stock farming, he introduced increased numbers of purebred sires to upgrade the herd, and then turned to growing feed for animals being prepared for market in order to have an advantage over other cattlemen who were not yet utilizing those methods.

Not until two decades after Fulton's passing did the Taft Ranch, the "perfect principality," as President William Howard Taft referred to it, achieve a national and international reputation for its contribution to agriculture. Through its use of scientific farming and progressive techniques on large demonstration farms the ranch aided the development of the South Texas Plains. For farmers coming to the area the company provided information concerning crops known through experience to be productive or unprofitable. The aggressive leadership that won this recognition for the Coleman-Fulton Pasture Company, popularly known as the Taft Ranch, was given by Joseph French Green, who had outstanding talent for formulating progressive ideas to make the soil productive and who had also the energy to carry his thoughts to fruition. Without the seemingly unlimited financial backing of Charles Phelps Taft and Anna Sinton Taft of Cincinnati, the achievements Green gained would not have been possible. A great deal of credit for developing the region is shared with the highly capable assistance of Green's foremen and hundreds of independent farmers who migrated to South Texas in search of a new home at the time many of the large ranches disposed of their holdings.

Materials necessary for this study were gathered for the most part in the University of Texas Archives, in Taft, Texas, and in the Sinton and Rockport courthouses in San Patricio and Aransas Counties, respectively, with some information obtained in the Library of Congress, the National Archives, the Historical and Philosophical Society of Ohio Archives in Cincinnati, and in South Texas newspaper files. A special debt of gratitude is owed to Mr. Edward N. Tutt and Mr. C. J. Meyer of Taft for granting permission to use the Coleman-Fulton Pasture Company's official records and for giving freely of their time to discuss events on the ranch in days gone by. Unusually efficient cooperation was rendered by Dr. Dorman H. Winfrey and Mr. Charles W. Corkran of the University of Texas Archives, Dr. Llerena Friend of the Eugene C. Barker Texas History Center, Mr. James M. Day of the Texas State Archives, Mr. Alexander Moffit and Mr. Fred Folmer of the University of Texas Library, Dr. W. Neil Franklin of the National Archives, Dr. Louis L. Tucker of the Historical and Philosophical Society of Ohio, Mr. and Mrs. Keith Guthrie of the Taft *Tribune,* Mr. Jack L. Baughman of the Rockport *Pilot,* Mr. James Tracy of the Sinton *San Patricio County News,* Mrs. Velma Sherman, San Patricio County clerk, and Mr. W. E. Beasley, Aransas County and district clerk. A particular note of thanks goes to Mr. and Mrs. Walter C. Sparks, Jr., of Taft and to Mrs. May Mathis Green Watson of Corpus Christi for sharing helpful source material, and to Mrs. Frances V. Parker of Austin for making maps used in this study.

I am deeply grateful to the following persons for assistance in their own special way: Mrs. Hattie Gilleland, Mr. Paul Lott, and Mrs. Elinor Fulton Conger, Corpus Christi; Mrs. May Fulton Hoopes, Ingleside; Dean W. R. Woolrich and Dr. Mody C. Boatright, Austin; Mr. and Mrs. Claud Boykin, Mrs. Miller Harwood, Miss Ednus Marie Roots, Mrs. Jack Stapper, Mr. and Mrs. John William Albin, Mr. and Mrs.

Ben Ivey, Mr. and Mrs. E. W. Sandars, Mr. Ben H. Cummins, Mr. and Mrs. D. Lard, Mr. and Mrs. Dalton Green, Mr. and Mrs. Henry R. Moore, Mr. Ernest Guedin, Mr. and Mrs. W. Leroy Weber, Mr. Harry Mount, Taft; Mrs. Fay Green Hunt, Gregory; Mr. and Mrs. John Weber and Mrs. Maurice W. Cochran, Fulton; Mr. Henry Schmidt, Rockport; Mr. and Mrs. J. D. Moore, Mr. Bob Austin, Mr. and Mrs. Manton Williams, Judge James Colon Russell, and Sheriff S. Frank Hunt, Sinton; Mr. George H. Paul, Omaha, Nebraska; and in general to the people of Taft, Texas, who made a visiting student feel most welcome in their midst. Thanks are also rendered to Mrs. Curtis Varnell of Austin for proofreading and to Mrs. Norris G. Davis for typing the manuscript in final form.

The highpoint in recognition of professional services in an acknowledgment page such as this is reached when a student attempts to give credit to his supervising professor. To Dr. Joe B. Frantz goes this writer's heartfelt appreciation for expert and understanding guidance that has made the task of welding a mass of notes into a series of coherent chapters a pleasant one.

But the greatest degree of gratitude goes to my wife, Linda, who is deserving of some sort of medal for tolerating my lack of co-operation in the running of the household during the time this study was underway. Her continual encouragement and interest in the topic made the work seem lighter.

[illegible] Mr. and Mrs. L. W. Saunders, Mr. [illegible], Mr. and Mrs. [illegible], Mr. and Mrs. Dalton Green, Mr. and Mrs. Henry R. [illegible], [illegible] Mr. and Mrs. W. [illegible], Mr. [illegible], Mrs. [illegible], Mr. and Mrs. John [illegible] Mrs. Maurice W. [illegible], Mr. [illegible], Mr. and Mrs. [illegible] Moore, Mr. [illegible], Mr. and Mrs. [illegible] [illegible] Judge [illegible] and [illegible] to the people of [illegible], Texas, who [illegible] [illegible]. Thanks are also [illegible] [illegible] for [illegible] [illegible] for [illegible] and [illegible].

The [illegible] of [illegible] such as this is [illegible] [illegible] [illegible] [illegible] [illegible] [illegible] [illegible] that has [illegible] [illegible] chapters [illegible].

But the [illegible] of [illegible] [illegible] [illegible] [illegible] [illegible] [illegible] [illegible] [illegible] this work [illegible] [illegible] [illegible] work such [illegible].

CONTENTS

ILLUSTRATIONS

Following page 116

MAPS

THE TAFT RANCH: *A Texas Principality*

I. LIVE OAK PENINSULA—EMPORIUM OF THE SOUTHWEST

When George Ware Fulton decided to move his family from Covington, Kentucky, back to Texas, in 1867, after an absence of twenty-one years, one of his lifetime friends sent him an almost cautionary letter—a warning that went unheeded.

> Taking a speculative view of it, I am however gratified in not having had a prominent part in affording thee the opportunity to almost expatriate thyself, forsaking many of the comforts perhaps of civilized life (but possibly escaping some of the evils also) at some risk I am inclined yet to think from barberous man—*Texan* & perhaps Indian Thee has my sympathies in thy undertaking—hoping to hear occasionally from thee with a wish that we may yet meet in the land of the living.[1]

As the years passed, Fulton was assured that his decision had been wise and profitable.

Born in Philadelphia, Pennsylvania, in 1810, Fulton moved westward at an early age and was teaching school in Indiana when the Texas Revolution began.[2] A strong desire among the townspeople of Vincen-

[1] Samuel Jeans, Philadelphia, Pennsylvania, to George Ware Fulton, Sr., Covington, Kentucky, November 18, 1867, Fulton Collection (hereafter cited as FC).

[2] G. W. Fulton, Sr., Rockport, Texas, to John Henry Brown, Dallas, Texas, May 14, 1887, Brown Collection. All of Fulton's official correspondence was written from Rockport, Texas, unless specified otherwise.

nes, Indiana, to assist the Texans resulted in the creation of a company of volunteers, with Fulton the elected captain.[3] Arriving in the new nation in December, 1836, the Hoosiers became an integral part of an army composed of Texans and United States volunteers. Fulton, commissioned as a second lieutenant in the Army of the Republic of Texas, served in that capacity until he resigned May 31, 1837, one day before the Army was disbanded.[4] For approximately six months thereafter he was employed as a draughtsman in the General Land Office. During the next two years he served as customs collector of the District of Aransas with an office on the northernmost point of Live Oak Peninsula, on the Texas coast.[5]

As a reward for his service in the Republic of Texas Army, Fulton was granted 1,280 acres in San Patricio County, near Aransas City in Refugio County.[6] An acquaintance, Henry Smith, first Anglo-American governor of Texas from November, 1835, to March, 1836, was granted large tracts on Live Oak Peninsula, and hired Fulton and Willard Richardson of Galveston, later the publisher of the influential Galveston *Daily News,* to locate the claims for him.[7] Fulton, therefore, spent a number of years in that vicinity of the present state and came to know it quite well.

After a time in the unsettled regions of southwest Texas, Fulton moved to the lower Brazos River Valley and taught school at Bra-

[3] Reminiscences of G. W. Fulton written on the reverse side of Report to Stockholders of the Coleman-Fulton Pasture Company for January 1, 1892, FC.

[4] George Ware Fulton File, Audited Military Claims, Treasury Department, Republic of Texas.

[5] *Ibid.* Fulton served in the General Land Office under Commissioner John P. Borden from September 30, 1837, to February 13, 1838. Power of Attorney, G. W. Fulton, Sr. [n.p.], to Henry Smith [n.p.], October 24, 1841, *ibid.* Fulton to General H. G. Wright, Galveston, Texas, October 18, 1879, FC. Fulton to J. H. Brown, Dallas, July 7, 1889, Brown Collection. The District of Aransas included the territory between the Guadalupe River and the Rio Grande.

[6] Republic of Texas Land Certificate No. 666, issued to G. W. Fulton, Houston, Texas, December 2, 1837, State of Texas General Land Office.

[7] Affidavit of G. W. Fulton for *G. W. Fulton* ET AL. vs. *the Unknown Heirs of Thomas W. Johnson, Deceased;* suit pending in the District Court of Galveston County, Texas, 1890, FC. For a full story on Willard Richardson see Sam Acheson, *35,000 Days in Texas.*

zoria.[8] Meanwhile, he married Harriet Gillette Smith, a daughter of Governor Henry Smith, and lived near Brazoria until 1846. Mechanically apt, this cousin of Robert Fulton of steamboat fame went to Washington, D.C., to secure a patent on a device to improve boat power steam. With the aid of letters of introduction signed by Memucan Hunt and Henry Austin to President James K. Polk, Secretary of the Treasury Robert J. Walker, and United States Senator John C. Calhoun, Fulton was well received and in a short time was issued Patent Number 4710.[9] Although the title was "Improvement in Propelling Vessels," the patent pump was not limited to that class alone, as it was used later in the construction of steam fire engines. In 1859 Fulton entered into a contract with the Baltimore firm of Poole and Hunt for exclusive manufacturing rights of the invention, Fulton to receive fifty dollars for each engine using his pump.[10]

In 1846 Fulton moved with his family to Baltimore and for the following two decades worked as a newspaperman in Maryland and Ohio, as general superintendent for various railroads in Pennsylvania, Ohio, and Illinois, as a prospector for oil and lead, and as assistant engineer under John A. Roebling in the construction of the historic suspension bridge across the Ohio River at Steubenville, Ohio.[11] Henry

[8] Gene North, "A Historical Survey of the Taft Ranch" (M.A. thesis), pp. 16–17.

[9] Memucan Hunt, Galveston, to James K. Polk, Washington, D.C., March 21, 1846; Henry Austin, Brazoria, Texas, to Robert J. Walker, Washington, D.C. [undated, 1846?]; Austin, Brazoria, to John C. Calhoun, Washington, D.C. [undated, 1846?]; "Improvement in Propelling Vessels," Patent No. 4710, United States Patent Office, August 26, 1846; all in FC.

[10] Agreement of G. W. Fulton, Steubenville, Ohio, and Poole and Hunt, Baltimore, Maryland, September 24, 1859, FC.

[11] G. W. Fulton, Sr., to Brown, Dallas, December 20, 1886, March 8, 1889, Brown Collection. Fulton, York, Pennsylvania, to Eli Lewis, president of York and Cumberland Railroad Company [n.p.], June 27, 1851; George M. Gill, Baltimore, to James L. D. Morrison, Bel Ville, Illinois, February 11, 1853; Fulton to General H. G. Wright, Chief of Engineers, United States Army, Galveston, June 8, 1880; J. Edgar Thomson, Philadelphia, to Fulton, Steubenville, Ohio, October 2, 1856; Fulton, Cincinnati, Ohio, to Harriet Fulton [n.p.], August 29, 1860; John King, Baltimore, to Fulton, Covington, Kentucky, October 20, 1862; Internal Revenue License No. 1483 issued to Fulton, June 30, 1866; W. A. Roebling, Trenton, New Jersey, to Fulton, July 20, 1891; all in FC. Unlabeled, undated newspaper clipping in possession of Dean

Smith, Mrs. Fulton's father, died in the California gold fields in 1851 and left to his children his vast land holdings in Texas, most of it on the Gulf Coast in Refugio County. This land was of little importance until the post-Civil War period, when beef packeries were established in the area and the range-cattle industry became profitable. In 1867 Fulton returned to Texas and for several years was the executor of the Henry Smith estate.

Fulton redeemed large amounts of land that had been purchased by the state of Texas for non-payment of taxes by paying charges and costs. Two of Henry Smith's sons, John G. and James E., accompanied their father to California in 1849 and remained there after his death. Because they had no intention of returning to Texas and because the Fultons were looking after the family's affairs, the brothers deeded their property rights to their sister, Mrs. Fulton.[12] A third brother, William W. Smith, in 1856 conveyed all his title as an heir to the real estate to Joseph F. Smith, a cousin. From this kinsman Mrs. Fulton purchased the remaining claim and became sole owner of 11,314 acres in Aransas County, 12,106 acres in San Patricio County, 2,228 acres in Jackson County, and 2,534 acres in Galveston County.[13]

Fulton's move to Texas was motivated by reasons other than merely the desire to care for his father-in-law's estate. Interested in land speculation, he immediately organized the Aransas Land Company, also known as the Fulton Land Company and the Fulton Town Company. In December, 1867, twenty shares of stock worth one thousand dollars each were issued by the new company to George W. Fulton and Olive Livingston of Refugio County, Texas; Samuel Jeans of Philadelphia; Alfred Gaither, John M. Mueller, John Boyle, and David Sinton of Cincinnati; and William F. Schronmaker of Covington, Kentucky.[14]

W. R. Woolrich, University of Texas Department of Engineering, Austin, Texas.

[12] Transcribed Deed Records, Aransas County, April 21, 1870, Vol. TB, p. 170.

[13] Deed Records, Aransas County, September 7, 1872, Vol. C, pp. 180–181. Aransas County Tax Receipts, September 24, 1872; statement of taxes due on land in San Patricio County by Comptrollers Office, Austin, April 6, 1870; Jackson County Tax Receipt No. 534, for year 1878; Galveston County tax receipt for year 1871; all in FC.

[14] Stock Ledger, Aransas Land Company, FC.

The Fulton Town Company acquired 10,000 acres of land—2,000 on Live Oak Peninsula and 8,000 across Puerto Bay—at $2.00 an acre.[15] A town was surveyed and platted four miles north of Rockport on Live Oak Peninsula fronting on Aransas Bay. Lots in the new town of Fulton were placed on sale and for a time the market was brisk—so active, in fact, that in 1873 the company declared a dividend of $200.00 a share, and another in 1874 of $67.40 a share.[16] Prosperity seemed assured for the region but when the area's claim to industry—the beef-packing business—failed in the 1870's and the early 1880's sales of Fulton Town Company property slowed to the point that profits were insufficient to pay taxes on the land not yet sold.[17] Not until the land boom of the 1890's did the market for the lots revive.

Live Oak Peninsula lay in both San Patricio and Refugio Counties until 1871, when Refugio County surrendered its claim to newly created Aransas County. The peninsula was surrounded on three sides by water: Aransas and Copano Bays encompassed the jutting northern end while Aransas and Corpus Christi Bays enclosed the eastern and southern sides. San Patricio County, which extended into western Live Oak Peninsula, was also partially encompassed by water: Redfish and Corpus Christi Bays on the east, Corpus Christi and Nueces Bays on the south, Nueces River on the west, and the Aransas River across the northeast flowing into Copano Bay.

A short distance offshore were sandy islands, which protected the coast from severe wind and water action by the Gulf of Mexico, but which served as a hindrance in ocean-commerce enterprises. The only way to enter the sheltered bays was through Aransas Pass, a narrow, shallow inlet between Saint Joseph and Mustang Islands, and only vessels with shallow draughts could enter the natural gap, the depth of which varied occasionally because of wind and water erosion on the shifting sand.

Live Oak Peninsula increased in importance in the late 1860's, for at that time ranchers were looking for a market for the innumerable

[15] James C. Fulton, Rockport, to McCampbell and Welch, Attorneys, Corpus Christi, December 2, 1887, FC.

[16] Stock Ledger, Fulton Town Company, FC.

[17] J. C. Fulton, Rockport, to McCampbell and Welch, Corpus Christi, December 2, 1887, FC.

Longhorns scattered over the coastal prairies. Largely at the insistence of John M. Mathis and Thomas Henry Mathis, cousins who were partners in ranching, the Morgan Steamship Company extended its route of coastal trade in 1867 to include Rockport.

John M. Mathis, born in Henry County, Tennessee, on February 28, 1831, was in Texas at the time of the Civil War. When the Federal Navy blockaded the Texas coast, and the best means to sell Texas cotton was in Mexico, Mathis secured permits from the Confederate government to transport bales of cotton from Houston to Matamoros, Mexico, on contract from individuals in Texas.[18] Soon after the war ended he settled in Rockport.

Thomas Henry Mathis was born in Stewart County, Tennessee, July 14, 1834. Gradually drifting westward, he taught school in Kentucky and Arkansas, and moved to Gonzales, Texas, in 1859, where he started a cattle business. After moving to Victoria in 1861, Mathis entered the Confederate Army and served for the duration, then returned to South Texas.[19]

In 1867 the Mathis cousins consolidated property with James M. Doughty, a Rockport merchant and landowner, to ship cattle from the coast on the Morgan Line. Doughty owned land on a rocky point near the water's edge and had a beef pen situated there. John M. and Thomas H. Mathis connected a wharf to the enclosure for loading animals on steamers.[20] The Doughty and Mathis partnership soon ended and the property was divided; the wharf and warehouse were left to the Mathises, who continued to act as the Morgan agent.[21] The cousins advertised in the local paper:

We are authorized by Chas. A. Whitney & Co., for the Morgan line of

[18] *Mary Anna Bagley, Administratrix,* vs. *John M. Mathis,* Case No. 192; suit pending in District Court, Refugio County, February term, 1870, concerning sale of cotton to Mexico in 1864, FC. Taft (Texas) *Tribune,* October 26, 1922.

[19] "Josiah Mathis and His Descendants, a genealogical record of the Mathis family in the United States," unpublished mimeographed booklet compiled by Mrs. May Mathis Green Watson, Corpus Christi. Lewis E. Daniell, *Personnel of the Texas State Government with Sketches of Representative Men of Texas,* pp. 615–617.

[20] Transcribed Deed Records, Aransas County, August 24, 1867, Vol. TA, pp. 387–390.

[21] *Ibid.,* July 31, 1868, Vol. TA, pp. 432–433.

steamships, that the steamers, *Austin* and *Alabama,* are running to Rockport, each making one trip per week between New Orleans and Rockport, carrying freight at 90 cts. in U S currency per bbl. to the later place. And we will say to shippers generally that charges at Rockport will be 10 cents specie per bbl.—including Receiving, Forwarding, Wharfage, Advancing and Storage, if necessary.

J. M. & T. H. Mathis[22]

Livestock raising was the principal industry in Southwest Texas during the Reconstruction period. The unfenced coastal prairies extending from Aransas Pass to the Nueces and Aransas Rivers had multitudes of cattle but few people; however, the area gained in population as immigration to Texas increased in the 1870's. Most of the land was state-owned or had been granted to Texas veterans, who had not bothered to secure a patent on their property or even to locate it with a survey.

An early ranching family in the region was the Coleman clan. Youngs Coleman, originally from Virginia, immigrated to Liberty, Texas, and after a series of moves within the state settled in San Patricio County. A son, Thomas Matthew Coleman, born at Liberty in 1833, moved to the Coastal Bend with his family in the 1850's.[23] The Colemans were engaged in ranching in San Patricio County by 1854, when Youngs and Thomas M. recorded their marks and brands in the county clerk's office.[24]

The large supply of cattle in Southwest Texas in the ante-bellum period unfortunately had no local market. Texas livestock were shipped on ocean-going vessels and driven overland to New Orleans, but it was not until the late 1850's that cattle started up the long trail to the Midwestern cities. Thomas M. Coleman was one of the first to use this method to find a market when he was a party on three such cattle drives to Chicago in 1857, 1858, and 1859.[25]

[22] Corpus Christi *Advertiser*, August 21, 1869.

[23] Interview with Mrs. Maurice W. Cochran, Fulton, Texas, July 28, 1961. Mrs. Cochran, a great-granddaughter of Youngs Coleman, has done extensive genealogical research on Coleman family history.

[24] Marks and Brands, San Patricio County, May 9, 1854, Vol. "A–B–C," p. 17.

[25] Thomas Atlee Coleman, San Antonio, Texas, to Anna Margaretta Coleman Born [Rockport?], undated, unpublished letter.

After service in the Confederate Army, Thomas Coleman returned to his ranching activities, and worked also as deputy inspector of brands for San Patricio County under J. Myrick. He inspected cattle being sold, and certified that the brands were correct when the bill of sale was recorded in the stock-sales book in the county courthouse.[26]

Five men, full of determination for material success according to the American dream and endowed with strong wills to pursue their goals, were thrown together in South Texas by circumstances in the Reconstruction period, and sought to accomplish their aims by uniting into a single business. "Coleman, Mathis and Fulton, Dealers and Shippers of Live Stock," declared the letterhead on the stationery of the partnership that formed in 1871 with headquarters in Rockport.[27] An express purpose for the consolidation of interests was

> to offer equal if not better facilities for the disposition of their [local stock raisers'] cattle and relying for our profits entirely upon the additional value we may give them by a few months in our pastures—we will offer a steady market instead of the intermitting one as now— . . . our present business will be to purchase lean cattle—fatten and ship, or sell to packers.[28]

The partners, and the proportion of property owned, were: Youngs Coleman and Thomas Matthew Coleman, one-third; John M. Mathis and Thomas Henry Mathis, one-third; and George Ware Fulton, one-third.[29]

These men, who joined with the express purpose of dealing in livestock, were necessarily well informed on the industries which complemented their own business. Of particular interest to them was the earliest industry on that part of the Gulf Coast—meat packing.

Although cattle were plentiful, the market for them, either trailed or shipped, was practically nonexistent. Enterprising ranchers and Northern capital turned to transporting animal carcasses in cans or casks. Coleman, Mathis, and Fulton sold beeves to the numerous pack-

[26] Stock Sales Book, San Patricio County, April 25, 1871, Vol. A, pp. 194–198.

[27] Charles M. Holden, Fulton, Texas, to Coleman, Mathis, and Fulton, Rockport, March 24, 1873, FC. Deed Records, San Patricio County, June 3, 1871, Vol. 5, pp. 429–430.

[28] G. W. Fulton, Sr. [addressee unknown, ca. 1871 or 1872], FC.

[29] Deed Records, San Patricio County, Vol. 3, p. 633.

eries between Rockport and Indianola, as did other cattlemen. Businessmen experimented with meat preservation. When business slackened, the plants turned to processing hide and tallow.

A great amount of excitement occurred in Texas and the nation when the beef factories started operations. Ranchmen realized that they would share a home market for their products if this industry proved successful, and that the long, dangerous drives to the North would be unnecessary. The San Antonio *Daily Herald* proclaimed the good news and hinted that the state's citizens were rejoicing over this new means to prosperity.[30] *Flake's Bulletin* of Galveston chimed in that as the industry seemed assured of success the people of Texas should not stand by and see Northern capital make all the profits. The exhortation was referring to a Baltimore company's clearing $10,000 a month on a $200,000 investment. "Now if this can be done, why do not the people of Texas avail themselves of it and instead of selling their beef cattle at one or two cents per pound, get six or eight or even higher prices for it."[31]

Experiments in meat preservation proved ineffective although a wide variety of processes were attempted. All other modes of preserving meat fell into disuse in favor of a more acceptable way—the use of artificial cold.

Mechanical refrigeration, a product of American ingenuity, had its first successful application in 1851.[32] John Gorrie, a Florida physician, designed a machine to condition air for hospital patients and secured a patent in 1851. Mechanical modifications during the 1850's and 1860's resulted in refrigeration units that could make ice for a large market in many Southern cities. It was not, however, restricted to that use alone. Alert minds saw the possibility of utilizing the artificial cold in the beef-packing industry. In 1869 George Ware Fulton of Fulton, Texas, secured from the United States Patent Office Patent Number 92,035 for "Improvement in Apparatus for Slaughtering and Curing Meat." Fulton's plan called for building an abattoir with double walls with a space between them in which to place non-heat-conducting ma-

[30] San Antonio *Daily Herald*, November 9, 1866, June 14, 28, 1867.

[31] *Flake's Bulletin* (Galveston), September 28, 1870.

[32] W. R. Woolrich, "Mechanical Refrigeration—Its American Birthright," *Refrigerating Engineering*, Vol. 53, No. 3 (March, 1947), p. 196.

terial in order that the room within could be kept cooler. An apparatus would discharge cool air into the slaughterhouse, enabling a carcass to be moved from room to room throughout the building without an increase in temperature.[33]

Practical application of Fulton's plan began in 1871 when three Holden brothers—Daniel Livingston, Elbridge Gerry, and Charles M. —opened an artificially cooled abattoir in Fulton, Texas, the first of its kind in the nation. They prepared beef not only for American markets, but also for world markets.[34]

Suppliers of cattle to the meat-preservation establishments on the Gulf Coast were the local and inland ranchers. The Coleman, Mathis, and Fulton firm was such a company and was organized for the purpose, in part, of supplying livestock. In answer to an inquiry, addressed to the local newspaper in Rockport, concerning ranching activities in the Rockport-Fulton region, G. W. Fulton intimated in a letter that his company relied heavily on the sale of beef to packeries and expected the demand to increase with the use of refrigerated ships.[35]

Although artificially cooled vessels were still under experimentation in the 1870's, the firm of Coleman, Mathis, and Fulton looked upon this means to a market as more desirable than driving its animals on the long trail to Kansas. Evidence of expected profits and expenses entailed from such a venture is shown by a notebook kept by Fulton for a shipment of cold-storage beef to London.[36]

Cost of beef to net 660 lbs	$24.00
Proceeds of 660 lbs—10 cts	$66.00
Proceeds of Hide tallow &c	6.00
	$72.00

[33] United States Patent Number 92,035, issued to G. W. Fulton, Fulton, Texas, June 29, 1869, for the "Improvement in Apparatus for Slaughtering and Curing Meat," FC.

[34] Woolrich, "Mechanical Refrigeration," *Refrigerating Engineering*, Vol. 53, No. 3 (March, 1947), p. 246.

[35] G. W. Fulton, Sr. [addressee unknown, ca. 1871 or 1872], rough draft of a formal letter answering an inquiry about the Texas cattle industry, FC.

[36] George Ware Fulton Notebook [1879?], FC. Fulton must have omitted an item in his calculation because the column entitled "Expenses" totals $38.00. If the cost of the animal is included as an expense, the sum is only $62.00.

Expenses	
Freight & Refrigeration	13.20
Commission 5 pr c on 66	3.30
Agent 1 pr c	.66
Storage 30 days	1.25
Insurance	.28
Slaughtering	1.50
Profit	17.81
	$72.00

deduct $7.81 for contingencies expenses leaves $10 profit pr Steer on purchased animals. C.M.& F. purchased 50.000 in 1876 and sold 75.988 on cargo of beef say 200 tons

say 700 steers $24. pr head cost	$16.800—
proceeds at $34 p h	23.800—
net	7.000

above for purchased cattle

Steers raised on pasture will cost, including interest taxes and other expenses say $15 pr head yielding profit pr cargo of 760 = $13.300

produce of pasture three cargoes of anm—	$85500
profit on 17 cargoes purchased cattle—	253.000
	$338.500

four ships of 2000 tons burthen—each touching at Galveston for general freight, would make 6 trips pr annum and carry the carcasses of 1500 steers, or say, 20 cargoes pr annum of 1500 each—60,000 beeves

1500 steers cost $15	$22500
" " net London	51.000
net	28.500
	3
produce of pasture	$85.500
three cargoes pr ann	253.000
profit on 17 cargoes purchased cattle	$338.500

This arrangement for shipping refrigerated beef must have occurred in early 1879, for a letter written by Fulton at that time to a person in

London directed the ships where to dock. Coleman, Mathis, and Fulton arranged for the wharf and slaughterhouse owned by the Boston Meat Packing Company to prepare the experimental cargo. The best time for the trial to take place, according to Fulton, would be during the summer months, when nine or ten feet of water usually covered the sand bar at Aransas Pass as opposed to only eight feet during the remainder of the year. This was a departure from the usual killing time of October to July. Coleman, Mathis, and Fulton were prepared to slaughter as fast as the ships could receive, or an estimated two hundred tons of meat a day. As the cattle were fattest in the summer, Fulton suggested that the work be done at that time.[37]

Despite all the elegant preparations by South Texans with livestock and despite the Northern businessmen with capital to make beef packing prosper, little came of the venture. A satisfactory preservation mode was not found that would handle the tens of thousands of available marketable animals. Besides, Chicago and Saint Louis were gaining in importance as livestock centers—and they were nearer to the heavily populated areas of America. During the 1880's the beef-packing plants began to decrease in output, until their business dwindled to the point where they were forced to cease operations. Southwest Texas continued to send live cattle by ship to New Orleans and Havana and to drive them to Kansas markets until railroads penetrated the range. This new mode of transportation enabled the companies to send live animals to Kansas City, Saint Louis, and Chicago, causing the other forms of marketing previously used to fall by the wayside. The packeries closed and disposed of their properties. As the excitement caused by possible industrial development for South Texas abated, the people returned to a pastoral life. Time, town improvements, and tropical storms have erased all evidence of the once-thriving industry of meat packing from the face of the earth, leaving only memories in the minds of the few survivors of that era.

[37] G. W. Fulton, Sr., to Henry Kaming, London, February 1, 1879, FC.

II. LONGHORNS AND ACRES

THE PRIMARY REASON for the founding of the Coleman, Mathis, and Fulton partnership was to raise cattle on their own property, to provide a market for livestock from local, smaller ranches, and to lease pasturage for other persons' animals.[1] A favored location was obtained for this enterprise. Based at a natural harbor on Aransas Bay and serving as agent for a large ocean transport company, Coleman, Mathis, and Fulton handled nearly all the shipments of cattle produced west of the Guadalupe River.

Soon after organization in 1871, Coleman, Mathis, and Fulton stretched its range to cover 115,000 acres in San Patricio and Refugio [later Aransas] Counties. Natural water boundaries on the north, east, and south and a thirteen-mile-long fence on the west from Nueces Bay to Chiltipin Creek enclosed approximately 200,000 acres of land including Live Oak Peninsula, where the towns of Rockport, Fulton, and Ingleside were situated. The north, east, and south limits of the ranch were natural boundaries—Chiltipin Creek, Copano Bay, and Corpus Christi Bay, except for a fence eight miles long from Puerto Bay to

[1] George Ware Fulton, Sr., Rockport, Texas [addressee unknown, ca. 1871 or 1872], rough draft of a formal letter answering an inquiry about cattle industry in Texas, Fulton Collection (hereafter cited as FC). All of Fulton's official correspondence was written from Rockport, Texas, unless specified otherwise.

Corpus Christi Bay cutting off the point of the peninsula and creating a 115,000-acre pasture.[2]

The area thus enclosed was a treeless, level, coastal prairie with no gullies and no rocks, but with occasional swales and intermittent streams. A gentle rise in elevation occurred as one proceeded from the shore farther inland to a maximum height of fifty-five feet at present Taft, the greatest altitude above sea level in a twenty-five-mile circle. Some rank vegetation grew along the coast, primarily live-oak trees, which were stunted and bent by the constantly blowing wind from the Gulf of Mexico, and which extended inland only a short distance. For the most part the plains were covered with a heavy sod of curly mesquite grass, also with scattered bunches of prickly pear, chaparral, tasajillo, and catclaw. In the 1860's the mesquite tree was confined to western San Patricio County in a thirty-square-mile area known as the Brasada, a territory of dense growth unsuitable for farming until the trees were cleared away. Later, however, the mesquite spread over the entire Coastal Bend region.

The soil of the coastal plains was a black, waxy, extremely fertile ground, the chief composition of which was Victoria clay. The temperate climate, the approximately thirty inches of annual precipitation, and the long, sometimes frost-free, growing season allowed for the production of almost any variety of plant. Rarely did a drouth occur, but when dry seasons or freezing winters came they were usually quite severe. During normally wet years the native grass on the Coleman, Mathis, and Fulton range was sufficient to fatten an estimated 41,000 to 50,000 beeves for the market each year;[3] however, this figure was drastically reduced in later years.

Water was well dispersed over the whole tract, according to Fulton, and the company had plans to sink wells and erect windmills if water should become deficient. In 1871 cattle could drink in streams bordering or traversing the range and at a large number of "sinks" or depressions where water stood after a rain.

In order to separate the company's livestock from that of other

[2] *Ibid.* Map of parts of San Patricio and Refugio [later Aransas] Counties, February, 1872, Record Group 28, United States Post Office Department Records.

[3] G. W. Fulton, Sr. [addressee unknown, ca. 1871 or 1872], FC.

ranchers, Coleman, Mathis, and Fulton erected barriers of smooth wire or plank, which served as the principal building material until barbed wire was introduced in South Texas. One such fence of lumber was built north of the town of Fulton on land owned by George W. Fulton and leased to William S. Hall. The contract signed by these two men on March 20, 1871, stated that they would erect

> . . . a good and substantial plank fence, with cedar posts, not more than eight feet from center to center of post, and six planks in height (including cap) each plank to be 6 inches wide and 1¼ inch thick, except top string under cap which may be 3 inches wide—and well nailed to cap—with good and substantial gates, when required, and strong and permanent pickets extending into the Bay at either end of fence so as to effectually prevent the passing of horse or cattle.[4]

The northern tip of the peninsula between Copano and Aransas Bays was hemmed in by Hall; but at the end of the lease period the improvement became the property of Fulton.

Work on the Coleman, Mathis, and Fulton western boundary line began in October, 1871, and was completed in May, 1872.[5] The eastern and southeastern fence, extending from Puerto Bay to Corpus Christi Bay, was constructed at the same time for an average cost of $600 a mile. Natural boundaries, such as creeks and bays, constituted the remaining limits of the range. In 1872 Coleman, Mathis, and Fulton sold a narrow strip of land outside the encompassed pasture to Pryor Lea, president of the Aransas Road Company and a promoter of Aransas Pass improvement, and with it a one-half interest in the fence. Each was to pay half of the maintenance cost on future repairs.[6]

A joint boundary fence was not the customary practice of the Coleman, Mathis, and Fulton firm, although it could not be avoided at times. It is evident that disagreements could arise over who was to do the repair work and what the share of the cost should be. To forestall this unpleasant arrangement the company made it a uniform rule to place the wires fifteen feet inside its line as a means of preventing

[4] Contract for lease of land and building of fence between G. W. Fulton and William S. Hall, "both of Refugio County, Texas," March 20, 1871, FC.

[5] George Ware Fulton Notebook, FC.

[6] Deed Records, Aransas County, November 28, 1872, Vol. B, pp. 217–218.

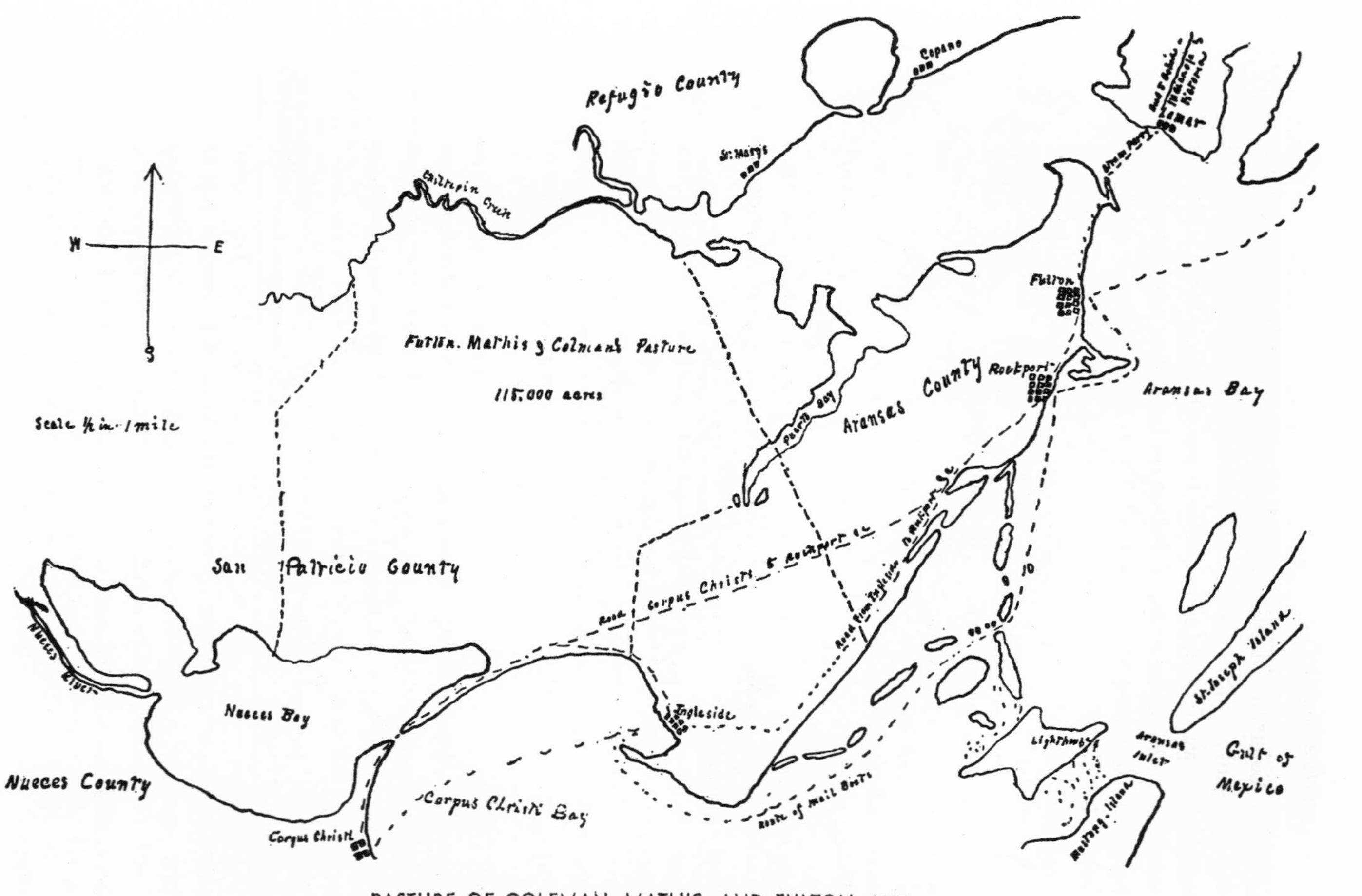

PASTURE OF COLEMAN, MATHIS, AND FULTON, 1872
Map from United States Post Office Department Records, National Archives

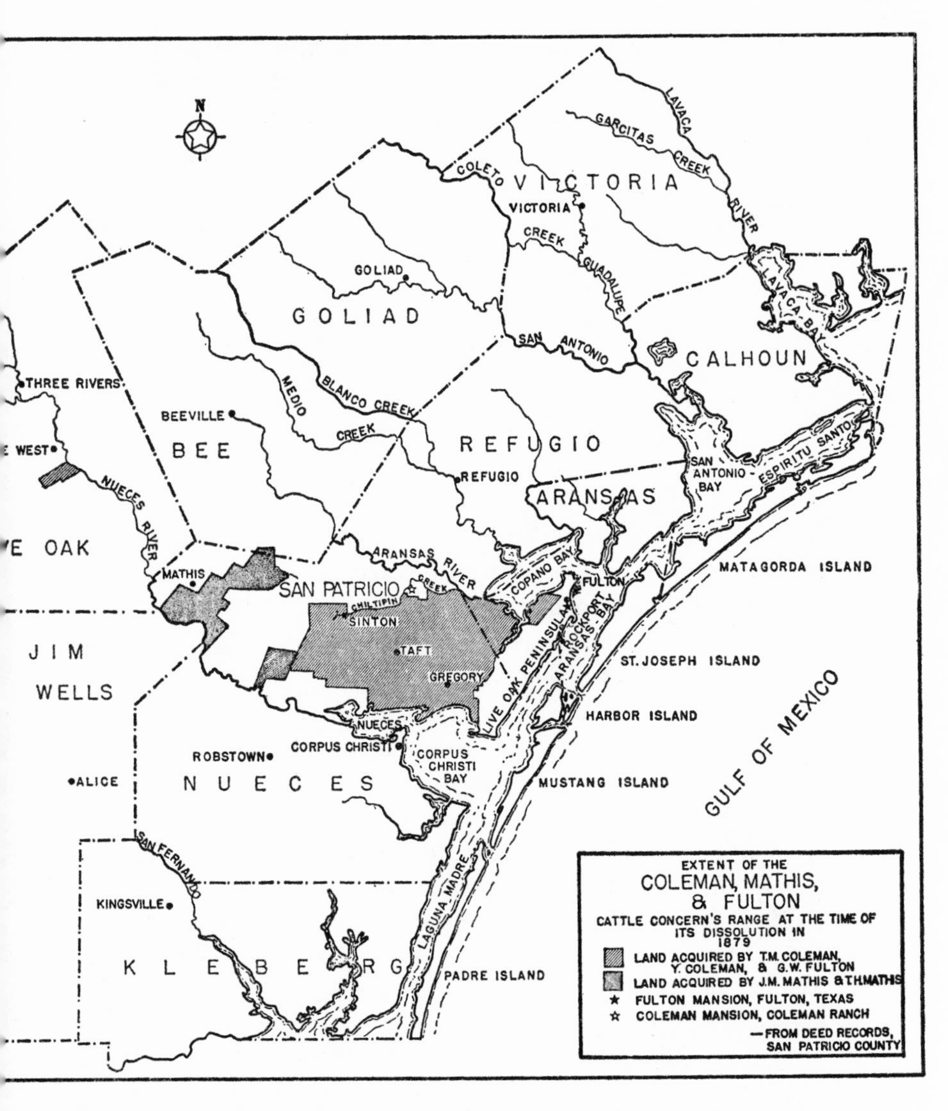

juncture with other parties.[7] A second reason for this practice was to keep livestock in different pastures from fighting and tearing down a fence. Gradually the firm subdivided the range into smaller plots for better handling of stock, thus enabling it to concentrate its herd after

[7] G. W. Fulton, Sr., to George Vinyard [Ingleside, Texas?], October 1, 1890, FC.

rains upon lots with the least natural-water facilities. Smaller enclosures would allow the ranchers to improve the quality of their animals through controlled breeding, a practice impossible on the open range.

To facilitate shipping their cattle and those consigned to the partnership to sell on a commission basis, Coleman, Mathis, and Fulton purchased a two-ninths interest in a wharf at Rockport owned by J. M. Doughty. The dock, warehouses, beef pens, office, and real estate must have been regarded as a good investment, because the small share sold for $5,000.[8]

Immediately after organization the ranch started purchasing property adjoining and already encompassed by it. The Republic of Texas had awarded Headright, Bounty, Donation, and Script certificates, which gave the holder the right to possess acreage out of the vacant and unappropriated public domain. Later the state government enacted a homestead or pre-emption law under which a person might live on the ground for a minimum of three years and then receive a patent as legal evidence of ownership.[9] As the eastern part of the state was settled, additional grants were given from the vacant land further west, most of which was not occupied by the 1870's, especially if it was located away from streams or rivers. Because of this law Coleman, Mathis, and Fulton were able to use thousands of acres for grazing purposes without buying. From time to time the company purchased scattered tracts in its enclosure if the original grantee or his heirs could be located and persuaded to sell. Most nonresidents with rights to acreage in San Patricio and Aransas Counties were willing to dispose of their property as this was their first opportunity to sell since the Revolution. June 3, 1871, is the date of the first purchase by Coleman, Mathis, and Fulton, when 1,476 acres were obtained for $430, an average of $0.29 an acre.[10]

During the next several years the enterprise continued to buy real estate, but the amounts varied in size and cost. For a league of land the company paid $1,550 in gold, at an average of $0.35 an acre. Price

[8] Deed Records, Aransas County, December 5, 1873, Vol. B, pp. 410–411.

[9] John T. Simmons, Jr., "A Search of the Records of the General Land Office," *Report of the Fifth Texas Surveyors Short Course* (February, 1952), p. 39.

[10] Deed Records, San Patricio County, June 3, 1871, Vol. 5, pp. 429–430.

ranged up and down from that figure, in one case as low as $0.15, to as high as $0.48.[11] The last sum was for 1,280 acres originally granted in 1838 as a bounty land warrant to Sam Houston, hero of the Texas Revolution, and sold by J. Carroll Smith, executor of Sam Houston's estate.

During the 1870's the ranch continued to acquire land by spreading out over San Patricio County and western Aransas County. Plots of ground measuring from a quarter section to several thousands of acres in each transaction were bought at prices ranging from $0.35 to $2.45 an acre.[12] Occasionally acreage was gained outside the immediate area of the home range. The company purchased 612 acres along Papalote Creek in Bee County for $1.00 an acre in 1877, and during the same year it added property in Live Oak County to its vast holdings.[13] While procuring real estate, the firm secured from the Toyah Creek Irrigation Company, Incorporated, not only its 640 acres but its right granted by the state to construct canals and ditches for navigation and irrigation.[14] Although this privilege was never exercised, the company obtained it in order to gain possession of the ground for grazing purposes.

Soon after the partnership was formed, its own business associates began selling land to it. Youngs Coleman conveyed 4,033 acres for $4,033 to the ranch, most of it choice property on Corpus Christi Bay.[15] Thomas M. Coleman deeded 200 acres on Nueces Bay for $600, and 7,419 acres adjacent to Chiltipin Creek and in the Brasada Pasture at $0.77 an acre.[16] Thomas M. Coleman and John M. Mathis jointly owned 1,920 acres in the northern part of San Patricio County on the south bank of the Aransas River and sold it to Coleman, Mathis, and

[11] *Ibid.*, September 19, 1871, Vol. 3, pp. 502–506; July 22, 1871, Vol. 3, pp. 509–511; February 7, 1872, Vol. 5, pp. 407–408.

[12] *Ibid.*, December 5, 1872, Vol. 3, pp. 508–509; April 15, November 10, 14, 1873, Vol. 3, pp. 514–515, 633–634, 636–638; May 22, September 28, 1877, Vol. 7, pp. 29–30, 93–95.

[13] *Ibid.*, July 7, 1877, Vol. 7, pp. 68–70. Atlee McCampbell, Corpus Christi, Texas, to James C. Fulton, Rockport, Texas, March 4, 1900, FC.

[14] Deed Records, San Patricio County, August 17, 18, 1877, Vol. 7, pp. 73–75.

[15] *Ibid.*, March 15, 1873, Vol. 5, pp. 395–397.

[16] *Ibid.*, April 6, 1873, Vol. 5, pp. 393–395; October 30, 1873, Vol. 6, pp. 74–76.

Fulton in 1873 for $0.35 an acre.[17] The last acquisition the company made was one week before it dissolved in 1879 when approximately 2,000 acres, including a wharf, pens, buildings, and town property in Rockport owned by Thomas H. Mathis and John M. Mathis were purchased for $22,260.[18]

By far the largest landholders that transferred property to the ranch were George W. Fulton and his wire, Harriet, daughter and heiress of Henry Smith. A total of 31,381 acres in Aransas and San Patricio Counties—on Nueces, Aransas, and Puerto Bays and on the inland—were deeded to the parent firm in the 1870's for a total of $27,794, an average of $0.885 an acre.[19]

The cattle company extended its holdings past the western boundary fence in San Patricio County, set in 1872 by the purchase of 9,133 acres in what was known as the Brazada, Brasada, or Brush Pasture. On March 1, 1875, it purchased 4,528 acres from Joseph F. Smith, cousin of Mrs. Fulton, and Willard Richardson, editor and publisher of the Galveston *Daily News*. The price paid for this brushy area was $1.50 an acre; but when an adjoining league and *labor* were added to the pasture less than eight months later only $0.62 an acre was paid to A. H. Phillips, the owner.[20] Immediately after the Brasada was purchased, it was fenced—a process that took from May 7 to July 1, 1875, to complete.[21] Within twenty years this land with its dense growth of mesquite trees and underbrush became virtually impregnable and was worthless for grazing purposes. Later 10,000 acres of it were conveyed to a company as a bonus for constructing a deep-water harbor, but, when the ocean port was not attained, approximately two-fifths of the area reverted to the ranch after a law suit. The remainder, which became the Welder and Odem subdivision of San Patricio County, was sold to farmers and made a productive agricultural region after the brush was cleared.

As the furthest point on the range was approximately forty miles

[17] *Ibid.*, October 30, 1873, Vol. 6, pp. 72–73.

[18] Deed Records, Aransas County, August 1, 1879, Vol. C, pp. 598–599.

[19] Deed Records, San Patricio County, May 12, June 2, 1873, January 10, 20, 1876, Vol. 5, pp. 507–510, Vol. 6, pp. 66–71, 77–78, Vol. 7, pp. 632–634.

[20] *Ibid.*, March 1, 1875, Vol. 6, pp. 354, 459; Deed Records, Aransas County, October 22, 1875, Vol. B, pp. 647–648.

[21] George Ware Fulton Notebook, FC.

from the shipping pens at Rockport, the distance was too great for trailing marketable cattle in one day. Animals lost weight on a forced drive of that duration, while some escaped in transit causing loss of valuable time to return them to the bunch. Regular work demanded of cowboys went undone temporarily because many men were needed to keep the herd orderly. To facilitate marketing livestock Coleman, Mathis, and Fulton purchased a 3,660-acre lot on the Copano Bay side of Live Oak Peninsula and named it the Little or Shipping Pasture.[22] From there the animals could be rounded up and driven the couple of miles to the place of embarkation in Rockport with two or three days' notice, a distinct advantage when one must watch a vacillating market and place beeves on it at the proper time in order to turn a profit.

Within the enclosure in San Patricio County were four leagues donated to the county by the state of Texas for education. Surveyed in 1858, and deeded to the county in 1862, the 17,712 acres of land was sold to Coleman, Mathis, and Fulton in 1878 for $1.00 an acre.[23]

In the late 1870's, when the South Texas Plains gained in population, demand for services such as roads and schools caused county officials to search through property records for land with delinquent taxes so that they could sell it to gain revenue. Lots of 160 to 640 acres went on the auctioneer's block and were struck off to the highest bidder. For 640 acres, back taxes were $2.80, costs accrued thereon were $2.00 plus $2.00 for the deed, with a total of $6.80 for a section of land, little more than one cent an acre. For the 2,096 acres obtained by Coleman, Mathis, and Fulton on July 1, 1879, from the San Patricio County tax collector, an average of approximately two and one-half cents an acre was paid.[24]

With the acquisition of property the company purchased cattle to place on it. Dogged by hard times, the ranchers' difficulties were particularly increased by the harsh winter of 1872–1873, which took a toll of the livestock, and by the financial depression of 1873, which started

[22] Deed Records, Aransas County, April 19, 1875, Vol. C, pp. 269–272.

[23] Surveyor's Records, San Patricio County, January 22, 23, 27, 1858, Vol. 1, pp. 103–107. Deed Records, San Patricio County, June 18, 1862, Vol. 7, pp. 126–128; February 11, 1878, Vol. 8, pp. 177–180; September 28, 1915, Vol. 58, pp. 66–67. Commissioners' Court Minutes, San Patricio County, October 6, 1877, Vol. 1, pp. 191–192.

[24] Deed Records, San Patricio County, July 1, 1879, Vol. 7, pp. 324–338.

in the Northeast but reached its dark hand of economic gloom into Texas. Outlets to the North were dried up as banks closed, and money was difficult to come by in the Midwestern cattle-buying centers. Texas ranchers were forced to sell more and more of their livestock to relieve the strain on dry pastures and to gain revenue.[25]

Coleman, Mathis, and Fulton bought many small herds and with the transactions went the brands. One such transfer occurred in 1873, when Thomas O'Connor of Refugio County sold his *THC* (connected) brand to them for $30,000.[26] O'Connor did not handle the trade himself but commissioned Robert and Jeremiah Driscoll to do it for $5,000 or 5,000 acres of land.[27] In the year 1875 alone the Coleman, Mathis, and Fulton firm purchased 264 brands with marks from neighboring ranchers, added a *T* on each animal's jaw to indicate the new owner, then turned the livestock onto their range.[28] Calves yet unbranded received the main brand of the firm, *CMF* (connected), which was registered in the counties in which the company operated.[29]

As livestock matured and became marketable, they were sold to packeries or to neighboring ranchers for a northern drive, or sent via ship to New Orleans or Havana. No evidence exists of cattle drives to Kansas by the Coleman, Mathis, and Fulton firm, but an accurate record was not kept before October 3, 1872.[30]

Texas coastal towns served as shipping points for beeves during the Republic period and early statehood. As the population shifted westward and livestock raising spread, ports such as Indianola and Matagorda became important, although traffic was not substantial until after the Civil War.[31] Texas beef was carried primarily to the cities of New

[25] J. Frank Dobie, *A Vaquero of the Brush Country,* pp. 22–23.

[26] *Ibid.*, p. 120.

[27] Sister Margaret Rose Warburton, "A History of the O'Connor Ranch, 1834–1939" (M.A. thesis), p. 20.

[28] Marks and Brands, San Patricio County, December 13, 1875, Vol. "A–B–C," pp. 234–237. The Marks and Brands book for Aransas County has long since been lost or misplaced.

[29] *Ibid.*

[30] Shipping Register, 1872–1881, Coleman-Fulton Pasture Company Records (hereafter cited as CFPC).

[31] U.S. Department of the Interior, Census Office. *Report on the Productions of Agriculture as Returned at the Tenth Census, 1880. . . . (House Miscella-*

Orleans, Mobile, and Havana by the Morgan Steamship Company. The Morgan Line monopolized those markets by charging exorbitant rates and by not permitting goods to be shipped to those ports unless first sold to the ship company.[32] The only outlet for cattle during the Civil War when the United States Navy blockaded Texas ports was overland to the Confederate Southeast or to California. The result of a restrained market was large numbers of cattle on hand when the conflict ended.

As the Morgan Line operated the principal freight service from the Texas coast, it profited greatly during the Reconstruction years transporting Texas cattle. The steamers, outfitted to carry animals between decks and on deck, used elevators to lower them to pens in the vessels. Trips to New Orleans took two days, and those to Havana required four. Hay was placed in the ships for cattle to eat and also scattered on the floors to prevent slipping.[33]

Coleman, Mathis, and Fulton contracted with the Morgan Line to transport its cattle during the 1870's. From October, 1872, to July, 1878, when the Aransas Pass inlet became too shallow for steamships, a total of 104,600 beeves, cows, calves, and yearlings were billed to New Orleans from Rockport. This number constituted about one-third of the firm's entire shipments, the balance sent from Indianola, principally to Havana.[34] The United States Census Report for 1880 states that cattle shipped to Cuba were

> purchased and transported, under contract with the government of that island, by the Morgan Steamship Company. The special means of transportation furnished by this line of vessels, added to the quarantine restrictions on returning transports, has driven all lesser competitors out of the business, and the Cuban live-stock industry is now mainly under its control.[35]

---

neous Documents, 47th Congress, Second Session, Serial No. 2131, Doc. No. 42), III, 965, 976 (hereafter cited as *Agricultural Census for 1880*).

[32] Joseph G. McCoy, *Historic Sketches of the Cattle Trade of the West and Southwest,* pp. 19 ff.

[33] *Agricultural Census for 1880,* III, 976–977.

[34] Coleman and Fulton, Rockport, to Thomas S. Sedgwick, Assistant Engineer, Corps of Engineers, Galveston, Texas, June 30, 1880, in *House Executive Documents,* 46th Congress, Third Session, Serial No. 1954, Doc. No. 1, pp. 1249–1250.

[35] *Agricultural Census for 1880,* III, 976.

The Shipping Register of the Coleman, Mathis, and Fulton ranch states only that a contract was made with C. A. Whitney and Company, New Orleans agent of the Morgan Line, to send cattle to Havana as well as to New Orleans without mention that the freight company bought them first. The intimation is that the livestock were only consigned to the Morgan Company's care. Over 10,000 head, mostly beeves, were sent to Havana alone during the period November, 1875, to June, 1876.[36] Steamships employed in hauling livestock were the *Aransas, Austin, Clinton, Gussie, Harlan, Harris, Hewes, Hutchinson, Mary, Morgan,* and *St. Mary.* Although these side-paddle wheel vessels had a shallow draught, they still carried a large cargo. For example, the *Harris* carried 133 beeves and 241 calves in addition to necessary hay on a trip from Rockport to New Orleans in January, 1877.[37]

Controversy arose between the Morgan Line and Coleman, Mathis, and Fulton concerning shipment of cattle. The Corpus Christi agent would telegraph Rockport how much space was available on a particular ship going to New Orleans. The cattle would be brought from the Little or Shipping Pasture and placed in pens near the dock. If the cattle were not ready to be loaded when the vessel arrived, the captain sometimes would depart without receiving the cargo. When the ship was late or not ready to take the cattle on schedule, the livestock necessarily were kept in pens for a day without water or grass.[38] The cost to the ranchers was thirty dollars a day besides damages to the wild and frightened animals in the small enclosure and besides loss of weight by the cattle. The inefficiency of the Morgan Line—the result of confusion over who had authority to set the time of egress, the ship's captain or the head office in New Orleans—was causing unnecessary expense.

Another complaint was voiced by the Rockport agent for the maritime company. Texas coastal residents were dependent on the Morgan Line to transport their freight, as no other vessels came to that region.

[36] Shipping Register, 1872–1881, CFPC.

[37] Coleman, Mathis, and Fulton, Rockport, to C. Mehle and Company, New Orleans, January 17, 1877, CFPC, I, 313. All of the official correspondence of Coleman, Mathis, and Fulton was written from Rockport.

[38] Coleman, Mathis, and Fulton to C. A. Whitney and Company, agent, Morgan Line, New Orleans, October 12, 1876, CFPC, I, 151.

But the company was inconsistent in picking up proffered freight, sometimes choosing not to do so, especially from small customers.[39]

Although Coleman, Mathis, and Fulton was selling cattle on out-of-state markets, not enough money was coming into the company treasury to carry on the vast program of land and cattle buying. The recourse was to mortgage the range on a short-term basis to have funds to continue empire building. On May 5, 1874, a loan of $100,000 was obtained from Thomas O'Connor of Refugio County in return for a deed of trust to 120,000 acres in San Patricio and Aransas Counties.[40] Payment on the promissory note was due in four years, with 10-per-cent interest. A clause stated that if the interest were paid the note could be extended for two years.

In order to gain additional revenue the ranch shipped bones to the North to be made into fertilizer.[41] To obtain the maximum revenue from its pasture, the Rockport cattle concern allowed neighbors to pasture their livestock upon its range for a fee.[42]

Soon after the partnership was formed, it began upbreeding the herd. Fulton had resided in Covington, Kentucky, for several years and in 1875 he corresponded with a Kentucky friend about purebred bulls to be used in Texas.[43] The company's records do not mention when blooded stock was first introduced, but at the time of dissolution in 1879 several dozen full-blooded Durhams were on hand.

The extremely dry fall of 1876 resulted in a lack of grass for fattening beeves for the market. In order not to sell at a loss, the company held over at least 12,000 head until the following spring. As fall turned to winter, continued dry weather prevented the firm from marketing its cows and beeves, which caused its money matters to be rather

[39] *Ibid.*, November 14, 1876, CFPC, I, 192.

[40] Coleman, Mathis, and Fulton to Thomas O'Connor [Refugio, Texas?], found in Deed Records, San Patricio County, May 5, 1876, Vol. 6, pp. 20–24; in Deed Records, Aransas County, May 5, 1874, Vol. B, pp. 505–509.

[41] S. Bentz, near Hoods Mill, Maryland, to G. W. Fulton, Sr., Rockport, May 1, 1875, FC.

[42] Sidney G. Borden, Sharpsburg, Texas, to J. C. Fulton, Rockport, April 9, 1876, FC.

[43] James W. Peel, Lexington, Kentucky, to G. W. Fulton, Sr., Rockport, June 12, 1875, FC.

tight. The company, in an attempt to forestall creditors, requested delays in meeting payments due, telling them that everything would be fine when spring came.[44] Nevertheless money became scarce in the office till, and $10,000 more was borrowed at 18-per-cent interest on a ninety-day note from a Corpus Christi banking house to tide the ranch over until spring.[45]

Natural increase alone did not account for the abundance of marketable beeves on hand. The ranchers purchased animals to pasture a short time on the home range and to sell when fat. By September, 1876, prices had risen from the $12.00 per head for beeves and $8.00 for cows as in 1872 to $20.00 for beeves and $12.00 for cows.[46] Stock purchased locally during the summer of 1876 at $15.00 a head delivered at the company's pasture strained the capacity of the range. The ranchers further burdened it by purchasing a multitude of Mexican cattle that they hoped to fatten and sell. As water and grass began to wane in September, 1876, the partnership decided that even the low cost of $11.25 a head, with prospects of selling in six months at almost 100-per-cent gain, was too much to pay until grass and water, essentials in livestock raising, increased.[47] Although the firm cancelled most of its shipments, it sent a few token loads to New Orleans during the winter of 1876–1877. Beeves in prime condition, sometimes rare that season, commanded a top price of $25.00 each.[48]

Cold cash was an important item to these stockmen at that time. The firm made small shipments of beeves valued at $20 to $27 a head, yet the obtained prices were not sufficient to maintain regular operations. Charles Morgan of New York, head of the Morgan Line of steamships, advanced $30,000 in January, 1877, on a six-month note at 10-

[44] Coleman, Mathis, and Fulton to E. Ray, Rayville, Texas, December 25, 1876, CFPC, I, 270; to W. A. Pettus, Goliad, Texas, December 15, 1876, CFPC, I, 239.

[45] Coleman, Mathis, and Fulton to Doddridge and Davis, Corpus Christi, December 27, 1876, CFPC, I, 277.

[46] Shipping Register, 1872–1881, CFPC. Coleman, Mathis, and Fulton to F. J. Carrillo [n.p.], [September, 1876], CFPC, I, 131.

[47] Coleman, Mathis, and Fulton to F. J. Malone [n.p.], September 13, 1876, CFPC, I, 103; to James Nichols, Helena, Texas, August 4, 1876, CFPC, I, 28.

[48] Coleman, Mathis, and Fulton to C. Mehle and Company, New Orleans, December 24, 1876, CFPC, I, 269.

per-cent interest, and took as security a deed of trust for 4,000 head of beeves on the range.[49]

Other sources were tapped but the interest rate came high. E. Ray of Rayville, Texas, advanced a smaller sum for a short-term loan but obtained 12-per-cent interest.[50] Security for borrowed money was often made in land. Coleman, Mathis, and Fulton offered Francke and Danneel, of New Orleans, a mortgage on 45,000 acres described as the best mesquite grazing land in the country, including the Brasada Pasture, in return for $20,000, but these financiers were not interested.[51] Again the reason for borrowing at that time was to hold over a large number of animals which, by early summer, would bring at least $10 more on the New Orleans market and $7 or $8 more in Havana. Joseph Friend and Samuel Cahn, Corpus Christi banking partners, advanced $15,000 but only in return for a deed of trust for the 3,660-acre Little or Shipping Pasture on Live Oak Peninsula, near Rockport, and for their choice of 2,000 cows.[52] A hint of prosperity allowed the mortgagee to pay off some of its debts in 1877, but the following year it was forced to ask for credit again with a $10,000 loan from Friend and Cahn.[53]

Part of the $100,000 mortgage for 120,000 acres, executed in 1874 to Thomas O'Connor, was paid when it came due in May, 1878. A new note had been made in April, this time for $40,000 at 12-per-cent interest with all *CMF* (connected) cattle offered as security.[54] For a full description of the several stocks ranging in San Patricio, Aransas, and Refugio Counties, with their marks and brands, O'Connor was referred to the editions of the Rockport *Transcript*, a local weekly newspaper.

Times must not have been as hard as the several large debts would

[49] Deed of Trust Records, Aransas County, January 16, 1877, Vol. A, pp. 235–239.

[50] Coleman, Mathis, and Fulton to E. Ray, Rayville, Texas, January 25, 1877, CFPC, I, 321.

[51] Coleman, Mathis, and Fulton to Francke and Danneel, New Orleans, February 3, 1877, CFPC, I, 346–347.

[52] Deed of Trust Records, Aransas County, February 6, 1877, Vol. A, pp. 252–253.

[53] *Ibid.*, August 17, December 12, 1877, Vol. A, pp. 261, 269–270; March 9, 1878, Vol. A, pp. 275–277.

[54] Deed of Trust Records, San Patricio County, April, 1878 [day not cited], Vol. A, pp. 130–134.

indicate, for Coleman, Mathis, and Fulton declared a $214,634.19 dividend on April 30, 1878.[55] Each partner was to share according to the extent of his ownership in the firm; for example, Fulton's undivided one-third interest amounted to $71,544.73.

Five months prior to January, 1879—the date when the company would be released from the mortgage to Anderson and Simpson of New Orleans on the Henry Bend Pasture—the firm gave a deed of trust to E. D. Sidbury of Corpus Christi for the same property to secure a note in the sum of $14,665.98.[56] This last debt became necessary as cattle shipments were halted in the summer of 1878, when a yellow-fever epidemic broke out in New Orleans, and a subsequent quarantine stopped all communication by steamer with Texas. In November livestock were again permitted to leave the coastal ports for market.[57]

Since the 3,660-acre Little or Shipping Pasture on Live Oak Peninsula was choice property, the ranch had no difficulty in getting loans, using this lot as security. When the March 9, 1878, notes held by Friend and Cahn were paid on February 20, 1879, Coleman, Mathis, and Fulton mortgaged the pasture and 2,000 head of cows four days later to other Corpus Christi banking partners, Perry Doddridge and Allen M. Davis.[58] The $10,000 loan was comparable to opening a checking account, because the bank was to furnish funds and cash the ranch's drafts.

Although cattle sales were sufficient to pay off the mortgage to E. D. Sidbury on the Henry Bend Pasture in 1879, nonetheless that tract was again put up as security on a loan of $15,000 from D. Sullivan of Indianola, at 12-per-cent interest, in order to continue the program of land buying and, as it seems, to meet other notes coming due.[59] With

[55] J. C. Fulton, Rockport, to R. W. Stayton, Corpus Christi, March 16, 1903, FC.

[56] Deed of Trust Records, San Patricio County, August 1, 1878, Vol. A, pp. 151–154; January 10, 1879, Vol. A, pp. 167, 169.

[57] George S. Whitney, Rincon Ranch, to John Tinney [n.p.], July 30, 1878, CFPC, III, 30; to John M. Mathis [Indianola, Texas?], November 15, 1878, CFPC, III, 39. Neill C. Wilson and Frank J. Taylor, *Southern Pacific: The Roaring Story of a Fighting Railroad*, p. 70.

[58] Deed of Trust Records, Aransas County, February 20, 24, 1879, Vol. A, pp. 307–311.

[59] Deed of Trust Records, San Patricio County, August 1, 8, 1879, Vol. A, pp. 198–206.

funds from the new mortgage the debts to Doddridge and Davis and to Thomas O'Connor were absolved.[60]

Most ranches were defined on the extremities by a drift fence separating cattle of different owners. By finding a gap in a fence or by tearing it down in order to get on the other side, cattle wandered oftentimes far from the home range. They were, of course, branded, and at a glance one knew to whom they belonged. At the spring and fall roundups strays could be cut out of the herd and held for the owner to claim. Coleman, Mathis, and Fulton employed individuals to attend each gathering and paid twenty-five cents for each head under its brand returned home.[61] A more strenuous way of collecting one's estrayed stock was to hire a person to scout over adjoining regions in search of cattle wearing particular brands and to return them for the reward of one dollar a head.[62]

A major purchase of real estate other than those tracts previously mentioned, which were by and large in a proximity, was the acquisition of the Henry Bend Pasture in the northwestern part of San Patricio County. In 1876 Walter Henry sold for one dollar an acre the four leagues and *labores* of the Delgado survey situated in a deep bend of the Nueces River adjoining the town tract of San Patricio.[63] In order to pay for the property, on the day it was bought Coleman, Mathis, and Fulton gave a mortgage on the Henry Bend Pasture to Anderson and Simpson, bankers at New Orleans, in return for a loan of $18,420.[64] By having a large pasture away from the main range, the company was allowed to separate portions of its herd and to keep an exclusive area for beeves or for cows as appeared necessary.

Headquarters of the sprawling Coleman, Mathis, and Fulton ranch were at Rockport, but the operational center for normal day-to-day activities was at a place known as Rincon Ranch, west of Live Oak Peninsula across Puerto Bay. Other ranches named after persons who

[60] *Ibid.*, October 24, 1879, Vol. A, pp. 215–217. Deed of Trust Records, Aransas County, September 26, 1879, Vol. A, pp. 335–336.

[61] Coleman, Mathis, and Fulton to A. J. West, Refugio, Texas, November 22, 1876, CFPC, I, 201.

[62] Dobie, *A Vaquero of the Brush Country,* p. 119.

[63] Deed Records, San Patricio County, February 9, 1876, Vol. 6, pp. 453–456.

[64] Deed of Trust Records, San Patricio County, January 10, 1879, Vol. A, pp. 167–169.

once owned the land or by natural features were the Brasada, Big Pasture, Stockley, Henry Bend, Cruz Lake, Mesquite, Pistola, Mud Flats, Consado, Puentez, Doyle Water Hole, Gollege, and Indianola Prairie. In the late 1870's George S. Whitney was foreman, and from the Rincon he commanded a host of employees, who did the riding, cooking, fencing, milking, and other chores necessary on a cattle spread. Wages received by the foreman in 1879 were $83.33 a month, while $15 seemed to be the prevailing rate for those engaged in more routine tasks of little responsibility.[65]

As a supplement to the food rations of milk cows and of horses, kept at the various camps on the range and at the Rincon, corn was raised. In 1878 a bumper crop harvested at the Rancho Del Rincon was sufficient to supply all the needs of the Coleman, Mathis, and Fulton firm. Fifty-three acres of the staple were planted in 1879 but no attempt was made to mass feed all cattle on the range.[66]

During periods of drouth large numbers of livestock perished for lack of grass and water. Writing about "the great die-up" of 1878–1879, two studies reported that an eighteen-month drouth ruined many small ranchers on the coastal prairies and depleted the herds of Coleman, Mathis, and Fulton.[67] However, this natural disaster is not mentioned in the correspondence of the company, and the foreman's record of an abundant growth of corn, a commodity that definitely needs rainfall to subsist, gives the opposite impression.

In the latter 1870's the five partners were not as cordial in their relationship as they were when the business began. They purchased, with speculations of turning a profit, one thousand head of beeves, which were to be sold immediately. J. M. Mathis, for the partnership, sold them to the C. A. Whitney and Company, New Orleans agent of the Morgan Line, and delivered them at Guadalupe Station on the railroad leading into Indianola. Contract price to the transportation

[65] Rincon Ranch Pay Roll, March, 1879, CFPC, III, 95–97.

[66] G. S. Whitney, Rincon Ranch, to M. Thomas, Cumingsville, Texas, July 4, 1878, CFPC, III, 29; to James M. Doughty [Rockport ?], July 27, 1879, CFPC, III, 73.

[67] North, "A Historical Survey of the Taft Ranch" (M.A. thesis), p. 43. May Mathis Green Watson and Alex Lillico, *Taft Ranch: A History of the Fifty Years of Development sponsored by Coleman-Fulton Pasture Company with sketches of Gregory and Taft, the two towns it created*, p. 2.

company was two and one-eighth cents a pound for beeves, while calves and young cows sold by the head at $5.50 and $12.00 respectively.[68] Fulton and the Colemans did not hesitate to say that Mathis should not have accepted this low price. The other partners felt a better price could have been received and that the least Mathis could do would be to consider or consult them. "Partners should be more open-mannered in business," Fulton emphasized.[69] Mathis agreed to accept full responsibility in the matter and signed an affidavit stating that the firm of Coleman, Mathis, and Fulton would not be liable for any loss or damage that might result from the Whitney-Morgan contract.[70]

The uncordial atmosphere in the partnership resulted in its dissolution on August 7, 1879. At that time Thomas M. Coleman had an interest of three-twelfths in the business; Youngs Coleman, one-twelfth; Thomas Henry Mathis, two-twelfths; John M. Mathis, two-twelfths; and George Ware Fulton, four-twelfths.[71] Thomas M. Coleman had increased his holdings by purchasing an additional one-twelfth interest from Youngs Coleman, his father, in 1874.[72]

An inventory was taken to determine the amount of property the firm owned as of April 30, 1879. At that time it was estimated that the company possessed approximately 200,000 acres under fence and an additional 15,000 acres not enclosed. Horses, mules, and jacks were counted and evaluated, as were cattle at the several camps. The business closed with fifty-six full-blooded Durham bulls and cows on hand, along with a small herd of mixed stock. Naturally, the largest number of bovines in the pastures were the Longhorn, native, Mexican, or Texas breed. On the home range the combined Big Pasture, Rincon Ranch, and Brasada Pasture held the most cattle, although over 7,000 head roamed the leased prairie land near Indianola.[73] The values placed on the animals were $100 for Durham bulls, $60 for Durham cows, $12 for native beeves, $20 for half-breed beeves, $15

[68] J. M. Mathis, Indianola, to C. A. Whitney and Company, New Orleans, March 22, 1879, FC.

[69] G. W. Fulton, Sr., to J. M. Mathis, Victoria, May 18, 1879, FC.

[70] Affidavit of J. M. Mathis, witnessed by G. S. Whitney at Rincon Ranch, June 26, 1879, FC.

[71] Deed Records, San Patricio County, August 7, 1879, Vol. 7, p. 342.

[72] *Ibid.*, July 24, 1874, Vol. 6, p. 122.

[73] Coleman, Mathis, and Fulton Journal, 1878–1879, CFPC.

for cows with calves, $11 for dry cows, and a sliding-scale value for calves, while the price on yearlings depended upon their ages.[74] In eight years the firm of Coleman, Mathis, and Fulton became a big business in South Texas as evidenced by the estimated value placed on all the horse stock, cattle stock, and real and personal property. When the inventory was completed and the books closed on April 30, 1879, the debit and credit columns balanced at a little over one million dollars.[75]

The five partners divided the property on an equitable basis. On August 7, 1879, they decided that Thomas M. Coleman, Youngs Coleman, and George W. Fulton were to gain possession of the main range in San Patricio and Aransas Counties, while Thomas H. Mathis and John M. Mathis were to be given land in the areas more remote from Rockport. The new partnership of Coleman and Fulton, in which Thomas M. Coleman had an undivided three-eighths' interest, Youngs Coleman one-eighth's, and George W. Fulton four-eighths', received 166,636 acres in San Patricio and Aransas Counties on the main range. This area contained the huge continuous block of land from Corpus Christi Bay on the south, Nueces Bay and a fence on the west, Chiltipin Creek on the north, and Copano and Puerto Bays on the east. The Rockport dock with the land on which it stood, including the real and personal property connected with it, went to Coleman and Fulton, as did 3,700 acres in Aransas County and 2,500 acres in San Patricio County not connected with the main pasture. Coleman and Fulton received also 6,081 acres in Live Oak County, for a total of 178,917 acres awarded to the new partnership.[76]

All of the cattle belonging to Coleman, Mathis, and Fulton went to Coleman and Fulton, as well as the horse stock, crops, agricultural implements, ranch fixtures, and all improvements on the transferred land.[77] Also all debts of the ranch went to its successor, except those owed to R. Runge and Company, bankers of Indianola; D. Sullivan of Indianola; W. B. Baker; Lane and Payne of Goliad; and John S. Mc-

[74] *Ibid.* Deed Records, San Patricio County, August 7, 1879, Vol. 7, pp. 344–345.

[75] Coleman, Mathis, and Fulton Journal, 1878–1879, CFPC.

[76] Deed Records, San Patricio County, August 7, 1879, Vol. 7, pp. 345–351.

[77] *Ibid.*, p. 351.

Campbell of Corpus Christi. These debts, amounting to $31,972.76, were to be paid immediately from the proceeds gained from selling cattle on the Henry Bend Pasture before the old firm dissolved. The remaining $274,687.41 of the indebtedness and liabilities was to be paid by Coleman and Fulton.[78]

Thomas H. Mathis and John M. Mathis jointly received 37,676 acres in the western part of San Patricio County, most of it being the Henry Bend Pasture and adjoining surveys.[79] An 11,000-acre lot transferred to the Mathis cousins bordered the Big Pasture and the Brasada Pasture on the west side. Maintenance and repair costs on the boundary fence were to be borne equally and to be considered community property so far as the lands owned or controlled by the parties were contiguous. Undoubtedly, it was felt that the division of assets was not as equal as it should be, for Coleman and Fulton executed a promissory note to the party of T. H. and J. M. Mathis for $15,191.67, payable in six years at 10 per cent.[80] Security for the debt was a mortgage on the Big Pasture. Coleman and Fulton were not prohibited from giving other deeds of trust to portions of the same property to obtain loans to discharge the firm's indebtedness, but the Mathis cousins reserved the right to have precedence over other lienors.

The agreement of dissolution ended eight years of united effort to build an empire of land and cattle in South Texas. During that time the cattle kingdom grew, the packing-house era reached its peak and started to wane, barbed wire was invented and effectively used to enclose vast ranges, upbreeding of livestock became a practice rather than a dream, and other innovations occurred to change the lives of those in rural communities. The Western Union Telegraph Company extended a line to Rockport and Corpus Christi during the early 1870's, after the citizens of each town raised separate subscriptions of $6,000.[81] Subscribers received rebates on telegraph rates by paying only

[78] *Ibid.*, pp. 343–344.

[79] *Ibid.*, pp. 352–356.

[80] *Ibid.*, pp. 356–357. T. H. Mathis, of Aransas County, and J. M. Mathis, of Victoria County, issued a Release of Mortgage on August 29, 1885, certifying that the debt was paid in full. See Deed Records, Aransas County, August 29, 1885, Vol. K, pp. 389–390.

[81] John Van Horne, Louisville, Kentucky, to G. W. Fulton, Sr., Rockport, January 8, 1871, FC.

one-half the cost of each message sent until the amount originally paid was refunded. Distances to the more densely settled regions of the nation were spanned, enabling persons in South Texas to be aware of events thousands of miles away from their homes in only minutes. Of particular interest to the cattle industry, ranchers and packers alike, was the price of beef in New Orleans and in the other livestock centers of the country, which could be reported promptly by telegraph, allowing owners to get their stock to market at the proper time.

The telephone was another invention that was put into use soon after it was placed on the market. Coleman, Mathis, and Fulton is credited with the pseudo honor of being the first to introduce windmills, barbed wire, purebred cattle, and the telephone to South Texas. Available evidence does not reveal who received the first shipment of these items. One is led to believe that the Pasture Company was not racing to be the first firm to bring these products to South Texas; rather it desired to put these innovations to practical use immediately, for a purpose—that of making life more enjoyable and of increasing the profit side of the ledger through the adoption of progressive ideas.

Alexander Graham Bell uttered his well-known phrase, "Mr. Watson, come here, I want you," on March 10, 1876. Within two years Coleman, Mathis, and Fulton put into operation a telephone circuit which connected the Rockport office with the Rincon Ranch and with Thomas M. Coleman's home on the Chiltipin.[82] Unnecessary delays could be avoided in sending or receiving messages; from the Rincon Ranch George S. Whitney, the foreman, could order supplies over the telephone, rather than dispatching a man on horseback on a ride that would consume an entire day. In a matter of seconds the Rockport office could request that a number of cattle be sent to the shipping pens, thus saving valuable time in order to take advantage of a flexible market.

In these ways and others, post-Civil War Texas was dominated by change. Large ranches were carved from the public domain or from unoccupied territory, and what can be called the "Cattle-Baron Era"

[82] Arthur B. Homer, Galveston, to G. W. Fulton, Sr., Rockport, March 19, 1878, FC. G. S. Whitney, Rincon Ranch, to Tom M. Coleman [Chiltipin Ranch ?], April 4, 1878, CFPC, III, 3; to Coleman, Mathis, and Fulton, April 30, 1878, CFPC, III, 22.

was ushered in. Vast holdings of land and cattle gave prestige and status to those in the favored positions. These stockmen became leaders in their communities, built fine homes, sent their children to schools in the eastern United States, and in general did more in developing their region than anyone else.

Two of the finest homes built on the South Texas coast during this era were constructed by George W. Fulton in Fulton and by Thomas M. Coleman on his Chiltipin Creek ranch, approximately thirty miles west of Rockport. Fulton, a civil engineer by training and occupation before he turned to livestock raising, is said to have designed the plans for his four-story dwelling situated near the water's edge on Aransas Bay between Fulton and Rockport.

Beginning in 1872 work on the Fulton dwelling continued for four years before the family moved in. Excavations were made for a basement, a concrete foundation was laid, and construction begun. Thick walls were designed to withstand tropical storms that frequently hit that region of Texas. Stories conflict concerning the exact thickness of the mansion's walls, but an account told by a lineal descendant of Fulton states that:

> Hard pine planks ten inches wide and two inches thick were dipped in tar, laid flat and spiked together, both for outside walls and partitions. The outside boards of cypress were placed vertically, and corners were reinforced with thick cypress blocks, giving the impression of stone walls. The interior walls were lathed with specially sawed cypress, plastered and calcimined white.[83]

Apparently, the architect intended for the house to stand against wind storms, but if it should fall it would go over in one piece.

Water for the house came from two sources. A windmill nearby filled a tank on the roof and a motor pump forced water into a second tank from a cistern by the side of the structure. The well water was used for water closets, laundering, and other rough use, while the rain water in the cistern was used for household purposes.[84]

In the basement were the kitchen, a laundry room, a trough of circulating water for cooling food to prevent spoilage, and a furnace

[83] [Mrs. Gladys Gibson], "Authentic History of Fulton Mansion Told by Descendant," Rockport *Pilot*, March 26, 1959.

[84] G. W. Fulton, Sr., to William H. Lock, Buffalo, March 21, 1891, FC.

that forced warm air through ducts leading to all the rooms in the house, coming out in mock fireplaces. This device was used for air conditioning in the summer by forcing cool air into the vents. A gasoline-powered generator shipped from New York on the Morgan Line produced lights for the house, as well as heat for the laundry and cooking.[85]

Shipped from New Orleans were doors, sashes, shutters, Venetian blinds, stairways, and door trimmings of black walnut, as well as window glass, ornamental gateposts, and screens. The final bill for all the interior finishings in the mansion amounted to $11,586.08.[86] The main floor contained a large hallway, dining room, library, and plant conservatory. On the second and third floors were seven bedrooms, each with its own fireplace through which warm or cool air, depending on the season, came from the basement. Marble mantels, slate hearths, and hearth tile were purchased in New York and shipped by sea to Fulton.[87] A small room, used as an observatory, was built overlooking the bay, and served as the fourth story of the mansion. From that vantage point one could see for miles. Between the third and fourth levels a small concealed room opening into the back side of closets was used to store valuables.

A copper mansard roof covered the structure. Plumbing supplies were obtained in New York. The initial order called for French tubs, a fifty-gallon copper boiler for hot water, French closet bowls, fourteen-inch marble basins, and black-walnut stands.[88] The bathrooms at the Fulton abode were not only functional but attractive! A dumb waiter ordered from New York allowed food cooked in the basement kitchen to be served in the dining room in minimal time and with little effort. New furniture for the house was purchased in Cincinnati. The receipt of goods shipped on December 27, 1876, in-

[85] Receipt to G. W. Fulton, Sr., by O. Tirsill, New York, August 12, 1876; Fulton to Waters Pierce Oil Company, Galveston, June 30, 1891; Fulton to Herman Westervelt, Corpus Christi, June 4, 18, 1890; all in FC.

[86] George Purves, New Orleans, to G. W. Fulton, Sr., December 11, 1876, May 16, 1877, FC.

[87] Penrhyn Slate Company, New York, to G. W. Fulton, Sr., August 10, 1876, FC; Miller and Coats, New York, to Fulton, December 2, 1876, FC.

[88] Miller and Coats, New York, New York, to G. W. Fulton, Sr., August 18, 1876, FC.

cluded such items as a cedar chest, writing desks, leather lounge chairs, French bedsteads, spring and hair mattresses, love seats, a parlor suite, rocking chairs, chess table, veranda chairs, bookcases, hatracks, and other necessary things for housekeeping, totaling $3,582.35.[89]

Expensive carpeting and draperies were purchased in New York; a custom-made silver tea-service set and silver table utensils, complete with a silver bell for signaling the servants, were ordered from a New York silversmith; new bedding supplies were sent for; crystal chandeliers were designed and blown just for the occasion in New York; specially made doorknobs came from Philadelphia; lawn equipment and plants for landscaping were brought in from New Orleans; house paint was shipped on Morgan steamers from Baltimore and New York—all with apparent disregard for cost.[90] The result was a beautiful structure that still stands almost a century later with no sign of exterior disrepair, although vandals have marred the bedrooms and upstairs hallways. Fulton in his correspondence did not state the total expense for erecting and furnishing his mansion, but a local newspaper editor in 1891 estimated the cost to be $100,000.[91]

A housewarming and reception was held for the Fultons in their new home after it was completed and everyone was shown through the rooms for a personal inspection. A spark of jealousy was kindled in the wife of one of Fulton's business associates. On the way home after the reception Mrs. Thomas M. Coleman informed her husband that she liked the house; in fact, she liked it so well that she wanted one built just like it, only larger and more ornate.[92]

Construction started immediately at the Coleman Ranch, on Chiltipin Creek, and by 1880 the home was finished. One informant says that the Colemans tallied up to $80,000 and then quit counting. An-

[89] Meader Furniture Company, Cincinnati, to G. W. Fulton, Sr., December 27, 1876, FC.

[90] Alexander T. Stewart and Company, New York, to G. W. Fulton, Sr., December 4, 1876; Gorham Manufacturing Company, silversmith, New York, to Fulton, August 10, 1876; Mitchell, Vance, and Company, New York, to Fulton, August 11, 1876; William W. Fulton and Son, Philadelphia, to Fulton, September 6, November 10, 1877; J. Muller, New Orleans, to Fulton, January 20, 1876; C. P. Knight, Baltimore, to Fulton, November 1, 15, 1877, May 9, 1878; all in FC.

[91] Aransas Harbor (Texas) *Herald*, November 12, 1891.

[92] Interview with Mrs. Maurice W. Cochran, Fulton, July 28, 1961.

other account states that the total sum was $150,000.[93] Elaborate furnishings were brought in; landscaping for a mile around the house was attended to by persons employed for that purpose alone; stables, hunting dogs, and pens were installed for the benefit of ranch occupants and guests; fountains and statues were placed in the gardens. All this extravagance of both mansions spoke of the carefree, reckless abandon that characterized the cattle-baron era in Texas.

The period of range and cattle empires did not end with the dissolution of Coleman, Mathis, and Fulton. Rather, a new and larger venture awaited those who retained possession of the ranch carved from the wilderness. During the next half century a big business enterprise, led by the remnants of this firm, sponsored the settlement of the area and was largely responsible for the economic development of the South Texas Plains.

[93] *Ibid.* Coleman McCampbell, *Texas Seaport: The Story of the Growth of Corpus Christi and the Coastal Bend Area*, p. 60.

III. THE GREAT PLAINS BUBBLE

EXUBERANCE in the cattle kingdom during the early part of the 1880's was unmatched by any other period before that time and possibly since then. In this era ranchers over the entire Great Plains region increased their herds and extended their ranges. A shortage of cattle led to higher prices, which in turn attracted American and foreign capital to the West, as huge fortunes seemed within the grasp of enterprising individuals. This boom might well be described as the "Great Plains bubble," because investments soared beyond the realm of economic reality before a drouth and overgrazing led to a forced readjustment in ranching practices. Progressive techniques—improved water facilities, enclosed ranges, upbreeding of livestock—became the key to the future, and forward-looking ranchers met the challenge. An organization caught up in this boom was the Coleman and Fulton firm, a partnership cattle business in South Texas formed at the time the bonanza started, which operated in grand style while the tide of prosperity was strong.

On August 7, 1879, the Coleman and Fulton company was formed from the remnants of the Coleman, Mathis, and Fulton firm. The original partners in the new organization, Thomas M. Coleman, Youngs Coleman, and George W. Fulton, were joined on August 25, 1879, by the latter's son, James C. Fulton, who received an undivided one-sixteenth part in the real and personal property of Coleman and Fulton.[1]

Born in Baltimore, Maryland, on January 2, 1848, the younger Fulton received training as a civil engineer in Kentucky and Ohio before moving to Texas with his parents in 1867. For a time he was associated in a mercantile firm with John G. Caruthers and Charles M. Holden in the town of Fulton; later he assisted his father in business affairs in Coleman, Mathis, and Fulton, and then became a partner in Coleman and Fulton.[2]

In order to obtain funds to begin operation the Coleman and Fulton company mortgaged 29,000 acres in the Brasada Pasture, the brushy area on the western side of its range, to Joseph Friend and Samuel Cahn of Corpus Christi.[3] Business was sufficiently prosperous during the fall of 1879 to allow the Brasada mortgage to be liquidated within six months.[4] The 3,660 acres in the Little or Shipping Pasture in Aransas County were mortgaged to another Corpus Christi banking house, Doddridge and Davis, for a second time to provide funds for cashing checks of Coleman and Fulton.[5]

Although an estimate of livestock on hand was made when the Colemans and Fulton severed relations with the Mathis cousins, the first order of business for the new concern was to have an exact count. All the brands owned by Coleman and Fulton were published in the Rockport *Transcript* so that neighboring ranchers would be able to know the ownership of the company animals. R. R. Mitchell, a Rockport ranch hand, was employed to search the South Texas prairies for estrayed livestock and to return them to their owners for a fee.[6]

The tradition of Coleman, Mathis, and Fulton of buying real estate

[1] Deed Records, Aransas County, August 25, 1879, Vol. C, pp. 621–622.

[2] Transcribed Deed Records, Aransas County, May 2, 1870, Vol. TB, pp. 102–103. James C. Fulton, Rockport, Texas, to R. W. Stayton, Corpus Christi, Texas, March 16, 1903, Fulton Collection (hereafter cited as FC). Lewis E. Daniell, *Personnel of the Texas State Government with Sketches of Representative Men of Texas*, pp. 19–20.

[3] Deed of Trust Records, San Patricio County, August 28, 1879, Vol. A, pp. 206–209.

[4] *Ibid.*, February 5, 1880, Vol. A, p. 209.

[5] Deed of Trust Records, Aransas County, September 27, 1879, Vol. A, pp. 328–330.

[6] *Ibid.*, September 24, 1879, Vol. A, pp. 326–327.

was maintained by its successor. In addition to land, other property was purchased. Doddridge and Davis, Corpus Christi bankers, owners of the Rockport Wharf Company, sold it to Coleman and Fulton in February, 1880.[7] Coleman and Fulton then became agents for the Morgan Line in Rockport and used the pier to ship their cattle, as well as livestock and freight consigned to them. The company sold land for additional income. One of the larger transactions was a purchase by Thomas P. McCampbell, San Patricio County rancher, of 5,500 acres in the southeastern corner of the Coleman and Fulton range for $2.08 an acre.[8]

Although the four associates of the enterprise enjoyed harmonious relations, they wanted to curtail any disagreements that might arise in their partnership. As all members were pecuniarily liable for the actions of one colleague, they decided to remove this risk by forming a joint-stock company. A fifty-year charter was filed in the Office of the Texas Secretary of State on May 1, 1880, and notice was given to the public that the Coleman and Fulton partnership would become the Coleman-Fulton Pasture Company, a private corporation organized under the laws of the state of Texas.[9] The announced purpose was for the

> . . . breeding, buying and selling, of Horses, Meat, Cattle, Sheep and goats, and for shipping the same to home or foreign ports, either alive, or the products thereof after slaughter, and for the purpose of carrying on the above described business to own pasture lands, Wharves, Slaughter Houses and vessels of transport, or other apurtenances required for the convenient carrying on of the same.[10]

Within a short time after the joint-stock company was formed, the associates inventoried the real and personal property and then transferred it by deed from the partnership.

Thomas M. Coleman, Youngs Coleman, George W. Fulton, and

[7] Deed Records, Aransas County, February 12, 1880, Vol. C, pp. 711–712.

[8] Deed of Trust Records, Aransas County, April 26, 1880, Vol. A, pp. 363–364; December 4, 1880, Vol. A, pp. 371–372; December 24, 1880, Vol. A, pp. 390–391.

[9] Coleman-Fulton Pasture Company, Charter No. 1206, May 1, 1880, Office of the Texas Secretary of State.

[10] *Ibid.*

James C. Fulton surrendered their claim to 165,940 acres in Aransas and San Patricio Counties with improvements—including seventy miles of plank and wire fences, six artificial lakes for watering stock, and seventeen miles of telephone line between the Rockport office and the Rincon Ranch—8,435 head of cattle and 1,500 head of horses and mules, all of the wagons, harness, and agricultural implements, and a five-sixths' interest in the Rockport Wharf Company owned jointly with the King Ranch—all for the sum of $334,000.[11] Rather than in cash, payment was made in shares of stock valued at $100 each. In the distribution of the capital stock Thomas M. Coleman received 1,252 shares, Youngs Coleman, 418, George W. Fulton, 1,570, and James C. Fulton, 100—a total of 3,340 shares valued at $334,000.[12] This amount was slightly under half of the total authorized capitalization of $750,000. The corporation arrived at the sum of $334,000, representing net capital, by figuring the value of assets at $501,000 minus the indebtedness of $186,100 which it inherited from the Coleman and Fulton partnership.[13]

The initial directors listed in the charter were George Ware Fulton, Thomas Matthew Coleman, and James C. Fulton. At the first meeting of the Board of Directors, on January 14, 1881, George Fulton was elected president, Thomas Coleman became superintendent, and Sam J. Seymour of Rockport, was appointed secretary and treasurer.[14] James C. Fulton, one of the original directors when the corporation was formed

[11] Deed Records, San Patricio County, January 5, 1881, Vol. 7, pp. 544–548. Deed Records, Aransas County, January 5, 1881, Vol. D, pp. 61–66.

[12] Deed of Trust Records, Aransas County, January 5, 1881, Vol. A, pp. 386–388. [George Ware Fulton], *Organization, Charter and By-Laws of the Coleman-Fulton Pasture Company, Rockport, Texas*, pp. 3, 11. Minutes of the Coleman-Fulton Pasture Company Board of Directors' Meeting (hereafter cited as Minutes of Directors' Meeting), January 11, 1881, Coleman-Fulton Pasture Company Records (hereafter cited as CFPC).

[13] Deed Records, San Patricio County, January 5, 1881, Vol. 7, pp. 546–547. The indebtedness was to Thomas O'Connor for $120,000.00; John M. and Thomas Henry Mathis, $15,190.67; San Patricio County for school lands, $17,712.00; heirs of Joseph F. Smith in payment of land, $8,128.05; Doddridge and Davis on account, $5,000.00; also, sundry notes and liabilities amounting to $20,096.27; a total of $186,126.99. The Board of Directors, rounding off this sum to the nearest thousands figure, referred to the indebtedness as $186,000.

[14] Minutes of Directors' Meeting, January 14, 1881, CFPC.

on May 1, 1880, resigned to enter private business, and Youngs Coleman replaced him. Annual stipends were set for the president and superintendent at $4,800 each, with $3,000 for the secretary-treasurer.[15]

Articles of Organization and By-Laws were drawn up to serve as the basis for the company's operating procedure. Although the authorized capital was $750,000, the directors decreed that the number of shares issued at present would amount to $501,000. In addition to the 3,340 shares of common stock subscribed by the incorporators, 1,670 additional shares of preferred stock would be offered for sale. To induce investors the members agreed to award at least an 8 per-cent dividend to the holders of the special certificates before considering persons with common stock and stated this policy in the Articles of Organization.[16] The unissued 2,490 shares were reserved as a sinking fund for the extinction of the concern's indebtedness and as dividends if any shares remained after debts were paid.[17] Proceeds from the sale of preferred stock were to be used in purchasing cattle.

George W. Fulton, affectionately known as the "Colonel," a title of courtesy then commonly awarded to elderly men of standing in a community, was the author of the Articles of Organization and the By-Laws. The directors, who were responsible for the welfare of the business, were to be stockholders in the corporation, with authority to elect officers; the president was to come from their own number. Duties of the officers were spelled out in detail, but in general the By-Laws made the president responsible for the office work, while the superintendent was general manager of the ranches.[18]

A company seal, designed by Colonel Fulton, consisted of a head of a Longhorn steer with ears in the mark of the company, two underhalf crops, and the brand *T* underneath. In an outer circle was the name of the corporation with the words "of Aransas and San Patricio Counties, Texas" in an intermediate circle.[19]

The company immediately circulated a letter to interest purchasers in the preferred stock, and local residents and Northern capitalists quickly started buying the issues. The Rincon Ranch foreman, George S. Whitney, bought 50 shares. Colonel Samuel M. Mansfield of the

[15] *Ibid.* [16] *Ibid.* [17] *Ibid.*
[18] *Ibid.* [19] *Ibid.*

United States Army Corps of Engineers believed the investment to be so sound that he subscribed to 250 shares. Mansfield, in charge of harbor improvements on the Texas coast, was well acquainted with the potential success of a business of this sort: "I believe the investment will succeed by the land alone, situated as it is on what I believe will be the best harbor in Texas a year hence."[20] Moneyed men in Baltimore and Cincinnati were eager to obtain the preferred stock; the largest buyer, purchasing 500 shares, was David Sinton of Cincinnati, an Irish immigrant who became wealthy in the pig-iron manufacturing business during the Civil War and who invested also in Fulton's Aransas Land Company.[21] Other subscribers during the first year of the corporation's existence were Thomas M. Coleman, 230 shares; H. O. Sullivan of San Patricio, Texas, 50 shares; Joseph N. Kinney of Cincinnati, 100 shares; John S. Leib of Baltimore, 25 shares; A. H. Lewis of Cincinnati, 20 shares; and T. M. White of San Patricio County, Texas, 20 shares.[22]

The Board of Directors of the Coleman-Fulton Pasture Company, not relying solely on the United States mail to solicit stockholders, sent Colonel Fulton on a mission to sell the shares. Most of David Sinton's investment was made at the insistence of Fulton, who guaranteed to him in writing, while in Cincinnati in the spring of 1881, that dividends would be forthcoming and that the company would be operated on a sound, economically conservative basis.[23] Fulton, as president, agreed to limit the company's indebtedness to $50,000 after the present debt was extinguished. On this score the Colonel ran into disagreement when he returned home. After the other officers of the

[20] Samuel M. Mansfield, Galveston, Texas, to George Ware Fulton, Sr., Rockport, February 21, 1881, FC. List of subscribers to Coleman-Fulton Pasture Company preferred stock, January 14, 1881, FC.

[21] List of subscribers to Coleman-Fulton Pasture Company preferred stock, January 14, 1881, FC. Statement of Coleman-Fulton Pasture Company preferred stock held by David Sinton as of July 1, 1882, David Sinton Records, 1869–1900, p. 201 (Sinton Collection). "The Tafts of Cincinnati," *Life,* May 26, 1952, p. 108.

[22] List of subscribers to Coleman-Fulton Pasture Company preferred stock, January 14, 1881, FC.

[23] G. W. Fulton, Sr., Rockport, Texas, to David Sinton, Cincinnati, Ohio, May 2, 1881, FC. All of Fulton's correspondence was written from Rockport, Texas, unless specified otherwise.

corporation pointed out that the land-buying and cattle-buying programs would suffer if mortgages were limited to that low sum, the men in a compromise placed the ceiling on borrowing at $100,000.[24]

Profits began to come into the firm's coffers as a program of shipping cattle by steamer to New Orleans got under way. The Coleman-Fulton Pasture Company cattle, scattered over the ranges of South Texas, were returned to the ranch, where older cows were culled out and sent to market along with mature beeves. During the year of 1881 a total of thirty-four shipments by sea were consigned to C. Mehle and Company of New Orleans for gross receipts amounting to $61,077.[25] The Pasture Company sent other livestock to the commission houses of Aycock Mitchell and Company and of R. M. Flautt and Company in the same city.[26]

Scarcity of cattle was a problem when the Pasture Company began operations. Wanting to have the grass utilized until sufficient numbers of livestock could be purchased or grown to consume its maximum production, the Coleman-Fulton Pasture Company allowed neighbors to pasture their animals on its range for an annual fee of $1.50 for cattle and $3.00 for horses.[27] Officials of the corporation did not rely completely on natural increase to bolster their herd but began purchasing livestock where they could be found. Hide-and-tallow factories, meat-packing plants, ocean-going vessels, and the trails to Kansas depleted the number of Longhorns in Texas. A short-term investment in Texas beef was unfeasible because high purchase prices offset the profits to be realized from weight gained while the cattle were under one's care.

As Mexico was the closest place where less expensive animals could be obtained, the Coleman-Fulton Pasture Company bought large numbers there. In 1881 James M. Doughty was hired to go south of the Rio Grande on a buying mission.[28] Proceeds arising from the sale of preferred stock were invested in Mexican cattle, which were delivered

[24] Minutes of Directors' Meeting, May 24, 1881, CFPC.

[25] Sale of cattle in New Orleans by C. Mehle and Company, New Orleans, Louisiana, 1881, CFPC, "Accounts" Book, p. 240.

[26] Shipping Register, 1881–1886, CFPC.

[27] Pasturage Book, 1882–1886, CFPC.

[28] Minutes of Directors' Meeting, December 10, 1881, CFPC.

to the company's pasture at a price of $7 to $11 a head. After a short session on good grass in San Patricio and Aransas Counties, the same bovines were sold at a profit of 30 per cent.[29] In this way the Coleman-Fulton Pasture Company began to assure dividends for its investors.

Business was good during the initial year of operation; and, although the entire indebtedness was not retired, the consensus of the directors was that a distribution of the profits should be declared to bolster confidence in the firm. A 4-per-cent dividend was paid on July 1, 1881, receivable either in cash or in reserved stock;[30] the following January the amount was increased to 16 per cent, paid from earnings of the current six months.[31] The latter apportionment favored the holders of preferred stock, who received a 4-per-cent cash payment and 12 per cent in stock, while persons with common stock were given 1 per cent in cash and 15 per cent in stock.

During the first year the projects undertaken by the Coleman-Fulton Pasture Company had become so numerous that an assistant was needed to help the president care for the business in the main office at Rockport. Another son of Colonel Fulton, George Ware Fulton, Jr., was selected to head the newly created post of vice president, effective January 1, 1882.[32] Duties of the office were to serve in the absence of the president and to render assistance to the chief executive at all times, for which the annual stipend was $1,600.

The younger Fulton had been born in York, Pennsylvania, on February 2, 1853, had attended the University of Kentucky and the Harvard University Law School, and had then migrated to Texas in 1876.[33] He had tried his luck in a partnership law practice in Galveston in 1877–1878 with Robert V. Davidson, and in 1879 he had a practice by himself in Graham, Young County, Texas, approximately ninety-five miles northwest of Fort Worth.[34] After the young attorney re-

[29] [Fulton], *Organization, Charter and By-Laws of the Coleman-Fulton Pasture Company*, p. 12.

[30] Minutes of Directors' Meeting, June 3, 1881, CFPC.

[31] *Ibid.*, December 10, 1881, CFPC. [32] *Ibid.*

[33] Daniell, *Personnel of the Texas State Government*, pp. 250–252. Charles E. H. Glazbrook, Rincon Ranch, to Eugene A. Gilmore, Secretary, Harvard Law School, Cambridge, Massachusetts, June 4, 1896, CFPC, XVII, 287.

[34] George Ware Fulton, Jr., Graham, Texas, to G. W. Fulton, Sr., Rockport, January 10, 1878, December 4, 1879, FC.

turned to Galveston, the Colonel asked him to come to Rockport to be near his parents and those of his wife, the John Irving Caruthers of Ingleside; but George, Jr., had remarked that there were greater possibilities for financial reward at Galveston.

"How much do you make a year?" the elder Fulton had asked. The reply of a piteously low sum had netted a scoffing laugh by the cattle baron, who stated that he would guarantee the boy more than a Galveston lawyer received even if the work was nothing more than sweeping out the office of Coleman and Fulton.[35] A serious discussion had followed concerning the pecuniary potential of a capable person in Rockport, and George, Jr., had been convinced to seek his fortune in the Coastal Bend area. Locating in Rockport in December, 1879, he established a law practice in which he handled land claim suits and indebtedness claims, and represented the Coleman-Fulton Pasture Company in its court-at-law suits.[36] In addition to his private law practice, he became the Aransas County attorney in 1881. He was elected to the Board of Directors of the Coleman-Fulton Pasture Company in August, 1881, before becoming vice president of that corporation in January, 1882.[37]

Despite the prosperous times of the first year of the Coleman-Fulton Pasture Company's existence, the major debts were not extinguished. The extensive programs of real-estate improvement and cattle buying, coupled with the generous dividends to generate enthusiasm and good will among the stockholding public, were expensive.

Foreign investors, particularly British, were active in Texas and in the upper Great Plains region at that time, supplying capital for the establishment of their own spreads as well as loaning money for mortgages to ranchers. In 1882 Fulton induced the Dundee Mortgage and Trust Investment Company, Limited, of Dundee, Scotland, to loan

35 Interview with Mrs. May Fulton Hoopes, Ingleside, Texas, March 2, 1961. Mrs. Hoopes is a daughter of G. W. Fulton, Jr.

36 G. W. Fulton, Jr., Rockport, to Thomas Q. Muller [n.p.], September 25, 1880, CFPC, II, 25; to H. K. and F. B. Thurber and Company [n.p.], June 12, 1882, CFPC, II, 110.

37 G. W. Fulton, Jr., Rockport, to E. R. Rachal [n.p.], May 26, 1881, CFPC, II, 51. Minutes of the Coleman-Fulton Pasture Company Stockholders' Meeting (hereafter cited as Minutes of Stockholders' Meeting), August 3, 1881, CFPC.

$80,000, to be applied to the $120,000 debt owed Thomas O'Connor,[38] in return for a lien on 140,000 acres.[39] Edwin E. Wilson of the Kansas City Investment Company served as trustee for the Scottish group. With this capital in hand and with $40,000 from the sinking fund the Coleman-Fulton Pasture Company paid off its entire debt to Thomas O'Connor.[40] One month later another loan was given by the Dundee Company, this time for $20,000, making the entire debt equal to $100,000, with repayment of $20,000 annually beginning in 1885.[41]

Part of the expense of real-estate improvement originated from building fences to expedite the handling of livestock thus enclosed. In 1881 a fence of two ribbon and two barbed wires was stretched between the Brasada and Cruz Pastures in the western part of the range.[42] The following year the directors declared that "it is important to the interest of the Company, that a Separate pasture with good grass and water, be made for the purpose of holding and fattening beef cattle intended for Shipment," and they proposed that a fence be built "commencing at the line between the two Damion Surveys on the Chiltipin and running due South to Nueces Bay Near the Doyle Water Hole."[43]

Thus pastures formerly designated by their locations in various corners of the range became distinct entities when impregnable fences were constructed. The 1882 fence established a definite Beef Pasture from the Puentez Pasture and the Picatche Pasture, in the center of the range; other fences built in succeeding years formed the boundaries of the Rincon Pasture, in the northeast corner of the range on Copano and Puerto Bays, and of the Gregory Pasture, in the southeast corner

[38] Deed of Trust Records, San Patricio County, December 4, 1880, Vol. A, pp. 240–250. Deed of Trust Records, Aransas County, December 4, 1880, Vol. A, pp. 374–382.

[39] Deed of Trust Records, San Patricio County, May 1, 1882, Vol. B, pp. 36–40. Deed of Trust Records, Aransas County, May 1, 1882, Vol. A, pp. 418–423.

[40] Deed of Trust Records, San Patricio County, May 8, 1882, Vol. B, pp. 34–36. Deed of Trust Records, Aransas County, May 8, 1882, Vol. A, pp. 423–425.

[41] Deed of Trust Records, San Patricio County, June 5, 1882, Vol. B, p. 41. Deed of Trust Records, Aransas County, June 5, 1882, Vol. A, pp. 426–431.

[42] Minutes of Directors' Meeting, September 3, 1881, CFPC.

[43] *Ibid.*, July 1, 1882, CFPC.

fronting on Corpus Christi Bay. The Gregory Pasture was separated from the Beef Pasture by a cross fence on the north, built in 1885, from Alacran Mills to the back of Mud Flats Bayou.[44]

Land value, set at $2.34 an acre at the time of incorporation, was raised to $2.50 in 1882 as a result of the wire-stringing project. The firm's assets were thus increased $38,750; this amount was counted as earnings for dividend purposes although the actual cash did not come in.[45]

For the first half of 1882 business was good, even though the company's indebtedness was consolidated with the Scottish firm at the large figure of $100,000. Profits were sufficient to insure a dividend of 10 per cent, payable to holders of preferred stock on the scale of 4 per cent in cash and 6 per cent in reserved stock, and to those with common stock, 3 per cent in cash and 7 per cent in stock.[46]

After the midyear apportionments were made, some of the common-stock holders objected to the higher cash dividends paid to preferred-stock holders, saying the rates were discriminatory. Both groups had purchased stock at $100 a share. In order to justify the uneven distribution in cash, the Board of Directors considered charging $35 a share on future preferred-stock subscriptions.[47]

The liberal 18-per-cent dividend given for the second half of 1882, 4-per-cent cash on preferred, 3-per-cent cash on common, and the remainder in stock from the reserve,[48] caused David Sinton to question the propriety of making such large awards. He wondered if people would invest with a notion of receiving sums of that size each year and perhaps doubted that the future would be that generous to the company.[49]

Evidently the Board of Directors were of the opinion that providence would continue to smile upon them, for the large divisions continued. In order to provide a pool of reserved stock from which to

[44] Affidavit of D. Willis, Gregory, Texas, June 16, 1923, Deed Records, San Patricio County, Vol. 74, pp. 41–42; of R. K. Reed, April 25, 1924, Deed Records, Aransas County, Vol. M–2, pp. 542–543.

[45] Minutes of Directors' Meeting, July 1, 1882, CFPC.

[46] *Ibid.*, May 27, 1882, CFPC.

[47] *Ibid.*, July 1, 1882, April 7, 11, 1883, CFPC.

[48] *Ibid.*, December 2, 1882, CFPC.

[49] Sinton, Cincinnati, to G. W. Fulton, Sr., Rockport, December 18, 1882, FC.

draw, the Pasture Company stockholders elected to increase the capital stock from $750,000 to $1,500,000 in shares of $100 each.[50]

The severe winter of 1882–1883 halted cattle shipments from the Coastal Bend, causing financial difficulties for the ranch. Daily operations depended on sales of the only exportable commodity, livestock; and when not even token amounts were sent the company's bank account became exhausted. Secretary Seymour wrote that only "good fat will do—fair fat will lose money" and until the market improved the corporation needed $10,000 or $15,000 to carry it through until spring.[51] Despite the adverse condition that prevailed, Seymour exhibited a sense of humor by his statement that cargoes of livestock leaving the area were nonexistent: "There is nothing of movement transpiring here, except a very cold norther this morning."[52] Short-term loans were obtained occasionally by hypothecating the livestock or portions of the capital stock to get the corporation through temporary financial slumps.

By March, when shipments to New Orleans were picking up in tempo, the company's debt total was $34,211.90 in addition to the $111,980 mortgage.[53] David Sinton of Cincinnati, Ohio, who had written earlier that he felt Texas was a good place for investment owing to expanded railroad mileage and to increased immigration, both of which would cause land value to rise, now expressed his willingness to buy more of the company's certificates. He proposed that the combined total debts be paid off by converting them into shares, to be distributed pro rata to the stockholders, who would have the option of buying their allotted amount for cash. "I will further add that any Stock not taken as foresaid will be taken here."[54]

The Board of Directors sidetracked this proposal, as the members realized that they could not keep pace with Sinton's financial reservoir and that subsequently they might lose control of the corporation to the Cincinnatian. Instead, the Board decreed that the 425 shares of unsold

[50] Minutes of Stockholders' Meeting, December 2, 1882, CFPC.

[51] Sam J. Seymour, Rockport, to G. W. Fulton, Sr., Galveston, February 17, 1883, FC.

[52] *Ibid.*

[53] Sinton, Cincinnati, to G. W. Fulton, Sr., Rockport, March 22, 1883, FC.

[54] *Ibid.*, January 23, 1882, FC.

preferred stock would be sold at par plus a 35-per-cent premium. When informed that he could purchase if he so desired, Sinton wired, "Will take it have written today."[55] Another person from the Ohio city, Joseph N. Kinney, vied for the right to purchase the stock; the outcome was that Sinton took 325 shares, and Kinney got only 100.[56]

It is difficult to state exactly how judiciously the affairs of the company were conducted during the early years of its operation, for while dividends of 25 per cent were given in 1883, the officials at the same time borrowed $50,000 for the corporation's use.[57] The Board of Directors, however, did recognize the burden of a large debt and sought to reduce it by establishing a sinking fund for that purpose. At a meeting on December 1, 1883, it was stated that in the future,

> . . . before each semi-annual dividend shall be declared, Four per cent of the Net earnings shall be set apart . . . for the extinction of the indebtedness of the Company, Said Sinking Fund to remain invested in Cattle until required for payment of said indebtedness or any part thereof.[58]

The Board followed this provision at the next division of profits when an 11-per-cent dividend was declared: the first 4 per cent went to the sinking fund and the remaining 7 per cent was passed to the stockholders.[59] There was something special about this dividend, for despite the generosity displayed by the corporation to its owners for three years, it was fifteen years before profit sharing was resumed.

The sum loaned by Sinton to the Pasture Company in 1883 was increased whenever the ranch was caught in another financial squeeze. Sinton wrote that money was scarce in Cincinnati during the summer of 1884, but he would furnish the company with funds as best he could.[60] By October he held a series of small notes worth $30,500; then another note was negotiated to make a rounded-off figure of

[55] *Ibid.*, April 4, 1883, FC.

[56] Joseph N. Kinney, Cincinnati, to G. W. Fulton, Sr., Rockport, April 5, 6, 19, 1883, FC.

[57] Minutes of Directors' Meeting, June 2, August [?], December 1, 1883, CFPC.

[58] *Ibid.*, December 1, 1883, CFPC.

[59] *Ibid.*, June 7, 1884, CFPC.

[60] Sinton, Cincinnati, to G. W. Fulton, Sr., Rockport, June 12, 1884, FC.

$40,000, secured by a five-year mortgage on the 25,000-acre Brasada Pasture in the western region of the ranch.[61]

At the same time another source of revenue was tapped. The Coleman-Fulton Pasture Company borrowed $12,500 in ninety-day notes from its primary bank, the Whitney National Bank of New Orleans, hypothecating 159 shares of capital stock.[62] Part of the shares was intended for semiannual dividends payable in January, 1885, but harsh weather caused the directors to defer payments for the last half of 1884. Although the mortality rate for the cattle was low, the animals themselves lost much weight and were unmarketable for the present. The first payment on the Dundee mortgage was due April 1, 1885, and to that end the directors were looking when they decided to save the company's money to meet that debt.[63]

Adverse conditions in the cattle industry made it necessary to cut expenses during the winter of 1884–1885. At a stockholders' meeting on February 7, 1885, the number of salaried officers of the company was reduced when the offices of vice president and superintendent were consolidated. A reduction in stipends provided only $3,000 a year for the president, $2,000 for the combined vice president and superintendent, and $2,500 for the secretary-treasurer.[64] A power struggle developed when the consolidated position was to be filled.

For some time a rift had existed between Thomas Matthew Coleman and George Ware Fulton. Both appealed to Sinton, but the Buckeye banker refused to choose sides. Sinton wanted to keep both men in the organization because he needed experienced persons running the cattle business, a subject on which he admitted his ignorance. As Colonel Fulton was an expert at the management helm and as Coleman was an excellent cattle buyer, Sinton wrote that it was essential that both remain in the company to safeguard his investment.[65]

[61] *Ibid.,* October 20, 1884, FC. G. W. Fulton, Sr., to Sinton, Cincinnati, October 28, 1884, CFPC, IV, 110. Deed of Trust Records, San Patricio County, November 1, 1884, Vol. B, pp. 91–94. Minutes of Directors' Meetings, November 1, 1884, CFPC.

[62] G. W. Fulton, Sr., to Whitney National Bank, New Orleans, Ocotber 9, 31, November 6, 1884, CFPC, IV, 89–90, 114, 116.

[63] Minutes of Directors' Meeting, January 3, 1885, CFPC.

[64] *Ibid.,* February 7, 1885, CFPC. Minutes of Stockholders' Meeting, February 7, 1885, CFPC.

[65] Sinton, Cincinnati, to G. W. Fulton, Sr., Rockport, March 25, 1884, FC.

The By-Laws of the company as amended on July 5, 1884, gave the Board of Directors full authority to elect officers, but stated that the president and vice president must be chosen from their own number. Colonel Fulton, his son George, Jr., and Coleman were the members of the Board at the time of the reorganization. After the Colonel was re-elected as chief executive a contest developed for the second office. By a vote of 2–0, with Coleman abstaining, George W. Fulton, Jr., was elected as vice president-superintendent.[66]

Sinton and Kinney, both of Cincinnati and both with a large interest in the ranch, appealed to the Texans to get together and iron out their differences. Coleman and Fulton each wrote harshly of the other to Sinton, offering their stock for sale, but Sinton refused them, because he recognized that both men were needed to run the company and to keep public confidence in the value of the stock. "You and Mr. Coleman . . . both propose to sell me your Stock, my answer to which is I would not give Fifty Cents for the whole concern, providing I had to run it," he said.[67]

The primary reason for the break in relations between the ranchers was financial. Times were hard in the winter of 1884–1885. Money was scarce. Coleman drew heavily on the corporation's capital reserve to purchase stock in the company. His motive was to gain control of the Coleman-Fulton Pasture Company in order to oust the Fultons. To complicate the strained relations between the firm's executives, Coleman relatives attempted to draw money from the ranch office in Rockport for a pleasure trip to the World Exposition in New Orleans shortly after Coleman had practically exhausted the ranch's financial resources. Fulton became irritated at this apparent disregard for the welfare of the company during the period of enforced austerity, and swore that he would never permit Coleman to hold high office in the organization. In a letter to Sinton, Fulton announced that he had given Coleman an opportunity to arrange satisfactorily his family's money matters, but without success.

> It is a source of deep mortification to me to be compelled to adopt such a conclusion in regard to one that I had firmly believed to be correct in such

[66] Minutes of Directors' Meeting, February 7, 1885, CFPC.

[67] Sinton, Cincinnati, to G. W. Fulton, Sr., Rockport, February 21, 1885; J. N. Kinney, Cincinnati, to Fulton, Rockport, March 23, 1885; both in FC.

matters—But I am daily finding that the interests of the company have been made subservient to his projects.[68]

Sinton and Kinney appealed to Fulton not to let personal grudges harm their business interests but to go the second mile with Coleman by reinstating him as superintendent "with such salary as his service is worth . . . unless he has committed unpardonable transgressions."[69] Fulton refused to budge from his decision that son George would make a good superintendent. The Colonel's stubbornness led Sinton to comment that the boy was too young and inexperienced for such a position. "Let the young fellow earn his spurs before he wears them."[70]

When Coleman could no longer be an officer he chose to break all associations with the firm. He sold his stock to Sinton in June, 1885, and immediately resigned from the Board of Directors.[71] Sinton now became the largest shareholder; most of the company's stock stood in his and Fulton's names.

The big sale was an exciting event, especially since it occurred in the midst of a financial slump in the range-cattle industry. A story in a local paper gave a detailed account of the sale and some information on the ranch:

Recently T. M. Coleman, of Aransas County, sold his interest in the Coleman-Fulton Pasture Company to Mr. David Sinton, of Cincinnati, Ohio. By this sale Mr. Coleman disposed of 3,000 of the 8,000 shares which constitute the capital stock of the company, for which he receives $266,000. He reserves his elegant residence on the Chiltipin, with about 2,500 acres of land. The sale was made on a basis of about $3 per acre for the land and $12 for cattle. Mr. Sinton held a considerable quantity of stock in the company previous to his purchase from Coleman, and is now the owner of about three-fifths of the entire amount. The total stock is $800,000, divided into 8,000 shares of $100 each. Since its organization the Coleman-Fulton Pasture Company have been unusually successful, and the entire property now aggregates nearly $1,000,000.[72]

[68] G. W. Fulton, Sr., to Sinton, Cincinnati, February 20, 1885, FC.

[69] J. N. Kinney, Cincinnati, to G. W. Fulton, Sr., Rockport, March 23, 1885; Sinton, Cincinnati, to G. W. Fulton, Sr., Rockport, May 4, 1885; both in FC.

[70] *Ibid.*

[71] Minutes of Directors' Meeting, June 6, 1885, CFPC.

[72] Unlabeled, [Corpus Christi *Caller?*] undated [June, 1885?], newspaper clipping, FC.

A partnership with roots in the Reconstruction period came to an end. With the deterioration of business, once friendly relations became strained and then snapped. Coleman's sale to Sinton ended an era for the ranch when financial control was maintained in the home region, and policy could be made by those who gained their livelihood from the soil. Now, outsiders influenced decisions. This transfer of authority from the hands that shaped the ranch out of the wilderness occurred as the bonanza period ended. This was truly a time of change!

IV. READJUSTMENT IN RANGE PRACTICES

DAVID SINTON sought to make the ranch a profitable business by encouraging stricter economy. Upon becoming the corporation's major stockholder at the time when livestock prices were depressed, he exerted his authority toward improving the ranch's financial position by having a direct voice in company matters. Although slow to accept the new methods demanded in stock raising, he gradually permitted Colonel Fulton to make needed readjustments in range practices. In order to consolidate his control of the Coleman-Fulton Pasture Company, Sinton chose Coleman's replacement on the Board of Directors. The man elected had a tremendous influence on the Pasture Company during the next four decades and subsequently on South Texas. This new and important figure was Sinton's son-in-law, Charles Phelps Taft of Cincinnati, Ohio.

Born on December 21, 1843, to Alphonso and Fannie Phelps Taft, Charles grew up in Cincinnati and was graduated from Yale University at the age of twenty. After graduate work at Yale, where he received a master's degree in 1867, and at schools in Heidelberg, Berlin, and Paris, Taft married Anna Sinton, practiced law in Cincinnati, and became owner and editor of the Cincinnati *Times-Star*.[1] As Sinton grew older more of his business affairs were handled by his son-in-law.

[1] "Charles Phelps Taft," *Who Was Who in America*, I, 1213.

Shortly before Taft was placed on the Board of Directors of the Coleman-Fulton Pasture Company, the boom period of the range-cattle industry neared its end. The scarcity of stock on the grasslands of the Great Plains had led to reckless buying and overstocking of pastures. As grass became exhausted, more and more cattle were sent to market to thin out the herds; market conditions in turn caused prices to decline, thereby making it necessary to sell more animals to obtain funds for operational costs on mortgage notes. Many Western ranchers were ruined, while others, such as the Coleman-Fulton Pasture Company, were severely injured. The year 1885 marked what may be termed the turning point in the industry and closed the bonanza period.

An example of the overstocking of the Coleman-Fulton Pasture Company can be seen by an estimation of the number of acres allotted to each animal for grazing. On January 1, 1885, the ranch owned 32,224 head of cattle on approximately 170,000 acres.[2] That is an average of approximately one head to five acres, not including the numbers on the range owned by others who were paying a pasturage fee. At about the same time the King Ranch in South Texas owned 40,000 head of cattle running on 614,000 acres, an average of fifteen acres per animal. The XIT Ranch in the Texas Panhandle held 160,000 head of cattle on 3,000,000 acres, an average of one head to nineteen acres.[3] Some justification can be made when one compares the pastures owned by each firm: the King Ranch with sandy-loam land covered with some grass and a lot of mesquite trees, chaparral, and prickly pear; the XIT with short grass and little rainfall; and the Coleman-Fulton Pasture Company with usually abundant rainfall to nourish the lush growth of mesquite grass on fertile black land.

Livestock on the upper Plains suffered a high mortality loss during harsh winters, but the location of the coastal ranch, far enough south to escape the extreme effects of blizzards, enabled it to have a noticeably smaller loss. The foreman reported cattle deaths to the superintendent, who in turn deducted the number on the Cattle Register. Sin-

[2] Cattle Register, 1881–1898, Coleman-Fulton Pasture Company Records (hereafter cited as CFPC).

[3] Gilbert C. Fite and Jim E. Reese, *An Economic History of the United States*, p. 410. For particular accounts of the XIT and King Ranches see J. Evetts Haley, *The XIT Ranch of Texas and the Early Days of the Llano Estacado*, and Tom Lea, *The King Ranch*.

ton questioned the low mortality count made by Fulton in his annual reports, stating:

> I cannot see how you can count them or how you can count the carcasses of the deceased. I have read Books on the subject and if my memory serves me the smallest loss pr annum in Texas is 5 per cent which is far in excess of any allowance you have made.[4]

The average, annual death rate for the first four years of operation was 136, less than 1 per cent of the number on hand. This count was cut even further in 1885 when the loss was only 121 head. Colonel Fulton believed the low mortality rate, as compared to his neighbors' heavier losses, was a result of the improved water facilities, which increased the capacity of the pastures, and of the company's practice of selling old bulls and cows "before the time for natural dissolution."[5] The policy of keeping only the younger, healthier animals that could better withstand severe weather indicated good judgment in managing the range.

To lessen the burden on the pastures Fulton began an extensive program of selling in 1885. By advertising in the *Texas Live Stock Journal* published at Fort Worth, by writing to buyers in Texas and other states, and by shipping by steamer to New Orleans, he held the increase of the herd to a minimum.[6] In the communications Colonel Fulton made it a point to mention that the cattle were improved by crossing the native cows with Durham and Hereford bulls, a policy which meant better brood cows and a better fattening potential for the steers. The range delivery prices were $11 for one-year-old heifers and $15 for those

[4] David Sinton, Cincinnati, Ohio, to George Ware Fulton, Sr., Rockport, Texas, March 25, 1884, Fulton Collection (hereafter cited as FC).

[5] G. W. Fulton, Sr., Rockport, to Sinton, Cincinnati, February 26, 1885, FC. Sam J. Seymour, Rockport, to Davis Caden and Company, Corpus Christi, Texas, February 15, 1885, CFPC, IV, 254. Fulton, Rockport, to Sinton, Cincinnati, February 6, 1886, CFPC, V, 71–72. The correspondence of G. W. Fulton, Sr., and of Sam J. Seymour originated at Rockport, Texas, unless specified otherwise.

[6] G. W. Fulton, Sr., to *Texas Live Stock Journal,* February 9, 1885, IV, 244; to G. C. Howe, Logansport, Georgia, November 3, 1884, IV, 119; to Hudson Brothers and Walton, Burnet, Texas, February 28, 1885, IV, 170; to Robert W. Patterson, Ell Passo, Illinois, March 17, 1885, IV, 296; to Buoy, Lail, and Hamm, Albuquerque, New Mexico, March 29, 1885, IV, 307; all in CFPC. Seymour to A. Du Costa, Corpus Christi, Texas, June 9, 1885, CFPC, IV, 388.

two years old, while mixed yearlings went for $10 a head.[7] The Board of Directors never approved of driving cattle to market and did not propose to begin this practice, but rather relied wholly on selling to others for trailing to Kansas. The method of shipping to New Orleans and other ports was retained.

R. M. Flautt and Company, the ranch's chief consignee in New Orleans, would send a message by telegraph stating the number of cattle to ship within a week; Seymour in turn would wire A. Du Costa, the Morgan Lines agent in Corpus Christi, to save a certain amount of space on the eastward-bound ships. The ranch needed a notice from the commission agent three or four days in advance to have ample time to drive the cattle from the open range to the Little or Shipping Pasture, a distance of approximately twenty miles.[8] During the summer of 1885 shipments to the New Orleans market averaged two to three hundred head a week. As the ranch wanted to sell beeves more rapidly to get them off the overstocked pastures, Aycock Mitchell and Company, another commission agent in New Orleans, was temporarily contracted.[9] Besides the freight charges of the steamship company, the ranch had to pay approximately one dollar a head in charges to the consignee. An example is given for a shipment of sixty-nine steers in August, 1885:

Pen Fees added in freight	$ 6.90
Transfer	24.15
Driving	6.00
Stable Rent	8.40
Pasturage	17.95
Labor	5.00
	$68.40[10]

[7] G. W. Fulton, Sr., to Hudson Brothers and Walton, Burnet, Texas, February 28, 1885, CFPC, IV, 170; to Buoy, Lail, and Hamm, Albuquerque, New Mexico, March 29, 1885, CFPC, IV, 307.

[8] Seymour to R. M. Flautt and Company, New Orleans, Louisiana, February 22, 1885, CFPC, IV, 264; to Du Costa, Corpus Christi, June 4, 1885, CFPC, IV, 385.

[9] Seymour to Du Costa, Corpus Christi, June 9, 1885, CFPC, IV, 388; to Aycock Mitchell and Company, New Orleans, June 17, 1885, CFPC, IV, 395.

[10] Seymour to R. M. Flautt and Company, New Orleans, August 14, 1885, CFPC, IV, 479.

A barometer of the deflated boom in the range-cattle industry was the New Orleans market. After a brief flurry toward recovery in August, 1885, the indicators turned downward, apparently without limit. The following month Seymour wrote: "It seems as if the market of New Orleans is going to 'the bad'[.] And unless improvement takes place soon, the people will have to go hungry."[11]

Although the Coleman-Fulton Pasture Company suffered from the poor marketing conditions, it was not hit as hard as were the neighboring ranchers. For some time full-blooded Durhams and Herefords, costing from $100 to $250 each, were imported to improve the herd. By 1885 approximately three hundred of the purebred animals and a large number of mixed breeds were on hand. Because of the improved quality, the price in New Orleans for the Coleman-Fulton Pasture Company livestock was better than that for native stock. The company's average prices appearing on the 1885 market were "$22.42 for beeves, 11.20 for yearlings, 7.50 for calves, and 15.53 for cows when purchased by the head."[12]

Drilling water wells became a practice in the Coastal Bend as the ranges were well stocked, and as artificial lakes and streams proved incapable of supplying the increased numbers. Expenses for the wells came under the heading of "Real Estate Improvement," for they were intended not only as a temporary relief for the drouth conditions but also as a permanent program for increasing the value of the land. To carry on the expensive drilling operations the company borrowed money from the Whitney National Bank of New Orleans; but, as each note came due, the corporation was able to prevent foreclosure only by paying the interest due and by hypothecating more of its capital stock.[13] The hard times that pressed down on South Texas, as well as the agricultural West and Southwest, were characterized by Seymour when he wrote that a note owed by James C. Fulton could not be paid: "Collections with him as with any one else in this Section are hardly thought

[11] *Ibid.*, August 27, September 3, 25, 1885, CFPC, IV, 486, 500, 535.

[12] G. W. Fulton, Sr., to Charles Phelps Taft, Cincinnati, December 21, 1885, CFPC, V, 11–13; to Sinton, Cincinnati, January 8, 1886, CFPC, V, 28.

[13] G. W. Fulton, Sr., to Whitney National Bank, New Orleans, April 11, May 11, 1885, CFPC, IV, 327, 351.

of at present. All Seem to be waiting now for the good times coming when business will Spring up, and money more plenty than now."[14]

The expenses incurred in providing water for livestock were rewarding; by the end of 1885 sixteen windmills, scattered over the ranch were in operation, with four others bored and ready for the mill. One well near the bed of the Chiltipin Creek was free flowing. By damming the creek several miles downstream the company formed an artificial lake without the use of a pump. Two wells that proved unfit for stock were abandoned. Permanent improvements for providing water, in addition to the wind-powered equipment, were the Chiltipin Dam, forming a body of water approximately twenty miles in length and holding above tide 500,000,000 gallons of water; the Mud Flat Dam, backing up water approximately three miles; the Puerto Dam, holding a lake covering three hundred acres; the Gum Hollow Dam, converting a gully into a reservoir of approximately one hundred acres; and two smaller ponds.[15]

The winter of 1885–1886, the worst Fulton had witnessed since returning to Texas eighteen years earlier, was more intense than that of the previous year, causing an increase in livestock mortality. The range grass over the entire Great Plains region suffered from the extremely dry weather in the fall of 1885 and the ponds, after they began to dry up, left only useless or dangerous bogs. Although cattle losses were very heavy in Texas, New Mexico, and Kansas, the death rate of the herd of the Coleman-Fulton Pasture Company was slightly over 1 per cent; the majority of the animals lost were old and weak cows that bogged in the water holes. Fulton credited his firm's good fortune to the many wells the company had dug in the pastures.[16]

The year 1885 prostrated the cattle industry. Under the prevailing conditions the Board of Directors decided that the Coleman-Fulton

[14] Seymour to Rice, Born and Company, New Orleans, April 25, 1885, CFPC, IV, 348.

[15] G. W. Fulton, Sr., to Sinton, Cincinnati, March 1, June 18, 1886, CFPC, V, 28; to Coleman-Fulton Pasture Company Stockholders, January 1, 1886, CFPC, V, 61–64.

[16] G. W. Fulton, Sr., to Sinton, Cincinnati, March 1, June 18, 1886, CFPC, V, 114–115, 281. Edward Everett Dale, *The Range Cattle Industry: Ranching on the Great Plains from 1865 to 1925*, p. 92.

Pasture Company would withhold dividends in order to apply the net income to the payment of indebtedness and to permanent improvements. The first resolution Charles Phelps Taft offered upon becoming a director was to that end. As Sinton owned approximately 60 per cent of the capital stock, he wanted to put the corporation on a more nearly solvent basis. Through his influence Taft's motion that "all further cash dividends be hereby deferred until . . . [the company's interest-bearing] debts are liquidated" was approved.[17]

A further action by Sinton was to correct the faltering cattle firm by reviewing all business arrangements of the ranch. When cattle were sold, a duplicate sales receipt was sent to him, which he checked carefully.[18] The industrialist was consulted before major expenditures were made for permanent improvements or temporary relief. Sinton halted the practice of issuing capital stock, an expedient which Fulton used to obtain additional funds for purchasing cattle before the pastures were filled. Of the $1,500,000 of authorized capital, $883,800 had been bought at the time Sinton limited further subscriptions.[19]

Transportation was a major problem that faced the Coastal Bend area of Texas. Since railroads did not penetrate that region until the mid-eighties, ranchers were dependent on the Morgan Line. Building material and supplies were imported, while livestock was exported. The Coleman-Fulton Pasture Company acted as the Rockport agent for the steamship company, as had its predecessors, Coleman, Mathis, and Fulton and Coleman and Fulton. In addition to shipping its own animals, the corporation sold cattle for neighboring ranchers on a commission basis. Actual expenses encountered, such as feed, stable rent,

[17] Minutes of the Coleman-Fulton Pasture Company Board of Directors' Meeting (hereafter cited as Minutes of Directors' Meeting), June 11, 1885, CFPC. G. W. Fulton, Sr., to Coleman-Fulton Pasture Company Stockholders, January 1, 1886, CFPC, V, 61–64.

[18] Seymour to R. M. Flautt and Company, New Orleans, June 21, 1885; to Aycock Mitchell and Company, New Orleans, June 25, 1885; both in CFPC, IV, 401.

[19] Seymour to C. H. Brewster, Denison, Texas, September 30, 1885, CFPC, IV, 540. A letter from J. C. Fulton, Rockport, to G. W. Fulton, Sr., New Orleans, October 10, 1892 (CFPC, XIII, 149), lists the capital stock issued each year: 1881, 4,718 shares; 1882, 1,062; 1883, 1,773; 1884, 1,285; a total of 8,838 shares outstanding valued at $883,800 on January 1, 1892.

freight, and driving, were added to the 3-per-cent commission on gross proceeds received by the Coleman-Fulton Pasture Company.[20]

Rates for carrying stock from Rockport to New Orleans for a time were $5.00 for beeves, $4.00 for cows, and $1.75 for calves but in December, 1883, rates were reduced to $4.00 for beeves and $3.50 for cows.[21] On cattle shipments alone the Morgan Line received total freight payments of $605,432.51 from Coleman, Mathis, and Fulton; Coleman and Fulton; and the Coleman-Fulton Pasture Company for the period 1873 to 1883.[22] When the New Orleans market submerged below the point of dullness to practical nonexistence in 1885, the Rockport corporation approached the transportation company with a new scheme for selling its livestock.

> We see by the papers that you have perfected arrangements with the Jackson and Ill Central RRds for the shipment of cattle—As we have Beeves largely in excess of the New Orleans demands, Can you give us a low thro rate from Rockport to Chicago.[23]

The rate quoted for shipping cattle by water to New Orleans and from there by rail to Chicago was $80 a car with capacity for twenty head. Seymour stated that the price was a fair one but doubted whether the cattle could stand such a long journey. However, the Coleman-Fulton Pasture Company had no choice but to take the chance, because of the low prices and the limited capacity of the New Orleans market.[24] This arrangement proved only temporary, for within a year the Coastal Bend of Texas was directly linked to the Midwest by rail.

The breaking of the steamship company's transportation monopoly on the Live Oak Peninsula came none too soon for the Coleman-Fulton

[20] Shipping Register, 1881–1886, CFPC.

[21] Charles A. Whitney and Company, managers, office of Morgan's Louisiana and Texas Railroad and Steamship Company, New Orleans, to Coleman-Fulton Pasture Company, Rockport, May 31, 1882; Charles Fowler, agent of Morgan Lines, Galveston, to Coleman-Fulton Pasture Company, Rockport, December 26, 1883; both in CFPC (unattached letters enclosed in a letterpress book).

[22] Statement of freight paid to the Morgan Steamship Line on shipments of cattle from 1873 to 1883, FC.

[23] Seymour to J. G. Shriever, New Orleans, July 7, 1885, CFPC, IV, 415.

[24] Seymour to R. M. Flautt and Company, New Orleans, July 18, 1885, CFPC, IV, 435.

Pasture Company, which had several unredressed grievances. The most flagrant injustice occurred on January 14, 1885, when a ship that was half loaded with cattle was ordered by wire from the Galveston office to receive no livestock and to hurry back. The Coleman-Fulton Pasture Company officials indignantly telegraphed Charles Fowler, the agent in Galveston, "that *we must ship,* and . . . the Captn had no right to unload."[25] The captain of the *Aransas* waited three hours for a reply, but at 3 P.M., when still no answer had been sent, he unloaded the cattle and departed in order to clear the bar at Aransas Pass before dark. At half-past three a message came for the vessel to receive the livestock, but by then it was too late.

The cattle were driven back to pasture and then returned to the pens for the next weekly vessel on January 21. The wild, frightened animals, rebelling at the sight of the ship, were forced on board. Five head were taken out dead, and the ranchers feared that others might succumb before the destination was reached. As Seymour stated, "If our shipment could have went last week, all this would have been avoided."[26] The Coleman-Fulton Pasture Company asked for payment of damages amounting to $308.18, divided thus:[27]

Actual wages of 7 men 7 days	$ 40.83
Horses	49.00
Board	18.35
Damages	200.00
	$308.18

Fowler's reaction to all this was that the Coleman-Fulton Pasture Company had allowed the ship to leave before his telegram was received and therefore it was not "free from blame." Seymour answered, "You know as well as we do that we are styled agents of the M/L for Convenience *only* . . . and that we [do not] have, and are not expected to have, any power over the ship or Capt, *while in Port*. . . . Until we are given authority we don't propose to take it."[28] Because Fowler did

[25] Seymour to Doddridge and Davis, Corpus Christi, January 15, 1885, CFPC, IV, 206.

[26] Seymour to Charles Fowler, Galveston, January 21, 1885, CFPC, IV, 209.

[27] *Ibid.*

[28] *Ibid.*, January 29, 1885, CFPC, IV, 222–223.

not want the Morgan Line to stand the cost, he promptly laid the blame for the entire mess at the feet of the ship captain involved. The indomitable Seymour had the last word: "But if we might have a private opinion, we would say that to make the Capt responsible for damages (in our case) when he was obeying orders from his superiors is to say the least 'Small Potatoes'."[29]

Although other distasteful episodes occurred, the Coleman-Fulton Pasture Company had to get along with the Morgan Line as best it could. The ports of Fulton and St. Mary's thrived for a number of years after their birth, but gradually they were eclipsed by Rockport. By the mid-eighties the dock at Fulton utilized by the Morgan Line had fallen into disuse; St. Mary's only received freight, while the Rockport wharf owned by the Coleman-Fulton Pasture Company and by the King Ranch exported commodities from the large region. The following figures for the fiscal years ending June 30, 1885, and June 30, 1886, give an idea of the volume of trade of the three towns:[30]

Outward shipments:		1885	1886
Cattle	head	4,490	4,565
Horses	head	100	......
Fish and turtle	pounds	......	208,000
Merchandise	barrels	3,455	4,120
Cotton	bales	50	......
Hides	each	400	......
Inward Shipments:			
Merchandise	barrels	22,800	21,370
Lumber	feet	619,980	712,000
Shingles		533,000	520,000

No figure was given for the second year for shipment of hides, although cattle found dead on the range or bogged down in water holes were skinned, the hides cured, and then shipped. Thus part of the animal's value was salvaged.[31]

[29] *Ibid.*, February 5, 1885, CFPC, IV, 236.

[30] Seymour to Samuel M. Mansfield, Galveston, July 17, 1885, July 18, 1885, CFPC, IV, 434; July 14, 1886, CFPC, V, 309.

[31] Seymour to Davis Caden and Company, Corpus Christi, February 4, 1886, CFPC, V, 83.

During the winter and spring of 1885–1886 the Coastal Bend region suffered from a drouth so severe that the cattle shipments were reduced almost to a standstill. The dry, cold weather completely demoralized the market and reduced the Coleman-Fulton Pasture Company cattle in weight to such an extent that it was early summer before a semblance of normality returned. Local showers fell occasionally to bolster the hopes of the South Texas ranchers but the long-hoped-for general rain, one that Seymour wrote "would be worth hundreds of Thousands to the Section,"[32] did not come until the second week in June.[33] Twenty-two windmills dispersed over the ranch lessened the adverse effects of the drouth. The company expended approximately $80,000 on improved water facilities, additional division fences, and new buildings in order to handle its livestock more effectively when prosperity returned.[34]

One of the lasting tributes to this company was its progressive, professional rangemen and cattlemen, who stayed with the livestock industry through thick and thin and who realized that when good times returned they would be in a much better position because of the improvements. The presence of wells allowed dispersal of cattle over the pastures where drinking water was previously unavailable; also the wells provided for the upbreeding of the herds when enclosures with abundant water and grass permitted planned breeding.

The ranch was also improving its horse stock during the severe winter of 1885–1886. The Coleman-Fulton Pasture Company advertised its smaller mares for sale, keeping the larger and better animals for future breeding purposes.[35] Colonel Fulton reported in August, 1886, that the ranch was rid of all its Mexican horse stock.[36]

Persons who lived solely by the soil realized that the era of the range-

[32] Seymour to James M. Pagaud, Jr., New Orleans, May 28, 1886, CFPC, V, 242.

[33] G. W. Fulton, Sr., to Sinton, Cincinnati, June 11, 15, 1886, CFPC, V, 266, 272.

[34] G. W. Fulton, Sr., to Kansas City Investment Company, Kansas City, Missouri, April 12, 1886, CFPC, V, 180.

[35] G. W. Fulton, Sr., to J. W. Haley, Cleburne, Texas; to J. W. Burnett, San Antonio, Texas; both dated March 26, 1886, CFPC, V, 159.

[36] G. W. Fulton, Sr., to T. J. Barkley, Covington, Kentucky, August 26, 1886, CFPC, V, 380.

cattle industry was over and that new techniques must be perfected to survive. Colonel Fulton recognized this fact and stated in his report to the Pasture Company stockholders in 1886 that "a radical change in the Methods of Cattle raising is now demanded in this section."[37] Stock farming with tight enclosures and with better quality of animals, Fulton predicted, would replace the open range and the inferior grades that ranchers with no regard for anything but numbers allowed to roam at will. Fulton, with amazing foresight, wrote that his corporation must look to early marketing to get top prices for its products, and winter feeding to get the cattle fat before the market was glutted.[38] On this score he ran into trouble with Sinton, the Cincinnati industrialist, whose only "cow savvy" came from books on the subject. Sinton still clung to the old ways, and it took some time before Fulton convinced him that a new era was dawning in the livestock industry, an era requiring new methods.

In early 1886 the ranch sent token shipments to New Orleans in spite of the low prices received to obtain badly needed money and also to reduce the number of head on the overstocked range. A wage dispute between the Knights of Labor and coastal shipping firms in the spring of 1886 complicated the Coleman-Fulton Pasture Company's marketing problem.[39] When a strike by employees of the Morgan Line seemed imminent in February, 1886, a shipment of cattle from Rockport to New Orleans was halted in Galveston where the animals were sold at a fair price; thus a new market was accidently opened. It became so weak, however, that only an infrequent lot was sent there.[40] Seymour, in a letter to R. M. Flautt and Company, lamented the temporary loss of the New Orleans market: "We hope Strikers will 'Simmer' down after a while, and the Market *Simmer* up so that we can do a lively business with you after a while."[41]

[37] Report of G. W. Fulton, president, to the Coleman-Fulton Pasture Company Stockholders, January 1, 1886, CFPC, V, 61–64.

[38] *Ibid.*

[39] Corpus Christi *Caller*, February 4, 14, 21, March 14, 21, 28, April 25, 1886.

[40] G. W. Fulton, Sr., to Sinton, Cincinnati, March 1, 1886, CFPC, V, 114–115.

[41] Seymour to R. M. Flautt and Company, New Orleans, February 20, 1886, CFPC, V, 105.

The Knights of Labor struck against coastal railroads, also, and paralyzed shipments over the Southern Pacific Railway Company's track between Gliden, Texas, and Lafayette, Louisiana. G. W. Fulton, Jr., journeyed to San Antonio looking for buyers, but found none who would risk livestock on the railroad.[42] The disrupted shipping activities between Texas cities and New Orleans caused a complete demoralization of the cattle trade. Persons in debt to the Pasture Company could not pay because they could not sell their produce as expected; also, the ranch was hurt financially for the same reason. Normal coastal shipments were resumed in May, 1886, when the Knights lifted their boycott, but effects of the strike weighed heavily on the Pasture Company's fiscal condition.

The company renewed a promissory note from R. M. Flautt and Company replacing the one due, because it sold an insufficient number of cattle to bring in enough revenue to pay off the debt.[43] In order to have funds to use in normal daily operations until the marketing facilities improved, the ranch negotiated a $7,389.20 loan from its Corpus Christi bank and extended the payment of its $20,000.00 note to the Kansas City Investment Company for seven months.[44]

During the year 1886 the Coleman-Fulton Pasture Company embarked on a new program for getting maximum usage from its grass. It isolated poorer grades of heifers and cows at the spring roundup and employed a veterinarian to remove the ovaries of those females. A fat cow known to be not with calf brought a higher price from the butchers. D. J. Willis, a veterinary surgeon from Des Moines, Iowa, had spayed a large number for the neighboring Texas Land and Cattle Company of Nueces County with a low mortality rate, and President Fulton tried to get him to come to his ranch.[45]

[42] G. W. Fulton, Sr., to Sinton, Cincinnati, May 5, 1886, CFPC, V, 206. Fulton to John S. Leib, Baltimore, Maryland, April 29, 1886, FC. Corpus Christi *Caller*, March 21, 1886.

[43] Seymour to R. M. Flautt and Company, New Orleans, June 25, 1886, CFPC, V, 287.

[44] G. W. Fulton, Sr., to Edward E. Holmes, president, Kansas City Investment Company, Kansas City, Missouri, June 28, 1886, CFPC, V, 288. J. C. Fulton, Rockport, to Peter Doddridge and Company, Corpus Christi, June 21, 1886, FC. Sinton, Cincinnati, to G. W. Fulton, Sr., July 29, 1886, FC.

[45] G. W. Fulton, Sr., to J. Willis, Des Moines, Iowa, January 12, 1886, CFPC, V, 38.

Unsuccessful in the attempt to get Willis, Colonel Fulton accepted the services of Louis Brandt of Myersville, Texas; but whatever harmony prevailed when the veterinarian arrived at Rincon Ranch soon disappeared when many animals upon which he operated died. "We dispatched the old dutch humbug, who was slaughtering our cows while you were here," Fulton explained to Sinton, and "engaged a Kentucky V. S. who . . . opperated on some 250, to last evening, all of whom are doing well."[46] The new surgeon, a Dr. Bailey, was paid one dollar a head for the first 1,000 and fifty cents for all over that number. A total of 2,000 cows and heifers were spayed in 1886 with a loss of approximately 2 per cent, a good figure according to Colonel Fulton. Most of the deaths, besides the inefficiency of "the old dutch humbug," were caused by screwworms in the summer and cold weather in the winter. To deter the action of the devastating fly larvae, the ranchmen coated the wound with lard and tar until it healed.[47]

When the boom of the early 1880's was over and the prevention of overstocking became a primary concern, Sinton's curiosity was aroused as to the method Fulton used to estimate the number of head in the pastures. Sinton wanted an exact count made, but the Colonel pointed out that excessive handling would damage the cattle.

> The general rule, in Texas, for estimating the number of cattle on hand is to multiply the number of calves branded by 4. In the early days of our firm, we bought herds by this rule, and they largely over run the estimate, but beeves, were not then as closely sold, as at present.[48]

The Cattle Register was maintained in the Rockport office to keep an educated estimate of the number of livestock on hand. The purpose of the record, as written on the inside cover, was "to keep an approximate account of the cattle on hand, for the purpose of valuation; and to prevent danger of over-stocking the pasture."[49] As each new crop of calves arrived, the ages of the older animals were advanced on the book; thus,

[46] G. W. Fulton, Sr., to Louis Brandt, Myersville, Texas, January 25, February 18, 1886, CFPC, V, 54, 100; to Sinton, Cincinnati, May 5, 1886, CFPC, V, 207.

[47] G. W. Fulton, Sr., to George W. West, Lavaca County, Texas, December 10, 1886, V, 514; to W. L. Gatlin, Mount Calm, Texas, February 21, 1887, VI, 24; to Sinton, Cincinnati, May 5, 1886, V, 207; all in CFPC.

[48] G. W. Fulton, Sr., to Sinton, Cincinnati, February 6, 1886, CFPC, V, 73.

[49] Cattle Register, 1881–1898, CFPC.

at a glance one could see exactly the age and the number on hand in each category of calves, yearlings, cows, bulls, beeves, spays, and stags.

David Sinton had purchased controlling interest in the sprawling coastal ranch, sight unseen, in 1885; he then decided to visit Texas to see what he had. In April, 1886, he and his son-in-law, Charles Phelps Taft, partook of the well-known and well-dispensed hospitality of the Fultons, remaining three weeks as guests in the "Mansion-by-the-Sea." From there the two men were escorted over the range to get a close look at the rich, "hog-waller" black land, cattle roundups, ocean commerce, the revolutionary windmill, and the barbed-wire improvements. Convinced that he had a remarkable investment, Sinton returned with Taft to Cincinnati via Galveston and the health spa of Hot Springs, Arkansas.[50]

One can imagine that while the two older men were surveying the vast prairie land from a buggy seat, Fulton was pointing out to Sinton ideal places for selling cultivable land to farmers on the fringe of the ranch for the production of corn, sorghum, millet, and cured fodder that would be needed for supplemental feeding of the cattle during the coming winter in order to get them ready for early spring markets. Although Sinton was not convinced at the moment, the persistence of Fulton in letters written after they parted persuaded him to sell land to actual cultivators in July, 1886.[51] Immediately Fulton made a public announcement that the Coleman-Fulton Pasture Company would offer for sale approximately 10,000 acres in family-unit sized farms.

The new techniques of range management brightened the financial prospects for the corporation in the summer of 1886. Sinton's encouragement of stricter economy had provided more working capital and Fulton's progressive ideas had paved the way to higher profits. Also encouraging were the resumed cattle shipments to New Orleans. The long-hoped-for railroad connecting the South Texas coast with the cattle trading centers of the Midwest was inching its way to the Coleman-Fulton Pasture Company's range and promised a new era of prosperity. No longer would the ranch be totally reliant on the vacillating New Orleans market.

[50] G. W. Fulton, Sr., to Sinton, Cincinnati, June 18, 1886, CFPC, V, 280. Sinton, Cincinnati, to Fulton, Rockport, June 12, 1886, FC.

[51] Sinton, Cincinnati, to G. W. Fulton, Sr., Rockport, July 29, 1886, FC.

V. NEW MEANS TO NEW MARKETS

THE Coleman-Fulton Pasture Company experienced a shrinking of its purse as the drouth reached its lowest depths during the summer of 1886. In an attempt to escape the predicament of financial chaos corporation officials announced a new policy of selling land in family-size units. The ranch stood to profit not only by gaining revenue from the property, but also by having a local source for grain sorghum and coarse fodder-feed purchases. This produce, used in a winter-feeding program, would fatten animals for markets in early spring, at which time the Coleman-Fulton Pasture Company would be able to receive premium rates for its beef before a flooded market brought about lower prices.

Colonel Fulton believed that land would sell at that time because a railroad linking the Coastal Bend by rail with major cities in Texas and the United States was scheduled for immediate completion. Farmers, assured of adequate transportation for their crops, responded to Colonel Fulton's advertisement in such an enthusiastic manner that the old gentleman felt his faith in the new project was rewarded. In order to promote the success of its land scheme by encouraging the railroad to build in its direction, the Pasture Company promised a sum of money and a portion of its property as a right-of-way to the San Antonio and Aransas Pass Railway Company.

The actual building of a railroad to the Coastal Bend had roots in past decades. For several years the citizens of this region had hoped that a means to markets in other parts of the country would be a reality. When beef packing began on Live Oak Peninsula in the 1860's, the possibility of constructing a Pacific railroad from Aransas Pass through San Antonio was investigated by an agent from New York.[1] Apparently, this representative of Northern capitalists was not favorably impressed, because the scheme was abandoned. Perhaps the excitement of a rail line from Aransas Pass to connect the beef-packing industry with other cities helped sway Fulton to return to the Lone Star State in December, 1867, for, because of his long connection with railroads, he knew what impact a rail line would have in developing a region.

In 1871 the Rockport, Fulton, Laredo, and Mexican Pacific Railroad was chartered by the state of Texas. Citizens in the Coastal Bend hoped that the railway would make the Coastal Bend an important trade center.[2] According to the plan, the railroad would have a monopoly on the transportation of goods from the harbor at Aransas Pass along the proposed main artery of commerce between the United States and Mexico. George W. Fulton was the charter president; other officers were James M. Doughty, vice president; John M. Mathis, treasurer; and J. H. Hynes, secretary.[3]

Unfortunately, nothing came of this enterprise. Not until the promotion ability of Uriah Lott and the capital backing of Mifflin Kenedy united into one project, the San Antonio and Aransas Pass Railway Company, did rails extend to the Coastal Bend. Uriah Lott, a promoter par excellence, had come to Corpus Christi from Albany, New York, in 1868 and had spent several years espousing various transportation projects.[4] In 1884 he set out to span the distance between San Antonio to the port at Aransas by rail. Landowners whose property was adja-

[1] C. W. Eggery, St. Mary's, Texas, to George Ware Fulton, Sr., Covington, Kentucky, August 7, 1867, Fulton Collection (hereafter cited as FC).

[2] *Charter of the Rockport, Fulton, Laredo, and Mexican Pacific Railroad,* November 11, 1871, brochure originally in FC.

[3] *Ibid.*

[4] Saint Clair Griffin Reed, *A History of the Texas Railroads and of Transportation Conditions under Spain and Mexico and the Republic and the State,* p. 243.

cent to the proposed line received letters asking them to subscribe money and land for the road. Fulton was asked to contact his moneyed friends to donate toward the project.[5]

By June, 1884, persons of moderate means in San Antonio had subscribed a total of $178,000 and an estimated $172,000 more was expected from the capitalists and large property owners in that city.[6] On June 17, 1884, a large meeting was held at the Bexar County Courthouse, at which persons from all over South Central Texas were invited. Fulton was urged to bring his "influential friends" with him to help make final arrangements for the proposed organization.[7] Within a short time large bonuses were given; citizens in Corpus Christi gave $173,511.20 and Bee County donated $55,930.15.[8] There is no record of the amount the Coleman-Fulton Pasture Company contributed.

After a charter was issued by the state of Texas on August 28, 1884, plans got under way for actual construction. Work began the following year; but by January, 1886, only thirty miles had been covered and the San Antonio and Aransas Pass was stopped for lack of funds. Mifflin Kenedy, Corpus Christi, rancher, came to Lott's aid and pushed the road on to completion within the year.[9]

As the track extended toward the Coleman-Fulton Pasture Company, ranch officials became excited over the impact it would have on their marketing problem. Fulton selected a spot with good drainage for a shipping pen, in the northwest portion of the company pasture, near the site where the San Antonio and Aransas Pass railroad would enter the property, and persuaded Lott to alter the staked line to pass by it.[10] Both parties would benefit from the good location as the Coleman-Fulton Pasture Company intended to send a large quantity of livestock to market over the railroad.

[5] Theodore Raziene, San Antonio, Texas, to G. W. Fulton, Sr., Rockport, Texas, January 24, 1884, FC.

[6] *Ibid.*, June 10, 1884, FC.

[7] *Ibid.*

[8] Reed, *History of Texas Railroads*, p. 245.

[9] *Ibid.*

[10] G. W. Fulton, Sr., Rockport, to Uriah Lott, San Antonio, June 12, 1886, Coleman-Fulton Pasture Company Records (hereafter cited as CFPC), V, 268. All of Fulton's correspondence originated at Rockport, Texas, unless specified otherwise.

The Coleman-Fulton Pasture Company and the San Antonio and Aransas Pass Railway Company entered into a contract in July, 1886, whereby a right-of-way one hundred feet in width through all its lands, including land necessary for a railroad *Y* at Corpus Christi Junction, later named Gregory, was granted. Suitable depot grounds, not exceeding one acre, were reserved in a town to be established on the south side of Chiltipin Creek. The Pasture Company donated one square mile, 640 acres, for a townsite and gave the railroad company half the lots in an alternating pattern. The San Antonio and Aransas Pass was to install switches, erect station buildings and platforms, maintain a railway-express agency and a telegraph station, and also to put in a sidetrack in the center of the pasture for shipping cattle.[11] In return the ranch reserved the right to erect a warehouse at the sidetrack at Corpus Christi Junction and to build stock pens on a sidetrack for the exclusive use of the Pasture Company. Ranch officials were to have the privilege of free passage on the trains.[12] The railroad company was to build a ten-foot-high dam across Chiltipin Creek to hold water. The railway and the town had rights to use the area of backed-up water encompassed within eight hundred feet from the dam, and the Pasture Company would utilize the remainder.[13]

As the ranch had the privilege of naming the town on the south bank of Chiltipin Creek, Fulton began to search for a suitable name. In honor of his friend from Cincinnati the Colonel proposed "Sinton," and submitted the choice to the comrade. "We are to have the naming of the new town, and I propose, with your consent, to repair the oversight, which you have several times reproved, in the naming of "Fulton" by calling it "Sinton."[14]

[11] Contract of the Coleman-Fulton Pasture Company and the San Antonio and Aransas Pass Railway Company, July, 1886, FC. Deed Records, San Patricio County, January 27, 1890, Vol. 8, pp. 351–352; February 18, 1891, Vol. 8, pp. 562–563; October 26, 1894, Vol. M, pp. 127–129. Deed Records, Aransas County, February 18, 1891, Vol. M, pp. 351–353.

[12] *Ibid.*

[13] G. W. Fulton, Sr., to David Sinton, Cincinnati, Ohio, August 5, 1886, CFPC, V, 343.

[14] *Ibid.*, July 21, 1886, CFPC, V, 318–319.

Flattered, but trying to give the impression of giving in reluctantly, Sinton answered:

. . . As to the Town Site, I have no objection, but as to the name you propose to give it I would prefer that you call it Berlin, rather than Sinton, and I think it would be more attractive to the Dutch, and it is that class of men you want there, but I do not think it will ever become a very large city, but I will be satisfied with any name you may give it.[15]

That was all the encouragement Fulton needed to dedicate the town to his friend. "As regards the name of our new town, San Patricio (St. Patrick) the name of the county, is Irish all over, and I think "Sinton" will suit much better than "Berlin."[16]

Fulton's enthusiasm over the establishment of a town on his property was not caused wholly by the new shipping pens that would cut the distance necessary to drive cattle for loading. He thought also that there was a strong chance of changing the county seat to the new townsite. The ranch was located inconveniently far from the county records, which were in the town of San Patricio, on the Nueces River in the western part of San Patricio County. A move nearer the company office would save Fulton many trips on tax matters and other business. The distance in miles to "Sinton" from Rockport would be much shorter than that to San Patricio, and the traveling time would be cut as well, since the railroad was much faster than horse-drawn vehicles.

But Fulton had not overlooked the importance of the shipping pens at Sinton. Months before the road reached his pasture Fulton corresponded with commission agents in Saint Louis and Chicago to set up arrangements for marketing the company cattle when the time came.

We have, for several years, been shipping our cattle to New Orleans, pr Steamer. The Aransas Pass R. R. will within the next two or three months, be in operation from our pasture, when we will seek the most economical mode of reaching a market. We own the only cattle wharf on Aransas Bay, and without our shipments [it] would be greatly deteriorated in value. We are therefore desirous of being well posted in regard to the relative advantages or disadvantages of the change if we should determine to make

[15] Sinton, Cincinnati, to G. W. Fulton, Sr., Rockport, July 29, 1886, FC.
[16] G. W. Fulton, Sr., to Sinton, Cincinnati, August 5, 1886, CFPC, V, 343.

one. Please give us all the information, in regard to expense and other points, attending shipment by rail, that your extensive business arrangement will enable you to import. Our annual shipments will probably be from 6000 to 10000 head.[17]

The answer, $100 a carload to Saint Louis and $125 to Chicago, convinced Fulton that shipments by rail to the Midwest would be less expensive than those by steamer to New Orleans.[18] A person considering costs must compare the expense of trailing to Rockport from the pastures, a distance of approximately twenty miles, with that of driving the cattle to the nearby railroad shipping pens. If an animal escaped from a drive to the wharf on Aransas Bay, the cowboys' time in recovering it was equivalent to an average cost of $2.00 a head; if not brought in, the creature would eat grass until the next roundup and thus deprive immature livestock of the extra ration.[19] To be considered, also, was the fact that in Saint Louis, Chicago, and Kansas City, the cattle would be sold immediately, whereas in New Orleans there was a delay costing $1.00 to $1.50 a head in expenses.[20]

After the ranch received information on the Midwestern markets, Seymour bargained with the steamship company, announcing that if a reduction were not made in the charges on livestock "our shipments to New Orleans will be a thing of the past." The rates asked for were $3.00 on beeves, $2.50 on cows, and $1.35 on calves.[21] Existing records do not indicate that the Morgan Line lowered its freight cost, and most likely it denied Seymour's request, for during the next two years the Pasture Company sent only infrequent shipments by sea.

During the first week in September, 1886, the San Antonio and Aransas Pass tracks reached the ranch, thus liberating it from the Morgan Line monopoly on the Coastal Bend. The company men rejoiced on September 11, 1886, as the railroad received the first load

[17] G. W. Fulton, Sr., to Hunter, Evans and Company, Saint Louis, Missouri, July 5, 1886, CFPC, V, 297.

[18] G. W. Fulton, Sr., to T. J. Barkley, Covington, Kentucky, August 26, 1886, CFPC, V, 380.

[19] G. W. Fulton, Sr., to Sinton, Cincinnati, August 5, 1886, CFPC, V, 341.

[20] Sam J. Seymour, Rockport, to Whitney National Bank, New Orleans, Louisiana, August 27, 1886, CFPC, V, 383. All of Seymour's correspondence originated at Rockport, Texas, unless specified otherwise.

[21] Seymour to J. G. Shriever, New Orleans, August 15, 1886, CFPC, V, 358.

of Coleman-Fulton Pasture Company cattle at the Sinton shipping pens. For the occasion of the first shipment of livestock the seventy-six–year–old ranch president went to Chicago to conduct the sale personally.[22] By October 28, 1886, the remaining distance of twenty-seven miles to Corpus Christi was completed through the Pasture Company's range and across Nueces Bay.[23]

With the advent of rails Fulton began in earnest to encourage hard-working, thrifty persons to migrate to San Patricio County. In a public notice entitled "Important to Farmers" the Coleman-Fulton Pasture Company stated that it was releasing pasture land for cultivation purposes to procure suitable feed, other than grass, for fattening its cattle. The farms would be divided into tracts of one hundred acres each, four lots to a block, with each group separated by a thirty-foot road affording ingress and egress to the entire area. The price, to family men only, was $5 an acre, payable in installments, with 8-per-cent interest.[24] Payments could be made in cattle feed of all kinds providing it was acceptable to the ranch, at a rate equal to the nearest market price. If the tiller raised feed in excess of the required amount for meeting the installment payments he could sell it to the ranch for cash, thus assured of disposing all his surplus. Each farmer was required to erect a "comfortable dwelling" on the property as well as sufficient enclosures for all his own animals; the company would build barbed-wire fence around each tract.[25] To discourage speculators and to prevent the rise of large landholders on its borders, the Coleman-Fulton Pasture Company restricted sales to one lot to the customer, with an option for an additional one hundred acres after two years.

The ranch agreed to purchase, in addition to corn and grain sorghum, cottonseed for cattle feed.[26] With the ability of a promoter, Colonel Fulton pronounced the land the best in the state for cotton. The fleecy staple had been grown for a few years in the western part of

[22] Seymour to Sinton, Cincinnati, September 12, 1886, CFPC, V, 412. G. W. Fulton, Sr., to John S. Leib, Baltimore, Maryland, August 31, 1886, FC.

[23] James Lewellyn Allhands, *Uriah Lott,* p. 43.

[24] "Important to Farmers," announcement of the Coleman-Fulton Pasture Company to sell land to the public, October 22, 1886, CFPC, V, 455.

[25] *Ibid.*

[26] G. W. Fulton, Sr., to John H. Roberts, Courtney, Texas, December 7, 1886, CFPC, V, 510.

San Patricio County, chiefly around San Patricio and Sharpsburg. Sidney G. Borden, San Patricio County judge and large landowner, was one of the pioneers in promoting cotton culture in the Coastal Bend, shipping bales to market from the Coleman-Fulton Pasture Company wharf in Rockport.

The railroad had multiple advantages. In addition to stimulating the sale of farms, it shipped cattle out and carried foodstuffs into the region. Products could be imported quickly from San Antonio, Fort Worth, or Saint Louis, rather than solely from Louisiana.

Cargo billed for the range headquarters in the Rincon Pasture could be picked up at Gregory, formerly Corpus Christi Junction, and freighted by wagon only six miles to the ranch house. Through the old procedure supplies were transferred from a steamer, carried thirty miles by a lighter to a landing on Puerto Bay near Rincon Ranch, and then distributed by wagon to the ranches, camps, or to the company stores.[27]

Beginning in 1881 the company operated its own stores to provide employees and neighboring ranchers with merchandise.[28] When a tropical storm on August 19, 1886, undermined the warehouse at the Rincon landing, the building was moved to the ranch. The largest company store at that time was at the Rincon, quite a village in its own right. Situated on the ranch were, in addition to the commissary and warehouses, a two-story bunkhouse with a large dining room where single employees lived, separate houses for the married men, structures for the Mexican laborers, a large house for the superintendent, a smaller home for the foreman, a company office, a blacksmith and repair shop, necessary barns and corrals, and later a school building for the children in that vicinity of San Patricio County.[29]

During the fall of 1886 the Coleman-Fulton Pasture Company made only four livestock shipments by sea and then halted such shipments

[27] G. W. Fulton, Sr., to Woodward, Wight and Company, New Orleans, June 16, 1886, CFPC, V, 274.

[28] Coleman-Fulton Pasture Company, Amendment to Charter No. 1206, May 28, 1881, Office of the Texas Secretary of State.

[29] Unlabeled, undated [1952?], newspaper clipping in a scrapbook of Mrs. May Mathis Green Watson. John T. Luter, Rockport, to Heut and Son [n.p.], October 11, 1887, CFPC, VI, 194; to J. L. Quinn, Stockley Ranch, December 14, 1887, CFPC, VI, 246.

almost completely.[30] Concomitant with this desertion of the Morgan Line was the increased billing of railroad cars full of beeves. As the South Texas animals were well received in Midwestern markets, the ranch became a steady customer of Hunter, Evans and Company at the National Stock Yards, Saint Clair County, Illinois, across the Mississippi River from Saint Louis, Missouri.

The frequent carloads of cattle, rattling away from South Texas in the fall of 1886, bound for the National Stock Yards, boosted the company's financial status. Despite the declining price of livestock on the Northern market—a drop from $20.00 to $10.60 a head—and despite the adverse conditions that generally prevailed in the livestock industry, the Pasture Company was able to pay a number of its debts. Colonel Fulton exclaimed, "I feel that we are *out of the woods* financially,"[31] referring to the increased earnings of the company for the five months the railroad was in operation during the year, and to the reduction of the indebtedness by $80,000. A somber note was struck, however, when Fulton explained that this impressive record was made possible only by sacrificing dividends for the year.[32]

Most of the gross receipts of the Coleman-Fulton Pasture Company for the year came from the sale of cattle. By comparing the prices obtained in New Orleans with those in Saint Louis and Chicago, one can see why the South Texas ranchers heartily welcomed the railroad. In 1886 for the 1,963 calves, yearlings, cows, and beeves shipped by sea, the rancher received an average price per head of only $12.86, compared with an average of $13.83 a head for 2,694 cows and beeves sent by rail. The shipment of 24 calves to Galveston, 57 yearlings purchased by the railroad contractor, and 66 head bought locally by butchers amounted to 4,804 head, bringing an average price of $13.23.[33] The earnings of the ranch would have increased if marketing conditions had been more favorable to a large volume in sales during 1886; but, as it was, the weak demand permitted the shipment of only the

[30] Seymour to Sinton, Cincinnati, September 4, 17, October 4, 1886, CFPC, V, 404, 418, 435. G. W. Fulton, Sr., to R. M. Flautt and Company, New Orleans, December 25, 1886, CFPC, V, 524.

[31] G. W. Fulton, Sr., to Sinton, Cincinnati, December 3, 1886, FC.

[32] *Ibid.* G. W. Fulton, Sr., to Leib, Baltimore, November 27, 1886, FC.

[33] Gross receipts of the Coleman-Fulton Pasture Company during 1886, CFPC, "Accounts" Book, p. 267.

growth increase while the overall size of the herd remained the same.

As neighboring ranchers turned toward the railroad and away from the Morgan Line, the value of the Coleman-Fulton Pasture Company wharf diminished. Repair and maintenance costs of the dock were too expensive to allow for a profit from other business; therefore, the ranch officials were faced with a dilemma of what to do with it. The decision was further complicated when a hurricane hit Live Oak Peninsula on September 23, 1886, badly damaging the dock and shipping pens, besides inflicting widespread destruction over the entire region.[34] As the King Ranch had an interest in the Rockport Wharf Company, Fulton wrote to Robert J. Kleberg about the disposition of the property and asked, "What shall we do with the Elephant?"[35] Regardless of what the King Ranch decided, the Coleman-Fulton Pasture Company wanted to dispose of its interest in the wharf and notified the Morgan Line that the ranch would no longer be the agent in Rockport, effective December 1, 1886.[36]

"The Elephant," as Fulton described the wharf, was sold to the Southern Pacific Company, lessee of the steamship line, on December 4, 1886. For $3,500, the wharf, cattle pens, warehouses, and one acre of ground on Rocky Point in Rockport were conveyed by deed.[37] The amount due the Southern Pacific Company for ticket sales to date, $578.82, less $14.47 (2.5-per-cent commission for the ranch), was deducted from the $3,500; the remainder of $2,935.65 was divided on a five-sixths' and one-sixth basis between the Coleman-Fulton

[34] Seymour to G. W. Fulton, Sr., Cincinnati, September 24, 1886, CFPC, V, 428.

[35] G. W. Fulton, Sr., to R. J. Kleberg, Corpus Christi, October 21, 1886, CFPC, V, 456.

[36] Seymour to J. G. Shriever, New Orleans, October 23, 1886, CFPC, V, 460.

[37] Deed Records, Aransas County, December 4, 1886, Vol. E, pp. 57–59. Minutes of Directors' Meeting, November 30, 1886, CFPC. The Southern Pacific Company leased from the Morgan's Louisiana and Texas Railroad and Steamship Company all its steamships, tugs, piers, and landings from February 10, 1885, to February 15, 1887. At the time, C. P. Huntington and the Southern Pacific Company owned 95 per cent of the Morgan Line's stock, but the steamship company kept its corporate identity until 1934, when it was conveyed to the Southern Pacific System (Joseph L. Bart, Jr., Houston, public relations manager, Southern Pacific Company, to author, February 6, 1962).

Pasture Company and the King Ranch.[38] As a new agent was needed to operate the property, the Southern Pacific Company hired the efficient secretary-treasurer of the Pasture Company, Sam J. Seymour.[39] This was a good choice, because Seymour was thoroughly acquainted with the customers and with the manner in which business at the wharf had been conducted.

Although this new position was a promotion for Seymour, his resignation left the corporation without a secretary and treasurer. In order to save money the Board of Directors decided that Colonel Fulton would assume the role of treasurer, in addition to being president, and George Fulton, Jr., the vice president-superintendent, would be given the secretary's duties—neither person to receive an advance in pay for the additional responsibility.[40] But a short time later Colonel Fulton decided that the combined office of president-treasurer should carry a larger stipend than $3,000, and convinced the directors to raise it to $5,000.[41]

Fulton soon learned that he had acted prudently in selling the Rockport Wharf Company immediately after the railroad began transporting the region's cattle to market. A wharf in the bay deteriorates rapidly, and the company's property would have been valueless if the Southern Pacific Company had withdrawn its ships, as it did at Corpus Christi upon the purchase of the Rockport Wharf Company.[42]

The Coleman-Fulton Pasture Company, after disposing of its ocean-commerce agency, concentrated its attention on the cattle business. Although the ranch was selling farms for growing feed, Colonel Fulton felt that the harvest in the immediate future would not supply the need. To provide for this possible deficiency, he proposed to Sinton that the ranch break some land and use it for raising corn and grain sorghum. He also reminded Sinton that the ranch was now training oxen to work the plow for that purpose. Fulton stated that grass was good for raising

[38] Account of Southern Pacific Company with the Coleman-Fulton Pasture Company, December 1, 1886, CFPC, V, 504. G. W. Fulton, Sr., to Kleberg, Collins County, Texas, February 26, 1887, CFPC, V, 564.

[39] Minutes of Directors' Meeting, November 30, 1886, CFPC.

[40] *Ibid.*

[41] *Ibid.*, April 7, 1887, CFPC.

[42] G. W. Fulton, Sr., to Sinton, Cincinnati, April 5, 1887, CFPC, V, 593–594.

cattle, but since a large refrigeration abattoir was scheduled to be constructed at Houston he felt that "we must prepare to *feed beeves* to suit the demand."[43]

Sinton, still holding to the old methods of raising livestock for the market, regardless of the amount of fat on them, opposed the scheme and mentioned that feed farming on large spreads was not successful even in the corn belt of Illinois, and that it surely would not succeed in Texas.[44] Fulton countered with the theory that the ranch could realize larger profits if it irrigated, using the abundant and numerous windmills, and if it fattened beef with the artificially watered grain. The beef could be sold and processed in Texas and then sent North and East in refrigerated railroad cars, an advantage over shipping live cattle to Saint Louis or Chicago.[45] A sufficient number of wells had been bored to provide water for the attainment of the dual purpose of livestock and irrigation farming on a limited scale.

Water was a problem on the coastal prairies. Without wells ranchers had to rely on ponds and streams that often dried up during drouths. Drilling equipment was expensive, and once it was purchased the men had no assurance that they could locate good water. Often they struck brackish liquid and abandoned the effort. A device invented by James C. Fulton enabled the ranchers to drill wells through the salt water and rock formations to good water and to reach a depth greater than that previously possible, thus assuring an adequate supply at any point on the coastal plains.[46] The cost of a well, complete with pumping equipment and two ten-gallon tanks, was $2,000.[47] James C. Fulton, operator of the Pasture Company's drilling rig, later quoted the standard price as $5 a foot from machine level to lowest penetration of the auger.[48]

James C. Fulton, the South Texas agent for the H. Woodmanse Company of Freeport, Illinois, windmill manufacturer, handled towers,

[43] *Ibid.*, March 3, 1887, CFPC, V, 569–570.

[44] Sinton, Cincinnati, to G. W. Fulton, Sr., Rockport, March 28, 1887, FC.

[45] G. W. Fulton, Sr., to Sinton, Cincinnati, May 12, 1887, CFPC, V, 613.

[46] James C. Fulton, Rockport, to Kleberg, Collins County, Texas, March 9, 1887, FC.

[47] J. C. Fulton, Rockport, to Thomas P. McCampbell, Gregory, Texas, June 3, 1887, FC; to Kleberg, Collins County, Texas, March 9, 1887, FC.

[48] J. C. Fulton, Rockport, to P. F. Dunn, Corpus Christi, February 23, 1889, CFPC, VII, 61.

pumps, tanks, rods, pipes, tubing, and drinking fonts. By October, 1887, he had sold 65 mills to Coastal Bend ranchers: 30 to the Pasture Company, 14 to Samuel H. Smith, 8 to Thomas P. McCampbell, 9 to the Texas Land and Cattle Company, and 4 to the King Ranch.[49]

Several of the Coleman-Fulton Pasture Company's wells provided an apparent inexhaustible quantity, in one case, enough for three hundred head of cattle.[50] Another well reportedly was so limitless that it was adequate for 18,000 acres in the pasture.[51] Value of the land also was affected by drilling activity, for the price of real estate with water was one dollar an acre more than for waterless ground.[52]

Sinton became irritated at the expense for well boring and in March, 1887, ordered that it be stopped.[53] He did not realize the effects of a prolonged drouth or the problems of the ranchers without wells. After the hurricane in September, 1886, light showers fell to keep the grass green, but they did not provide enough precipitation for the water-storage areas. Stockmen in South and Southwest Texas turned their cattle on the open range because their ponds had evaporated or had been depleted, that is, all except those foresighted individuals who had windmills. Colonel Fulton quickly pointed out that over 50 per cent of his herd would have been lost if his company had relied upon precipitation alone. "Without our wells, I do not think we would have so much trouble to count our living cattle, if the stinck from the dead would permit us to see them. Fortunately we have provided wells in nearly any requisite locality."[54]

The winter of 1886–1887 was extremely severe in the northern Great Plains, and by the summer of 1887 ranchers from Nebraska and Colorado to Canada were shipping many of their surviving animals to market, thus depressing cattle prices still further.[55] In spite of the dry conditions and the weak markets that lingered during 1887, the

[49] Letter of introduction written by J. C. Fulton for Charles F. Deitrich, October 18, 1887, FC.

[50] J. C. Fulton, Rockport, to E. A. Pierce, Brownsville, Texas, June 7, 1887, FC.

[51] G. W. Fulton, Sr., to Sinton, Cincinnati, March 3, 1887, FC.

[52] *Ibid.*

[53] Sinton, Cincinnati, to G. W. Fulton, Sr., Rockport, March 28, 1887, FC.

[54] G. W. Fulton, Sr., to Sinton, Cincinnati, April 5, 1887, CFPC, V, 595–596.

[55] Edward Everett Dale, *The Range Cattle Industry: Ranching on the Great Plains from 1865 to 1925,* pp. 94–97.

Coleman-Fulton Pasture Company shipped cattle from the railroad loading pens at Sinton and at a siding in the center of its pastures known as "Mesquital."

The mature steers and the spayed cows were separated from the herd at roundups and placed in pastures near the railroad. In accordance with the custom of the livestock industry, cattle wearing strange brands also were set apart from the herd. The Coleman-Fulton Pasture Company superintendent notified neighboring ranchers that: "We will gather all estray cattle in our pastures and deliver them to owners at Rincon Ranch on April 30th inst. Please be prepared to receive yours at the time and place mentioned and oblige."[56] After spring roundup an initial shipment of 378 head of beeves and spays netted an $18.42 average, but subsequent prices declined because cattle raisers over the Great Plains flooded markets, seeking to relieve their parched ranges.[57]

Convinced that fattened spayed cows yielded a higher profit, the Coleman-Fulton Pasture Company continued its spaying program in 1887, but allowed its employees to do the operating. The cost was five cents a head compared to one dollar the previous year.[58] As the older cows suffered the highest mortality rate, the company made a distinction for those over ten years old, sending them "to a 'widows home' from which all bulls will be excluded and the cows fatten in peace."[59] In the belief that butchers preferred spayed cows and would pay more for them, the company made these animals recognizable by a brand on the jaw.[60]

To expedite transportation of livestock and supplies to divisions of

[56] George Ware Fulton, Jr., Rockport, to T. P. McCampbell, Gregory, Texas; to Borden and Coleman, Sharpsburg, Texas; to D. C. Rachal, Sharpsburg; to Thomas Henry Mathis, Rockport; to John J. Welder, Victoria, Texas; to George S. Whitney, Goliad, Texas; to John Woode, St. Mary's, Texas; to John Linned, St. Mary's; to Jerry Driscoll, St. Mary's; all written on April 16, 1887; all in CFPC, VI, 54–58.

[57] Sinton, Cincinnati, to G. W. Fulton, Sr., Rockport, May 24, November 18, 1887, FC.

[58] G. W. Fulton, Sr., to Sinton, Cincinnati, April 18, 1887, CFPC, "Accounts" Book, p. 276.

[59] G. W. Fulton, Sr., to Jim Martin, Collins, Texas, March 18, 1887, CFPC, V, 580.

[60] G. W. Fulton, Sr., to Hunter, Evans and Company, Saint Louis, Missouri, May 3, 1887, CFPC, V, 607.

the pasture, the ranch built a pen and loading chute at Gregory in 1887. Quite a village sprang up, consisting of buildings for the Coleman-Fulton Pasture Company horse ranch located there and of homes constructed by the railroad for its section hands. A post office was established with a ranch employee as postmaster. To connect Gregory with the Rockport and Rincon offices, a telephone line was strung, and extra transmitters were rented from the Erie Telephone and Telegraph Company of Austin, Texas, agent for the Boston-centered American Bell Telephone Company.[61]

The numerous wells on the Coleman-Fulton Pasture Company range were given credit not only for keeping the cattle alive during periods of drouth, but also for preventing disease among livestock. The water was impregnated with sulphur and iron, causing the hair to be lustrous and the hides free of vermin.[62] Of all the parasites in South Texas the tick caused the most damage. Imbedding itself into the skin, it made some animals ill, cut milk production of nursing cows, damaged hides, and sometimes caused death.

There were several theories about the source of "Splenic fever," as Colonel Fulton termed the disease after making an autopsy and finding the spleen to be destroyed; but not until the late 1880's was it discovered that the tick was the sole carrier of the fever. Cattle that drank water pumped from beneath the earth's surface, Fulton observed, had a death rate lower than that for animals in the same vicinity using earthen ponds. In one of his letters he stated: "I further believe the wells have eradicated 'Splenic fever' from our pastures."[63] But yet he was puzzled when imported cattle sickened and died after drinking well water and eating grass from the same pasture used by native cattle that escaped death. One of the great barriers to the success of the Texas livestock industry was the prevalence of southern, Spanish, splenic, Mexican, or Texas fever. Prejudiced Midwesterners did not want Texas cattle to enter their own settled areas because they feared

[61] Seymour to J. K. Dunbar, Austin, June 17, 1885, CFPC, IV, 394. G. W. Fulton, Sr., to Sinton, Cincinnati, March 25, 1887, CFPC, V, 586. Statement of disbursements during the year 1887, CFPC, "Accounts" Book, p. 283.

[62] J. C. Fulton, Rockport, to John Todd, Corpus Christi, April 9, 1888, FC.

[63] G. W. Fulton, Sr., to Hunter, Evans and Company, Saint Louis, April 19, 1887, CFPC, V, 602.

that the fever would be transmitted to domestic livestock. At the same time the Texans hesitated to import purebred bulls in large numbers to upgrade the herds because those animals frequently died shortly after arrival.

The United States government undertook a study of the cause of the disease in the 1880's. Largely through experimentation conducted by two scientists of the United States Department of Agriculture, Theobald Smith and Fred L. Kilborne, the tick was found to be the carrier of the fever.[64] Tick fever is characterized by high body temperature, destruction of red corpuscles, enlarged spleen, engorged liver, emaciation, and death. A particular kind of tick known to scientists as *Margaropus annulatus* lodges on an animal, and in the process of becoming engorged it deposits a microparasite that lives on the blood cells. When the female drops off she lays eggs and dies. Her offspring feed on vegetation for a limited time, then attach themselves to an animal's skin to keep the cycle going.[65]

The Department of Agriculture, finding that ticks survived winter only in a warm climate, established a quarantine line in 1889 to restrict the shipment of Southern cattle during the hot months except under special sanitary conditions.[66] The federal government experimented with methods of killing ticks and found that dipping livestock in a chemical solution was the most effective. Not until 1906 did Congress appropriate money for a national campaign to eradicate the fever tick.[67]

One of the techniques used to prevent cattle from succumbing to the illness was inoculation. Serum made from the blood of infected animals was given to other livestock in order to give them a mild case and thereby to immunize them. The Coleman-Fulton Pasture Company donated cattle to the Agricultural and Mechanical College of Texas for experimentation and persuaded the state veterinarian of Missouri

[64] T. W. Cole and William M. MacKellar, "Cattle Tick Fever," *Animal Diseases,* pp. 310–311. *Texas Almanac and State Industrial Guide, 1904,* p. 121. Arthur W. Sampson, *Livestock Husbandry on Range and Pasture,* pp. 315–316.

[65] Sampson, *Livestock Husbandry,* pp. 314–316.

[66] Cole and MacKellar, "Cattle Tick Fever," *Animal Diseases,* pp. 310–311.

[67] United States Department of Agriculture, "Tick Fever," *Farmers' Bulletin No. 1625,* p. 5.

to run tests.[68] The ultimate goal, of course, was to find a way to treat the cattle so as not to deprive the Pasture Company of shipments to Northern cities.

While the laboratory investigations were conducted, Fulton searched for a way to sell his cattle in spite of the quarantine line. Yet he did not want to be responsible for transmitting the Texas fever to other livestock. In the spring of 1889 the Coleman-Fulton Pasture Company entered into a contract with J. B. Taylor, San Antonio rancher and physician, whereby it would lease a 100,000-acre pasture of fine grass along the Devil's River in Sutton and Schleicher Counties, approximately 325 miles northwest of Rockport, and well above the quarantine line.[69] Rail transportation was not available to the area; therefore, rather than ship the four thousand head of beeves part of the way and drive them the remaining distance, ranch officials decided to trail them. Grass and water were plentiful along the way, the cost of driving would be cheaper, and the damage to the cattle would be less.[70]

As was his custom, Sinton objected to innovations in the livestock industry. Besides questioning the good sense of the whole scheme, he expressed fear that rustlers, or "cattle lifters," as he termed them, would steal the livestock unless an adequate number of competent men were sent along.[71]

The beeves transferred to the leased range did well during 1889 and were marketed in the spring of 1890 without any restrictions from the quarantine law.[72] Home pastures, relieved of the burden of carrying too many animals, thus had room for the natural increase of the herd.

[68] Paul Paguin, state veterinarian, Columbia, Missouri, to Dr. M. Francis, College Station, Texas, November 2, 1889, FC. M. Francis, Department of Veterinary Sciences, State Agricultural and Mechanical College of Texas, College Station, to G. W. Fulton, Sr., Rockport, November 6, 1889, FC.

[69] G. W. Fulton, Sr., to Edward E. Holmes, Kansas City, Missouri, March 22, 1889, CFPC, VIII, 30.

[70] G. W. Fulton, Jr., Rockport, to Benjamin Franklin Yoakum, San Antonio, April 1, 1889, CFPC, VI, 591–592. G. W. Fulton, Sr., to Sinton, Cincinnati, April 4, 1889, CFPC, VIII, 54. According to the statement of Coleman-Fulton Pasture Company for the month ending November 30, 1889 (FC), the drive cost an average of $1.11 a head.

[71] Sinton, Cincinnati, to G. W. Fulton, Sr., Rockport, April 30, 1889, FC.

[72] G. W. Fulton, Sr., to Sinton, Cincinnati, January 25, 1890, CFPC, VIII, 227–228.

Cattle retained in San Patricio and Aransas Counties were sent to New Orleans again when the quarantine prevented large shipments to Northern markets. Rumblings among ranchers concerning the rough treatment their livestock received aboard the trains indicated that the honeymoon with the railroad was over. Railways extending into new regions had been received with open arms and were allowed a virtual monopoly on transportation; but misuse of their power made some persons think twice before committing themselves entirely to the railroads. The Coleman-Fulton Pasture Company was caught in a dilemma. Considerable shrinkage on the Chicago trip, in addition to bruised and maimed cattle, forced the ranch to try the New Orleans market again but without success. "The New Orleans market has gone clean out," stated Colonel Fulton in 1889.[73]

The remaining hope of South Texas livestock raisers was a project espoused by the Texas Live Stock Association for slaughtering and packing beeves at home. The Houston Refrigeration and Canning Committee, of which Fulton was a member, raised over $500,000 in capital stock for the establishment of a cold-storage plant in Texas.[74] By 1889 one such business, in Galveston, was receiving the products of three dressed-meat firms in Columbus, Fort Worth, and Victoria, and through a contract with English parties it was to furnish six thousand carcasses a month. Fulton's objective in selling land to farmers for growing feed was to make cattle fat for this arrangement.[75] Although these firms in Southeast Texas absorbed a large number of the state's cattle, including those of the Coleman-Fulton Pasture Company, their large intake did not cause an appreciable difference in the number of live animals ordinarily shipped to Midwestern markets on the railroad.

The hard times in the late 1880's, when cattle markets were flooded and when a quarantine line was established, resulted in a company decision to sell less than the natural increase of the herd. Although dividends were deferred during those years, large expenditures were made for permanent improvements in real estate and for upbreeding of livestock. Repaying the mortgage to the Dundee Mortgage and Trust

[73] *Ibid.*, May 4, 1889, CFPC, VIII, 62.

[74] G. W. Fulton, Sr., to Hunter, Evans and Company, Saint Louis, August 19, 1887, CFPC, V, 655.

[75] G. W. Fulton, Sr., to Sinton, Cincinnati, May 4, 1889, CFPC, VIII, 61.

Investment Company, Limited, further drained the Pasture Company's capital—and at times it was unable to meet even these payments.

David Sinton, always coming to the rescue, became more and more the chief financial investor in the ranch. The note due the Scottish firm on April 1, 1886, was not settled until April, 1889, when Sinton paid the $20,000 principal and the $10,889 interest, receiving in return a mortgage on 75,000 acres in the northeast section of the ranch.[76] The pasture to the west of this mortgaged area, 31,138 acres in all, was placed under a lien at the same time to the Alliance Trust Company, Limited, successor to the Dundee Mortgage and Trust Investment Company, Limited, for $35,000 in order to pay the notes due in 1887 and 1888.[77] Both of these claims on the pasture land were payable in 1894. The ranch's indebtedness was increased in September, 1889, when C. Lowry of Austin, Texas, granted a loan for the ranch's bank checking account. Security for the promissory note was 1,748 acres on Copano Bay in Aransas County.[78] Credit was tight at that time; and, instead of the usual 8-per-cent interest on loans, a 12-per-cent rate per annum for three years was demanded.

By December, 1889, the corporation's indebtedness to the Dundee financiers was reduced to $25,000. To remove the account from the books the Board of Directors authorized a mortgage executed to David Sinton for that amount, secured by a lien on the Cruz Lake and Puentez Pastures in the northwest part of the range.[79] The Alliance Trust Investment Company, Limited, changed its American trustee in early 1890 from the Kansas City Investment Company to H. P. Drought, a San Antonio financier. With the funds obtained from Sinton in the early months of 1890, the corporation was able to retire the Dundee mortgage; Drought issued a release on April 1, 1890.[80] At this time

[76] Deed of Trust Records, San Patricio County, April 1, 1889, Vol. B, pp. 257–259. Sinton, Cincinnati, to G. W. Fulton, Sr., Rockport, April 30, 1889, FC.

[77] Deed of Trust Records, San Patricio County, April 1, 1889, Vol. B, pp. 288–289. G. W. Fulton, Sr., to H. P. Drought, San Antonio, April 3, 1889, CFPC, VIII, 41. J. C. Gilbert, *A History of Investment Trusts in Dundee, 1873–1938*, p. 64.

[78] Deed of Trust Records, Aransas County, September 5, 1889, Vol. G, pp. 74–79.

[79] Minutes of Directors' Meeting, December 10, 1889, CFPC.

[80] Deed of Trust Records, San Patricio County, March 11, 1890, Vol. B, pp.

a land boom was gaining momentum in South Texas. Taking advantage of the tide the ranch sold sections of its property and obtained sufficient revenue to retire all its indebtedness by July, 1890, except a $40,000 mortgage to David Sinton.[81] The new means to new markets had provided an upsurge of business activity for the Pasture Company, but it, to quote Colonel Fulton, was not yet "out of the woods financially."

During the decade of Sinton's and Fulton's association in the Coleman-Fulton Pasture Company, a multitude of emotions had been experienced—apparent prosperity, abject depression, and now buoyant hope for the future. A combination of livestock raising and diversified row-crop farming hinted at new success. The advent of the railroad increased transportation and communication to the Coastal Bend, and further improvement was promised during the following decade by the establishment of a deep-water harbor in that region.

298–300; April 1, 1890, Vol. B, pp. 300–303. Deed of Trust Records, Aransas County, April 1, 1890, Vol. G, pp. 103–105.

[81] G. W. Fulton, Sr., to Sinton, Cincinnati, July 16, 1890, FC.

VI. LAND BOOM AND NEW OPPORTUNITIES

DEMAND FOR LAND in South Texas rapidly increased when it appeared that the long-sought dream of a major port for ocean vessels would become a reality. In preparation for the expected influx of homeseekers the Coleman-Fulton Pasture Company extended its original 10,000 acres for sale by 5,000 in November, 1889.[1] This expansion was caused in part by the remarkable yield of cotton in the region. The Rachal Ranch adjoining the company's pasture on Nueces Bay raised a large crop that year; but the chief demand for cotton land increased when a party of prospective immigrants escorted by ranch employees found a stalk of cotton that had grown from an accidentally dropped seed, entirely without culture, containing eighty grown bolls. Colonel Fulton wrote to Sinton that "they started immediately for their families and farm implements."[2] Following this incident, additional one-hundred-acre lots were surveyed rapidly.

In 1888 South Texans received a stimulant to their hope for a deep-water harbor when the newly incorporated Aransas Pass Improvement Company announced its intention to perform a task left unfinished by

[1] James C. Fulton, Rockport, Texas, to C. W. Hill, Alvarado, Texas, November 29, 1889, Coleman-Fulton Pasture Company Records (hereafter cited as CFPC), VIII, 179.

[2] George Ware Fulton, Sr., Rockport, Texas, to David Sinton, Cincinnati, Ohio, September 21, 1889, CFPC, VIII, 144. All of Fulton's correspondence originated at Rockport, Texas, unless specified otherwise.

the federal government—creating a navigable channel at Aransas Pass.[3] This inlet separating Saint Joseph Island on the north and Mustang Island on the south had been the object of governmental attention for decades; but, despite large appropriations from Congress and private contributions from the Coleman-Fulton Pasture Company of Rockport and Mifflin Kenedy of Corpus Christi, no significant deepening of the pass had been achieved.[4] Now the Aransas Pass Improvement Company sought to tame the Gulf waves that had washed the shifty sand from the offshore islands into the pass, thus blocking the passage of all ships except those with shallow draughts. The proposed plan called for erecting jetties perpendicular to the mainland across the ends of Saint Joseph and Mustang Islands in order that natural scouring actions would be created by the ingressing and egressing tides and a deeper gap would be formed as the sand was carried further out on the continental shelf.

In preparation for the expected business expansion on Live Oak Peninsula the San Antonio and Aransas Pass Railway Company in 1888 extended its tracks to Rockport.[5] Property owners gave one-half of all unimproved lots to the railroad firm. Requests for land quickened as outsiders rushed in to buy farm lots and to obtain real estate for speculation. At that time James C. Fulton wrote that "we are in the midst of a *monster boom* in our town and neighborhood. My lands that two months ago I would have taken $5 pr acre for are now salable at twice that figure."[6] Because of this demand for property and because of Fulton's plan to raise feed for cattle, the Coleman-Fulton Pasture Company decided in the late 1880's to sell farm lots.

[3] Aransas Pass Improvement Company, Charter No. 3724, May 3, 1888, Office of the Texas Secretary of State.

[4] *House Documents,* 55th Congress, Third Session, Serial No. 3747, Doc. No. 2, pp. 1532–1533; 78th Congress, Second Session, Serial No. 10881, Doc. No. 544, p. 16. *House Executive Documents,* 42nd Congress, Second Session, Serial No. 1504, Doc. No. 1, p. 528; 48th Congress, Second Session, Serial No. 2279, Doc. No. 1, pp. 1313–1314. *Texas Land News,* April, 1892, p. 10. Minutes of the Coleman-Fulton Pasture Company Board of Directors' Meeting (hereafter cited as Minutes of Directors' Meeting), June 2, 1883, CFPC.

[5] J. C. Fulton, Rockport, to Woodmanse and Hewitt Manufacturing Company, Freeport, Illinois, April 16, 1888, Fulton Collection (hereafter cited as FC).

[6] *Ibid.*

As realty prices soared, so did the dreams and the hopes of the people ascend to unprecedented heights. Schemes to get rich were designed, for the period of prosperity seemed assured. James C. Fulton, one of the early speculators, planned to construct a fabulous hotel on Live Oak Point. After obtaining a 3,000-acre lot at the head of the peninsula from his parents,[7] young Fulton united with other individuals in 1889 to form the Ocean View Hotel Company.[8] The organization, built mostly on faith rather than on works, resembled a game of chance. If speculation of making a fortune were the angle, then Fulton was in the right crowd, for connected with this hotel company were such past masters at the promotion game as Uriah Lott, president of the San Antonio and Aransas Pass Railway Company; Benjamin Franklin Yoakum, long-time promoter of railroad schemes and currently the general manager of the San Antonio and Aransas Pass; and Reagan Houston, San Antonio lawyer.[9] The group planned to erect a structure valued at $50,000, exclusive of furnishings.[10] They felt that business would be profitable, since the area was already a sportsman's paradise and it would attract commerce and industry when the deep-water harbor became operative.

Colonel Fulton was one of those who hoped that manufacturers could be coaxed to the area. Expecting a large city to develop in that region, he approached Sinton with the idea of having their corporation assist such an enterprise by giving land for a townsite at an appropriate location of best benefit to the ranch. Sinton quickly vetoed that proposal. Geographically removed from the frenzy and the excitement that permeated South Texans, he did not share the belief that prosperity lay just around the corner. South Texas had no industrial activity, Sinton stated; it had neither fuel nor water power sufficient for manufacturing purposes. As its exports would consist of raw materials

[7] Deed Records, Aransas County, August 5, 1887, Vol. E, pp. 115–117, 122–125; December 12, 1889, Vol. K, pp. 554–555.

[8] *Ibid.*, January 6, 1890, Vol. I, pp. 556–558. Minutes of the Organizational Meeting of the Directors of the Ocean View Hotel Company, December 4, 1889, FC. Ocean View Hotel Company, Charter No. 4335, December 4, 1889, Office of the Texas Secretary of State.

[9] Minutes of the Directors of the Ocean View Hotel Company, December 4, 1889, FC.

[10] J. C. Fulton, Rockport, to Robert Laidlaw [n.p.], May 11, 1888, FC.

the endowment of ground for the establishment of a city would not pay.[11]

Sinton was logical, but South Texans were not looking for logic at the moment; rather, they sought a deep-water harbor and good times. In keeping with the spirit of the moment the Aransas Pass Improvement Company persuaded the residents of the town of Fulton to change the name of their village to "Aransas City." Such an avalanche of "Aransas" mail followed that postal clerks found it almost impossible to send mail to the correct, desired address; finally the citizens resumed the old title of Fulton.[12] Rockport was restyled "Aransas Pass" for a short time until its original appellation was restored. Along the coast south of Rockport, directly opposite the inlet, the short-lived town of Aransas Harbor was founded as a result of the boom.

Despite the Improvement Company's schemes for promotion and construction, it failed to obtain governmental permission to carry on the work. Rather, the Aransas Pass Harbor Company was chosen. This new firm had among its chief stockholders Uriah Lott and Benjamin Franklin Yoakum.[13] These gentlemen sought to connect the San Antonio and Aransas Pass Railway Company with the proposed port for the mutual advantage of themselves and Coastal Bend residents. In 1890 the plan went askew when their rail company went into receivership.

In order to keep the work going, citizens of Rockport formed a booster club which raised subscriptions from other South Texans, and subsequently purchased control of the Aransas Pass Harbor Company.[14] The Coleman-Fulton Pasture Company purchased $5,000 in stock and pledged 10,000 acres from its Brasada Pasture to the company that completed the harbor project and maintained a depth of water fifteen feet over the obstructive sand bar.[15]

[11] David Sinton, Cincinnati, to G. W. Fulton, Sr., Rockport, June 7, 1888, FC.

[12] G. W. Fulton, Sr., to Lewis M. Haupt, Washington, D.C., December 7, 1889, CFPC, VII, 211–212; to George T. Gregory, Kansas City, Kansas, December 27, 1890, FC.

[13] Aransas Pass Harbor Company, Charter No. 4520, March 29, 1890, Office of the Texas Secretary of State.

[14] Aransas Pass Deep Water Company, Charter No. 5289, October 8, 1891, Office of the Texas Secretary of State. *Texas Land News,* April, 1892, p. 1.

[15] Coleman-Fulton Pasture Company, Amendment to Charter No. 1206, December 26, 1882, Office of the Texas Secretary of State. Sinton, Cincinnati,

Officers of the merged firm solicited aid through delegations sent to San Antonio, Beeville, Corpus Christi, Portland, Gregory, Goliad, and Victoria. At a mass rally at Beeville on January 30, 1892, Colonel Fulton recalled that for decades Aransas Pass had served as the commercial center for the vast Southwest Texas region and for northern Mexico, and that the progress of that area had stopped when the harbor became landlocked in the late 1880's; but optimistically he assured his listeners that they were standing at the very threshold of unprecedented prosperity if enough money could be raised to continue the work on the inlet.

Other speakers also exhorted the people to contribute as the frenzy heightened. The reporter covering the meeting was impressed with the response, mentioning it in his article for the Aransas Harbor *Herald*: "Thousand dollar chunks of land and approved security were piled around him [Captain A. S. Jones of Beeville] so rapidly that doubt gave way to enthusiasm and the wildest excitement prevailed."[16]

Similar evangelical meetings were held throughout the Coastal Bend. At the Rockport gathering a few days later a scene all promoters dream of but seldom witness occurred. According to the newspaperman people lined up and

> . . . chipped in again with devotion ranging from five hundred to five thousand dollars and many other citizens of Rockport and Aransas Harbor added largely to their previous subscriptions. It was impossible for any one to keep track of the donations.[17]

The generous response at the various meetings enabled the officers to raise their self-imposed goal of $500,000 necessary to start the operations. On March 2, 1892, actual work began.[18]

Propaganda issued by the deep-water corporations attracted farmers and speculators to the region. Owners of large land blocks, such as the Coleman-Fulton Pasture Company, were in a good position to make tremendous profits selling property at inflated prices at the height of

---

to G. W. Fulton, Sr., Rockport, August 24, 1893, FC. Deed Records, San Patricio County, December 24, 1891, Vol. J, pp. 586–588.

[16] Aransas Harbor *Herald,* February 4, 1892.

[17] *Ibid.*

[18] *Ibid.,* August 25, 1892. *Texas Land News,* April, 1892, p. 1.

the boom. Inquiries about cultivable land on the Coastal Bend came in so fast that the Pasture Company hired a permanent secretary for the first time in four years to handle the correspondence.[19] James C. Fulton, the person appointed, prepared a mimeographed letter giving pertinent, general information.[20] The letter stressed the adaptability of the area as a winter garden, focusing on the point that with light frosts or none at all during the winter it would be possible to plant vegetables in the fall and to harvest early in the spring before markets were glutted and before prices declined. Prospective buyers were told that cotton, corn, and grain sorghum produced record yields in the deep black loam, that the climate was temperate in all seasons because of the constant sea breeze, that rails and sails met to provide adequate, inexpensive transportation, and that sporting facilities were abundant.[21]

Fulton printed also a descriptive folder with a general map of the ranch and the San Antonio and Aransas Pass rail lines in Texas, containing the same information but in a more dressed-up form. One idea added, however, was that citrus and other fruit trees planted on the Coastal Bend showed promise of producing in quantity.[22] This crop would open up a new line of agriculture for Texans, one with large profits on a few acres. The minimum price asked for land during the boom was $10.00 an acre for farming land in one-hundred-acre tracts and $25.00 an acre for ten-acre garden and fruit plots, payable on the installment plan if desired.[23] Some of this land which once sold for $2.00 an acre now brought as much as $78.12 an acre, depending on

[19] Minutes of Directors' Meeting, April 30, 1890, CFPC.

[20] Form letter from the Coleman-Fulton Pasture Company concerning soil, crops, weather, transportation, and price of land, date unknown [ca. 1890], FC.

[21] *Ibid.* J. C. Fulton, Rockport, to L. R. Potter, Chicago, October 24, 1892, CFPC, XIII, 167.

[22] *Homes in Texas! 160,000 Acres of the Best Land in Texas Are Now Ready for Occupancy,* brochure issued by the Coleman-Fulton Pasture Company, date unknown [ca. 1891], hereafter cited as *Homes in Texas!,* CFPC. J. C. Fulton, Rockport, to F. Davidson, Richmond, Virginia, March 25, 1892, CFPC, XII, 266.

[23] J. C. Fulton, Rockport, to J. W. Ruby, Vale, Runnels County, Texas, March 10, 1891, FC; to O. E. Gosdell, Lincoln, Nebraska, March 11, 1891, FC. *Homes in Texas!,* CFPC. J. C. Fulton, Rockport, to W. H. Levalon, Elmira, New York, January 28, 1892, CFPC, XII, 213. Minutes of Directors' Meeting, January 31, 1891, CFPC.

its location.[24] Bay-front property brought more than did similar soil farther inland; smaller tracts sold above the minimum price because of the increased costs of surveying and abstracting. From the beginning of the land boom until it began to wear off in late 1892, property sold for $10.00, $12.00, $15.00, $20.62, $25.00, $31.25, $50.00, and $78.12, with an average price by October, 1892, of $13.00 an acre.[25]

The Coleman-Fulton Pasture Company invited prospective buyers to come look at the soil and to enjoy the climate for a few days, advertising that if the parties came to terms the company would reimburse them for the expenses of the trip.[26] Land agents scattered over the nation received a commission of 5 per cent for each customer purchasing land.[27] At times the agent arranged for a colony of several families to come together, something of a transplanted community, to soften the hardships of moving to a strange place. One party in Meridian, Mississippi, asked for transportation for twelve families, stating that "the land . . . is worn out and that between the Democrats Republicans and *Nigers* the people are about discouraged," and adding "with a little effort we could easily get 500 or more families to immigrate to Texas."[28]

Sales were brisk during 1890 and 1891 until the acreage set aside for sale to farmers was practically gone. By and large, the San Patricio County property for sale was densely covered with chaparral and mesquite trees; although this land was unfit for grazing, it was valuable for cultivation when the brush was removed.[29] Of the 168,531 acres in possession of the company when its land was placed on the market,

[24] G. W. Fulton, Sr., to James M. Pagaud, Jr., New Orleans, May 3, 1890, FC.

[25] G. W. Fulton, Sr., to Sinton, Cincinnati, October 31, 1892, FC; to Samuel M. Mansfield, August 8, 1890, FC; to E. D. Allen, Corpus Christi, July 30, 1891, CFPC, XII, 62. Account Land Sales, 1890–1909, CFPC.

[26] J. C. Fulton, Rockport, to Adolf Pfund, Canarvan, Iowa, December 12, 1891, CFPC, XII, 162–163.

[27] *Ibid.,* November 12, 1891, CFPC, XII, 134. J. C. Fulton, Rockport, to John C. Smith, Denton County, Texas, CFPC, XII, 140; to J. W. Branch, Alvord, Texas, November 12, 1891, CFPC, XII, 133. G. W. Fulton, Sr., to N. Y. Bailey, Memphis, Tennessee, August 28, 1891, CFPC, XII, 75.

[28] J. C. Fulton, Rockport, to G. W. Fulton, Sr., New Orleans, September 24, 1892, FC.

[29] *Ibid.*

10,712 acres were sold in 1890, 2,834 in 1891, and 1,551 from January 1, 1892, to June 30, 1893.[30] By July 1, 1893, the ranch repurchased 1,046 acres from nonresidents unable to improve their property. The Coleman-Fulton Pasture Company bought the land back at an average of $6.63 and resold it at $10.00 to $12.00 an acre.[31] President Fulton's report to the company's stockholders in 1893 listed an additional 8,000 acres added to the assets of the firm as "Acres Estimated excess by Survey," thereby making a grand total of 164,031 acres owned at the end of the 1893 fiscal year.[32]

At the time negotiations for a deep-water harbor were in progress and as the land boom was in full swing, the San Antonio and Aransas Pass Railroad laid its rails northward on Live Oak Peninsula from Rockport to Fulton and graded a bed to Ocean View at the head of Live Oak Point in February, 1890.[33] Uriah Lott, president of the railroad and vice president of the newly chartered Ocean View Hotel Company, wanted the tracks extended to the site of his proposed hotel, thinking that visitors might flock to South Texas if a navigable channel was obtained.

Where the railroad crossed Coleman-Fulton Pasture Company holdings, a strip of ground fifty feet on each side of the center track was given free of charge as a right-of-way.[34] The rail extension benefited the owners of adjacent real estate, increasing property values far above the cost of the land donated.

With the coming of the railroad and with the voluminous advertising of tracts for sale, the population in Aransas County increased rapidly. Rockport, a thriving village in the days of the packeries, shrank in size when that industry disappeared; but with unusual vigor it sprang to life again in the late 1880's. By June, 1892, when the city was incorporated, 2,500 people lived within its corporate limits, with sev-

[30] Total land sales during the year 1890, CFPC, "Accounts" Book, p. 309. G. W. Fulton, Sr., to the Stockholders of the Coleman-Fulton Pasture Company, January 1, 1892, July 1, 1893, FC.

[31] G. W. Fulton, Sr., to the Stockholders of the Coleman-Fulton Pasture Company, July 1, 1893, FC.

[32] *Ibid.*

[33] G. W. Fulton, Sr., to Sinton, Cincinnati, February 19, 1890, CFPC, VIII, 258.

[34] Deed Records, Aransas County, March 9, 1891, Vol. M, pp. 459–460; December 9, 1891, Vol. N, p. 529.

eral thousand more persons on the surrounding garden and fruit lands.[35] In the same vicinity the Pasture Company owned 2,000 acres that it hoped to sell in small units at premium rates.

After the Aransas Pass Harbor Company was given the exclusive contract to provide a deep-water harbor at Aransas Pass, it organized a company to develop the town of Aransas Harbor, which it founded in 1890. The Aransas Harbor City and Improvement Company, a Kansas corporation, by and large had the same list of stockholders as the Harbor Company.[36] The fortunes of the town were so closely tied to the advancement of a navigable channel that both perished at the same time in the late 1890's. The present site of Aransas Pass, straddling the boundary line of San Patricio and Aransas Counties, is near the old location of Aransas Harbor but was started at a later date.

Although most of the colonization schemes were centered on the mainland adjacent to Aransas Pass, in 1890 a plan was formulated to build a town at Indian Point, which was the high bluff projected between Nueces and Corpus Christi Bays, directly opposite Corpus Christi. Rarely did the Coleman-Fulton Pasture Company sell land to anyone except individual farmers, but in 1890 and 1891 it sold 1,920 acres to three companies whose business was luring people to Texas. The New England Land Company purchased 640 acres at $75 an acre from the Coleman-Fulton Pasture Company in 1890 in the M. G. McLane survey, four and one-half miles west of Gregory on the San Antonio and Aransas Pass railroad, and established the town of Portland.[37] Later in that year this syndicate of Portland, Maine, merged with the New England Real Estate Company, and the two companies united their efforts to sell homesites on Corpus Christi Bay.[38]

Meanwhile, a Kansas firm, the Portland Harbor and Improvement

[35] Deed Records, Aransas County, June 3, 1892, Vol. M, pp. 325–326. J. C. Fulton, Rockport, to J. W. Ruby, Vale, Texas, March 10, 1891, FC; to O. E. Gosdell, Lincoln, Nebraska, March 11, 1891, FC.

[36] Aransas Harbor City and Improvement Company, Charter No. 526, August 21, 1890, Office of the Texas Secretary of State.

[37] New England Land Company, Charter No. 426, January 31, 1890, Office of the Texas Secretary of State. G. W. Fulton, Sr., to Mansfield, Boston, December 9, 20, 1890, FC.

[38] New England Real Estate Company, Charter No. 591, December 20, 1890, Office of the Texas Secretary of State. Aransas Harbor *Herald,* November 12, 1891.

Company, whose home base was Wichita, obtained a permit to do business in Texas on January 9, 1891, and opened offices in Portland, Corpus Christi, and Dallas.[39] With 640 acres purchased from the Coleman-Fulton Pasture Company, adjacent to that property owned by the Eastern syndicates, the Portland Harbor and Improvement Company began to subdivide its square mile and to develop an attractive townsite under the able management of John G. Willacy of Corpus Christi, later to become well known as a state senator and to have Willacy County named after him.[40]

Colonization attempts by the various promoters succeeded in attracting large numbers to the Coastal Bend. By 1892 population of the towns bordering the Coleman-Fulton Pasture Company were Rockport, 2,500; Fulton, 500; Gregory, 250; and Portland, 500.[41] A tremendous growth had occurred in the past decade. Rockport in 1880 had only 186 inhabitants of the 847 on all of Live Oak Peninsula; Gregory and Portland were yet unborn, but the census enumerator listed 177 persons living in "Coleman and Fulton's Pasture" and 43 in "Thicket Settlement," undoubtedly meaning the Brasada Pasture.[42] Figures that indicate the size of Sinton in the early 1890's are not available.

It will be recalled that the contract between the Coleman-Fulton Pasture Company and the San Antonio and Aransas Pass Railway Company in 1886 gave each party alternate lots in Sinton. Little planning was done to develop the town beyond the few structures initially erected for the railroad and the ranch officials. When the San Patricio County Courthouse burned in 1889 some of the county citizens began a movement to change the county seat from San Patricio to Sinton, for a central location for all. The necessary two-thirds' majority vote was recorded in 1893, and Sinton became the new seat of business for San Patricio County on June 28, 1894.[43]

[39] Portland Harbor and Improvement Company, Charter No. 600, January 9, 1891, Office of the Texas Secretary of State.

[40] Aransas Harbor *Herald,* November 12, 1891.

[41] J. C. Fulton, Rockport, to F. Davidson, Richmond, Virginia, March 25, 1892, CFPC, XII, 265.

[42] Tenth Census, 1880, San Patricio and Aransas Counties, Texas, Bureau of the Census, United States Department of Commerce.

[43] G. W. Fulton, Sr., to Sinton, Cincinnati, April 4, 1889, CFPC, VIII, 54. *San Patricio County News* (Sinton, Texas), September 29, 1938 (Century of Progress Edition, 1836–1938).

Inquiries for farms came in steadily to the Coleman-Fulton Pasture Company's office in Rockport, so many in fact that Secretary Fulton went North to confer with railroad officials, hoping to convince them to advertise the Texas real estate free of cost to the ranch.[44] The railroad would benefit from transporting commodities produced on the farms. On this trip the secretary interested Northerners in the Sinton townsite development, which the ranch was exclusively promoting, as well as in the garden and fruit tracts along Puerto Bay. Since the Missouri Pacific Railway Company advertised South Texas lands more than did any other rail line, the Pasture Company directed real estate agents to route settlers over the Missouri Pacific and its connections.[45]

At the time the ranch encouraged railroad officials to advertise the excellent farming land around Sinton, it subdivided two thousand acres into twenty-acre plots to be sold to actual settlers for $10 an acre. An agent, William J. Schofield and Company, of San Antonio, opened a Sinton office to sell lots for a 5-per-cent commission.[46] To assist in the town's development and to induce farmers and businessmen to live there, a corporation was formed known as the Sinton Town Company.[47]

Local ranchers and other community residents interested in the town's growth pooled their resources to buy the $6,000 capital stock divided into $100 shares. The incorporators were George W. Fulton, Jr., superintendent of the Coleman-Fulton Pasture Company; John J. Welder, large rancher in San Patricio and Victoria Counties; David Odem, long-time sheriff of San Patricio County; Darius C. Rachal, rancher and farmer near Sharpsburg on the Nueces River; Sidney G. Borden, San Patricio County judge and Sharpsburg businessman; William J. Schofield, L. N. Schofield, and S. W. McCall, of the William J. Schofield and Company of San Antonio; and S. D. Scudder of San Antonio.[48] The purpose of the syndicate was to erect buildings for

[44] G. W. Fulton, Sr., to Sinton, Cincinnati, September 28, 1893, CFPC, XV, 241–242.

[45] J. C. Fulton, Rockport, to G. A. Hurd, Chicago, November 14, 1893, CFPC, XV, 286; to D. J. Price, Palestine, Texas, November 16, 1893, CFPC, XV, 287.

[46] J. C. Fulton, Rockport, to William J. Schofield, San Antonio, March 24, 1892, CFPC, XII, 261–262.

[47] Sinton Town Company, Charter No. 6386, April 23, 1894, Office of the Texas Secretary of State.

[48] *Ibid.*

lease or sale, to loan money for such purposes, and to purchase, subdivide, and sell real estate within Sinton.[49] As soon as the Texas Secretary of State granted the charter the Sinton Town Company bought 333 1/3 acres from the Coleman-Fulton Pasture Company in the John Pollan and Archibald Herron surveys adjacent to the town and then began promoting its property.[50]

The Coleman-Fulton Pasture Company was quite successful in its land-selling program in the early 1890's and was able to resume dividends. Although the company did not have the actual cash in its till, it possessed enough vendor's lien notes to balance the liabilities.[51] Colonel Fulton credited his company's good fortune to the land boom and to the deep-water harbor under construction, and was so impressed that he wrote: "I have long since quit looking to cattle as the main object of our business."[52]

Dividends in cash and stock for the first four years of the company's operation had amounted to 80 per cent on the paid-up capital, but none had been declared since. During the late 1880's, while the beef market was demoralized, the firm paid much of its indebtedness and made extensive improvements such as fencing, increasing the water supply, and erecting ranch buildings. By 1891 average dividends for the decade amounted to 8 per cent.[53] The officials contemplated resuming dividends when increased land sales provided sufficient profit for the company, that is, until the drouth of 1891 and the adverse following years made postponement necessary.[54]

One of the reasons for waiting to declare dividends, aside from the decreased cattle value and sales, due to the dry conditions, was the uncertainty of how to handle the preferred stock. Fulton assumed the duties of treasurer when Seymour resigned in December, 1886, and in 1891 he was still performing those functions as well as those of the

[49] *Ibid.*

[50] Deed Records, San Patricio County, July 31, 1894, Vol. M, pp. 35–38.

[51] G. W. Fulton, Sr., to J. M. Pagaud, Jr., New Orleans, April 11, 1891, CFPC, XII, 2.

[52] G. W. Fulton, Sr., to Sinton, Cincinnati, October 31, 1892, FC.

[53] G. W. Fulton, Sr., to Mansfield, Boston, December 21, 1890, FC. J. C. Fulton, Rockport, to O. Newman, Tuxpan, Mexico, July 20, 1888, FC.

[54] Mansfield, Boston, to G. W. Fulton, Sr., Rockport, December 1, 1891, FC. Felix Agnis, Baltimore, to Fulton, Rockport, January 13, 1892, FC.

presidency without an increase in pay.[55] He felt he was entitled, because of his sacrifice, to a share of the profits on his common stock comparable to Sinton's share on preferred. The Articles of Organization of the company, dated January 5, 1881, stated that the preferred stock was to get an 8-per-cent dividend before any of the common stock was considered. Sinton offered to convert his 1,135 shares of preferred to common in order to place all stock on an equal footing for dividend payments if the company would first pay him $18,646.80, the sum he was entitled to, counting the years when dividends were deferred.[56] On October 1, 1891, the Board of Directors accepted this settlement, but did not complete the exchange of unconverted preferred stock for common held by other persons until two years later.[57]

Although the market was weak during these years, the company continued to sell its cattle, sending shipments by rail to New Orleans, San Antonio, Chicago, and Saint Louis. But the number of cattle in the pastures rose because the natural increase was greater than sales. On January 1, 1890, the ranch owned 44,026 head, and a year later 46,908. In 1892 the number decreased to 40,997 head and dropped further to 38,677 in 1893.[58] The Coleman-Fulton Pasture Company bought ten shares of stock in the American Live Stock Commission Company of Chicago and Saint Louis and consigned their animals to that firm. For each head sold, the Texas ranch received a dividend of twenty cents, a welcomed gain.[59]

During the drouth the Coleman-Fulton Pasture Company concentrated on ridding its pastures of old cows and the scrubby, native Longhorns to improve the herd further by limiting it to the more beefy English breeds; thus the firm would be prepared to obtain better prices when the market revived.[60] The absence of the older stock proved of

[55] G. W. Fulton, Sr., to Sinton, Cincinnati, November 19, 1891, FC.

[56] Sinton, Cincinnati, to G. W. Fulton, Sr., Rockport, June 18, 1891, FC.

[57] Minutes of Directors' Meeting, October 1, 1891, November 23, 1893, CFPC. G. W. Fulton, Sr., to Sinton, Cincinnati, June 11, 1891, CFPC, XII, 26.

[58] Cattle Register, 1881–1898, CFPC.

[59] G. W. Fulton, Sr., to Lasater Brothers, New Orleans, February 11, 1890, CFPC, VIII, 240. Report of G. W. Fulton to the Coleman-Fulton Pasture Company Stockholders, July 1, 1893, FC.

[60] J. C. Fulton, Rockport, to Thomas Dewese, San Antonio, February 17, 1891, FC.

benefit, because more grass was available for the other animals with a capacity for gaining weight. For 5,721 old cows and bulls sold in May, 1891, the ranch averaged $7 a head,[61] a low price, it is true, but a good sale when one considers that the reproduction potential decreases with age and that the ratio of loss is greater among older and weaker livestock during winter and drouth.

During 1891 the climb of the market price caused Colonel Fulton to remark that present conditions were "remindful of old times."[62] From the $0.08 to $1.00 a hundredweight in 1890, cattle prices rose to $2.80, $3.25, and $4.50 for steers during the following three years.[63] With all classes of cattle in demand and with each head worth approximately $25.00, the ranch lost no time in shipping while the market was encouraging.

For the first time in years "brushpopping," or rounding up cattle roaming in the brushy region, was profitable. Brushpopping was a dangerous affair at best, owing to the tremendous risk involved in riding among the brambles and the low-limbed trees after a longhorned steer. The animal might turn on the cowboy on horseback, far away from assistance of other riders, and gore him or his mount. Since cattle gathering in the brush was a slow process, it cost the ranchers valuable time spent by cowboys who could be rounding up the same number of head on the open range in less time. Dry weather was the best time to go brushpopping because the animals would have to venture away from their haunts to look for water tanks on the open prairie after the sloughs in the Brasada dried up.[64]

The number of head in the pastures decreased when accelerated shipping got under way. On January 1, 1892, the total livestock on hand was less than the number for the previous year, for the first time

[61] G. W. Fulton, Sr., to Sinton, Cincinnati, May 2, 1891, CFPC, XII, 11–12.
[62] *Ibid.*

[63] Sinton, Cincinnati, to G. W. Fulton, Sr., Rockport, December 16, 1890; J. B. Taylor, San Antonio, to J. C. Fulton, Rockport, July 21, 1891; J. C. Fulton, Rockport, to G. W. Fulton, Sr., New Orleans, September 19, 1892, May 22, 1893; Special Market Letter from Evans-Snider-Buel Company, National Stock Yards, Saint Clair County, Illinois, February 18, 1893; G. W. Fulton, Jr., Rincon Ranch, to G. W. Fulton, Sr., Rockport, April 30, 1893; all in FC.

[64] G. W. Fulton, Jr., Rincon Ranch, to G. W. Fulton, Sr., Rockport, May 3, 1893, FC.

since the Coleman-Fulton Pasture Company started; the decrease was caused by the sale of 7,776 head in 1891.[65] For the eighteen-month reporting period ending July 1, 1893, an additional 8,530 head were disposed of.[66] Occasionally a train hauling cattle was wrecked. In such cases the Coleman-Fulton Pasture Company placed claims against the railroad company for animals killed or injured, stating the loss according to the prevailing market price and the total sum expected.[67] The rail line would settle with the ranch after investigating the firm's record.

To assist in carrying on its cattle business, the ranch kept on hand a large number of horses, but it did not raise them for the market as such. At times, however, excess cow ponies were sold for approximately $30 to $40 a head.[68] Draft horses were kept in small numbers for the limited agricultural pursuits, chiefly the growing of corn at the Rincon Ranch and the Pocket Farm. In the early 1890's, when farmers who bought land on the coastal plains were demanding work animals, the Coleman-Fulton Pasture Company sold its surplus draft horses at $65 to $75 each.[69]

During the early 1890's the Coleman-Fulton Pasture Company continued sending its cattle to leased pastures in West Texas near Devil's River. One group was marketed for a profit of $27 a head in 1891, and another herd was driven to a range west of Kerrville and south of San Angelo.[70] As a measure of safety to relieve the dry Coastal Bend range, the Coleman-Fulton Pasture Company in 1892 sent five thousand head of cattle by railroad to green pastures in Indian Territory. George W.

[65] Report of G. W. Fulton to the Coleman-Fulton Pasture Company Stockholders, January 1, 1892, FC.

[66] *Ibid.*, July 1, 1893, FC.

[67] J. C. Fulton, Rockport, to John G. Taylor, General Live Stock Agent, Atchinson, Topeka, and Santa Fe Railroad, Frisco Office, Saint Louis, July 24, 1891, CFPC, XII, 54–55.

[68] G. W. Fulton, Sr., to Sinton, Cincinnati, May 2, 1891, CFPC, XII, 11. J. C. Fulton, Rockport, to H. D. Medearis, Fayetteville, Tennessee, December 12, 1891, CFPC, XII, 173. J. B. Taylor, Austin, to G. W. Fulton, Sr., Rockport, April 14, 1891, FC.

[69] J. C. Fulton, Rockport, to H. D. Medearis, Fayetteville, Tennessee, December 12, 1891, CFPC, XII, 173.

[70] G. W. Fulton, Sr., to Sinton, Cincinnati, May 2, 1891, CFPC, XII, 11–12; August 12, 1890, FC. J. B. Taylor, Austin, to J. C. Fulton, Rockport, July 21, 1891, FC.

Fulton, Jr., the ranch superintendent, leased land near Red Fork and Vinita from the Indian agent in Muskogee and remained in charge of the animals during the summer.[71] To get the livestock to Indian Territory by railroad, the ranch first was required to make a $20,000 deposit. This sum was borrowed from the Alexander, Rogers, and Crill Company, Union Stock Yards, Illinois, and secured by the Territory cattle.[72]

Indications pointed to an early marketing of the cattle placed on the well-watered, abundantly grassed range, but an unexpected pestilence hindered them from maturing rapidly. Small grey flies, not known in the Indian nation the year before, swarmed on the livestock, worrying them a great deal and causing them not to gain weight as quickly as they did ordinarily.[73] Only 25 per cent of the cattle were fit for market in September, 1892; because the Pasture Company did not want to buy hay for those remaining, it sold the entire herd "at very unsatisfactory figures."[74] The small grey fly migrated to South Texas and once again the cattle gained weight slowly, but fortunately its damage there was smaller than that in Indian Territory.[75]

Moving livestock to leased ranges prevented overgrazing of home pastures on the ranch during the drouth that continued through 1893 and 1894. Earthen ponds and dammed-up streams became dry because of insufficient precipitation. Taking advantage of the arid circumstances, ranch employees repaired and strengthened the company dams at Mud Flats, Gum Hollow, Cruz Lake, Puerto Bay, and Chiltipin Creek. Windmills again saved the ranch from a large loss in its herd,

[71] J. C. Fulton, Rockport, to Charles D. Kinney, Cincinnati, July 14, 1893, CFPC, XV, 154–156. G. W. Fulton, Sr., to J. Muir, San Antonio, March 9, 1892, CFPC, XII, 243; to Sinton, Cincinnati, April 4, 1892, CFPC, XII, 282; to Sinton, Cincinnati, May 9, 1892, CFPC, XIII, 5–7. G. W. Fulton, Jr., Red Fork, Indian Territory, to J. P. Hickinson, Jr., San Antonio, April 21, 1892, CFPC, X, 423.

[72] G. W. Fulton, Jr., Red Fork, Indian Territory, to Alexander, Rogers, and Crill Company, Saint Clair County, Illinois, May 23, 1892, CFPC, X, 454.

[73] J. C. Fulton, Portland, to G. W. Fulton, Sr., Rockport, May 25, 1893, FC. G. W. Fulton, Jr., Red Fork, Indian Territory, to G. W. Fulton, Sr., Rockport, September 13, 1892, FC.

[74] G. W. Fulton, Jr., Red Fork, Indian Territory, to G. W. Fulton, Sr., New Orleans, September 13, 1892, FC. Report of G. W. Fulton to the Coleman-Fulton Pasture Company Stockholders, July 1, 1893, FC.

[75] J. C. Fulton, Portland, to G. W. Fulton, Sr., Rockport, May 25, 1893, FC.

but neighboring stockmen were not so well prepared. The corporation estimated its loss during the dry winter of 1893–1894 at three thousand head, principally old cows and young cows with calves; but, as James C. Fulton admitted, this loss was "light compared to that of our neighbors owing to the fact of our having an abundance of water over our Pastures."[76]

Thousands of cattle were shipped to Indian Territory in early 1894 as the South Texas range gave out completely—then the rains came. James C. Fulton gave a dramatic account of the end of the drouth in his letter to Charles P. Taft: "Driscoll had forty-two Car loads at Corpus Christi just ready to ship when the rain came So after arranging satisfactionable with the Ry. people for expense Moving train he drove his cattle back to his pasture."[77]

When the Southwest was in the midst of the drouth, the federal government attempted to offset nature by producing precipitation with blasting powder. Senator Charles B. Farwell of Illinois, XIT Ranch cofounder, who was long interested in artificially produced rainfall by concussion, obtained $9,000 from Congress for experimentation.[78] In March, 1891, the Department of Agriculture started preparatory work, but needed a site to make the test. Rainy Washington was not a likely place. After invitations from many regions an offer by Nelson Morris of Chicago, owner of a ranch near Midland, Texas, was accepted. In August, 1891, in the middle of parched West Texas, a shower of one and one-half inches fell after dynamite-filled balloons were floated up into thin clouds passing harmlessly overhead.[79] The government crew moved to El Paso in September, 1891, and produced—or coincided with—a good soaking rain which fell on the town as well as on the country down the Rio Grande Valley.[80]

[76] J. C. Fulton, Rockport, to Joseph N. Kinney, Cincinnati, April 13, 1895, CFPC, XVI, 292–293.

[77] J. C. Fulton, Rockport, to Charles Phelps Taft, Cincinnati, April 7, 1894, CFPC, XVI, 122–123.

[78] *Senate Executive Documents,* 52nd Congress, First Session, Serial No. 2900, Doc. No. 45, p. 3. Charles Dudley Eaves and C. A. Hutchinson in *Post City, Texas: C. W. Post's Colonizing Activities in West Texas* reports that $19,000 was appropriated (p. 26).

[79] *Senate Executive Documents,* 52nd Congress, First Session, Serial No. 2900, Doc. No. 45, pp. 10 ff.

[80] *Ibid.*

An observer at the El Paso experiment was George W. Fulton, Jr., who represented a committee comprising officials of the Coleman-Fulton Pasture Company, Robert J. Kleberg of the King Ranch, and N. G. Collins, rancher at San Diego, Texas. That group of Coastal Bend ranchers invited the rain makers to come to their parched area; when they were told that federal funds were expended, they agreed to underwrite all costs. At Corpus Christi on September 26 bombs lifted into the air by balloons exploded as a cloud passed by. A heavy rain fell where no rain was falling before the concussion. After the Corpus Christi area became too wet for further tests, the crew sought a drier region.

On September 28, 1891, the equipment was set up at San Diego, fifty-five miles west of Corpus Christi, where the drouth was extremely severe. Just when the trial was about to begin, a dry norther blew in. One week later the wind returned from the south bringing with it small clouds from the Gulf. On October 10 the crew started to work. Balloons laden with bombs were anchored, six hydrogen generators were turned on, large stacks of dynamite were ready for detonation, the army from Fort Bliss placed mortars and cannons in position—at 9:45 P.M. on October 17, just as a little white cloud passed overhead, all hell broke loose. The night was lighted by the explosions, the ground was shaken for miles around, spectators became frightened and scurried home; but, before the night was over, one-half inch of precipitation fell on the embattled area, with several inches falling on the desert region southwest of San Diego toward Laredo.[81]

More precipitation would have occurred had not a norther blown in at the climax of the bombardment, shifting the rain clouds away. Skeptics claimed the norther brought the moisture, but those who believed in artificial rain making quickly pointed out that on the entire Texas plains the rain fell only where the tests were conducted. The financial supporters, Fulton, Kleberg, and Collins, agreed that their $1,533.52 was spent satisfactorily and that the trial was successful in producing rain artificially.[82] After the government funds and private subsidies were exhausted the Department of Agriculture team returned to Washington, and it conducted no further tests in South Texas.

The Coleman-Fulton Pasture Company, not wishing to be reliant

[81] *Ibid.* [82] *Ibid.*

completely on nature or on concussion for its water supply, began looking for other means to supplement its windmills. The success of D. M. O'Connor, Refugio County rancher, and of other persons over the state in discovering artesian water led the ranch to purchase artesian-well machinery. In the summer of 1892 the American Well Works of Aurora, Illinois, sold the ranch drilling equipment for $6,902.14;[83] the American Tube and Iron Company of Saint Louis provided well casings for $5,367.01.[84] When the shipment reached Gregory that winter, it was assembled at the Doyle Water Hole Farm, west of Portland on Nueces Bay. Actual drilling began on January 12, 1893.[85]

To a prospective buyer of company land, James C. Fulton, in charge of the operation, stated that

> . . . our object is to Irrigate our Bay Shore lands thereby eliminating all elements of uncertainty on act. of lack of Rainfall. Our lands on Nueces Bay are beautifully located being from 30′ to 50′ above the sea level and are mostly a deep black sand loam unsurpassed for fertility. We propose if successful in getting flowing water of suitable quality for Irrigation to cut these lands up into small tracts and shape it for fruit & garden lands and we feel safe in saying these lands with Irrigation will produce $250 to $300 or more per acre per annum with certainty.[86]

The drilling expenses were so great that the Coleman-Fulton Pasture Company contemplated increasing the price of its irrigated land to $100 an acre.

Fulton was successful in striking a strong flow of good water at 1,006 feet after six weeks' work, but before the strainer was inserted to wash out and to develop the well the casing broke 530 feet down.[87] The company salvaged that much of the tubing and began a new hole nearby

[83] J. C. Fulton, Rockport, to American Well Works, Aurora, Illinois, November 11, 1892, CFPC, XIII, 177. Report of G. W. Fulton to the Coleman-Fulton Pasture Company Stockholders, July 1, 1893, FC.

[84] J. C. Fulton, Rockport, to James B. Myers, American Tube and Iron Company, Saint Louis, Missouri, October 13, 1892, CFPC, XIII, 154. Report of G. W. Fulton to the Coleman-Fulton Pasture Company Stockholders, July 1, 1893, FC.

[85] J. C. Fulton, Rockport, to H. C. Clybourn, River Forest, Florida, January 11, 1893, CFPC, XIII, 241–242.

[86] *Ibid.*

[87] J. C. Fulton, Rockport, to James B. Myers, American Tube and Iron Company, Saint Louis, Missouri, February 24, March 25, 1893, CFPC, XV, 18, 44.

on March 25. On April 25, 1893, the bit was down 1,130 feet when water came gushing out stronger than it did at the first well. Remarkable features about this well, according to the driller, were:

> The 7″ casing is intensly Magnetic and there is an increasing flow of natural gass.—so much so that the water has the appearance of a vessel of boiling water I applied a light to it and the flame shoots up a foot or two and burns right along—. . . If the gass continues to increase with the full flow of water it will be valuable.[88]

Both the hydrogen gas and this second well were abandoned, for the gas was not in commercial quantity and hot salt water had seeped into the well and ruined it for all drinking-water purposes.[89] Excluding equipment, the cost of drilling the two shafts was one dollar a foot, and James C. Fulton believed this figure could be reduced on further tests.[90] On the suggestion of the ranch superintendent, George W. Fulton, Jr., the equipment was moved to Rincon Ranch, across Copano Bay from the site of D. M. O'Connor's three good artesian wells.

When Sinton learned of the two failures and of the cost of machinery, he fired a letter of protest to Colonel Fulton concerning the increased indebtedness.

> I cannot perceive any sufficient reason for the purchase of the above very expensive machinery etc. unless you intended to get up outside of the Company the business of boring Artesian wells For experimental purposes you could have employed persons who are engaged in this kind of business, and in my opinion at a much less cost than you have paid for simply boring without considering the cost of machinery, etc.[91]

He rambled on, remarking that there were no mountain ranges in the vicinity of the ranch which could provide a large artesian-water supply and surely not a supply sufficient for irrigation.

Since Colonel Fulton was severely ill when Sinton's letter arrived, James C. Fulton inherited the task of replying to the person who owned 51 per cent of the company's capital stock. As company secretary and

[88] J. C. Fulton, Portland, to G. W. Fulton, Sr., Rockport, April 26, 1893, FC.
[89] G. W. Fulton, Jr., Portland, to G. W. Fulton, Sr., Rockport, April 30, 1893, FC. J. C. Fulton, Portland, to G. W. Fulton, Sr., Rockport, April 30, 1893, FC.
[90] J. C. Fulton, Portland, to G. W. Fulton, Sr., Rockport, April 30, 1893, FC.
[91] Sinton, Cincinnati, to G. W. Fulton, Sr., Rockport, August 24, 1893, FC.

driller, young Fulton had been most responsible for persuading the Board of Directors to purchase the equipment. He wrote Sinton that obviously he did not realize the potentials of water wells on the Coastal Bend. The three O'Connor wells were flowing at a rate of 100,000, 200,000, and 500,000 gallons per day, respectively.[92] A wrong-sized strainer had been erroneously placed in the last well; otherwise it would flow at approximately 2,000,000 gallons a day.[93] Fulton pointed out that visible mountain ranges were not essential in Texas, mentioning the great volume of artesian water obtained in San Antonio and Waco.[94]

Progress was rapid on the third Coleman-Fulton Pasture Company well; by July 1, 1893, the depth was 1,172 feet, where the workers reached the same red-clay formation under which the O'Connor Ranch tapped good water. In the midst of the excitement about striking a flow at any time, the experiment was brought to a halt in September because the pond used in the drilling ran dry, forcing the crew to wait for rain to fill the tank.[95] Not until the following spring did a sufficient amount of rain fall to allow work to be resumed, but by then company policy was changed, no longer emphasizing artesian wells. The Pasture Company was unable to provide irrigation facilities for its purchasers of farming land, but it arranged other services.

Colonel Fulton's original purpose in disposing of land was to make certain the ranch would have a supply of grain for cattle feed. When an unexpected number of buyers appeared during the boom, the Coleman-Fulton Pasture Company permitted cotton cultivation on land it sold, agreeing at the same time to buy cottonseed for livestock rations. To stimulate the new industry, company officials in 1890 purchased one-half interest in a cotton gin. James C. Fulton arranged with B. A. Cross, a salesman, to transport a double gin in good running order to Gregory. A twenty-horsepower engine and boiler, a fifty-saw gin, a seventy-saw gin with condenser, a double-screw steam press, four-ton scales, a baler, and sixty feet of shafting one and 15/16 inches wide with suf-

[92] J. C. Fulton, Rockport, to Sinton, Cincinnati, September 1, 1893, CFPC, XV, 198–201.

[93] *Ibid.*

[94] *Ibid.*

[95] J. C. Fulton, Rockport, to J. I. Kirksey, Hillsboro, Texas, October 2, 1893, CFPC, XV, 247.

ficient belting for the machinery were valued at $2,800.[96] Cross was to be paid in land at the rate of $8 an acre after the machinery was delivered.[97]

Company records show no further mention of Cross or his gin, but Harrell and Boswell of Grandview, Texas, a partnership that erected the gin, might have been hired by Cross, or, on the other hand, might have bought his interest in the affair. The Coleman-Fulton Pasture Company signed a contract with Harrell and Boswell on May 28, 1891, to assemble the Gregory gin.[98] The agreement provided for the sale of four hundred acres of land, and also for a subsidy of $1,000 of the vendor's lien notes and $500 in Gregory lots. The Gregory subsidy was later changed, at Harrell and Boswell's request, to fifty acres or $500 of vendor's lien notes on land.[99] The gin, completed in September, 1891, could process ten bales a day, sufficient to handle the cotton grown in its neighborhood. Its capacity was to be twenty-five bales a day during the following year; indeed, it would be essential to meet that volume within six years before the $1,500 note held by the Coleman-Fulton Pasture Company would be cancelled.[100]

Emphasizing that cotton productivity was assured and that a gin had been constructed, the Coleman-Fulton Pasture Company immediately advertised to prospective buyers of its land the advantages of growing the fleecy staple along the coast. In addition to the benefit of having increased yields, freight costs for transporting cotton bales to tidewater were cheap. From the Coleman-Fulton Pasture Company region the charge was $1 a bale; from other points, such as Waco and Dallas, it was from $3.50 to $4.50 a bale.[101] Cultivators in the Gregory and Portland neighborhood quickly devoted more acreage to cotton production. James C. Fulton stated that there were 1,200 bales shipped

[96] Agreement between B. A. Cross and J. C. Fulton for Coleman-Fulton Pasture Company, witnessed by William C. Horgan, September 15, 1890, FC.

[97] *Ibid.*

[98] J. C. Fulton, Rockport, to Taft, Cincinnati, April 25, 1894, CFPC, XVI, 142; May 8, 1894, CFPC, XVI, 152.

[99] *Ibid.*, May 8, 1894, CFPC, XVI, 152.

[100] *Ibid.*, April 25, 1894, CFPC, XVI, 142; to L. H. Harrell, Nathan, Texas, January 20, 1895, CFPC, XVI, 234; to J. A. Harrell, Gregory, Texas, December 4, 1894, CFPC, XVI, 211.

[101] J. C. Fulton, Rockport, to Sinton, Cincinnati, September 1, 1893, CFPC, XV, 202–203.

from Portland the year after the gin owned jointly by the Coleman-Fulton Pasture Company and Harrell and Boswell began operation; he estimated that the 1893 crop would produce 3,000 to 5,000 bales and that at least one-third of it would be on lands sold by the Pasture Company.[102] This style of information undoubtedly persuaded many persons to come, look, and buy.

With money from land sales as well as that gained from the rise in cattle prices, the Coleman-Fulton Pasture Company met notes held by C. Lowry of Austin and by David Sinton.[103] The debt to Sinton was not paid off, however, for the company still owed him $18,646.80 payable in 1893.[104]

In the early 1890's the Coleman-Fulton Pasture Company performed various minor progressive measures that were indicative of the foresightedness of its officials. Believing good roads to be a prime necessity in an agricultural community, the ranch purchased a road-making machine that constructed access roads around the tracts sold to farmers. Increased prices for land during the boom returned manifold the company's investment in improving the lanes.[105] A hotel for use of prospective buyers while looking over the company's land, the Immigrants' Home, was built in Gregory at a cost of $1,087.21, surely a welcome place of rest for weary homeseekers.[106]

Some steps were taken to improve communications and transportation in the Coastal Bend. One big stride was purchasing the Rockport telephone exchange for $250 in order to have a continuous line from Rockport to Gregory. This provision left an eleven-mile gap in telephone connections between the ranch and Corpus Christi, the commercial and financial center of the Coastal Bend.[107]

Progressive action by the Coleman-Fulton Pasture Company in offer-

102 *Ibid.*

103 Deed of Trust Records, San Patricio County, September 12, 1891, Vol. B, pp. 441–442. Deed Records, Aransas County, December 12, 1892, Vol. O, p. 551.

104 Sinton, Cincinnati, to G. W. Fulton, Sr., Rockport, July 15, 1893, FC.

105 G. W. Fulton, Sr., to Mansfield, Boston, December 21, 1890, FC.

106 Report of G. W. Fulton to the Coleman-Fulton Pasture Company Stockholders, July 1, 1893, FC.

107 G. W. Fulton, Jr., Rincon Ranch, to L. C. Baker, Saint Louis, Missouri, December 23, 1890, CFPC, IX, 386; December 27, 1890 (telegram), CFPC, IX, 387.

ing a bonus for a second rail line through its range promoted additional transportational facilities in South Texas. The Saint Louis, Brownsville, and Mexico Railway Company, known also as the Pan American, surveyed a route southwest from Sinton that traversed Brasada Pasture. Landowners over whose property the road was to pass, encouraged by the prospects of real-estate-value increases, made donations to the Pan American. In 1891 the Pasture Company agreed to contribute $7,500 in eight equal installments for each ten miles of completed road from Victoria.[108] A main function of the corporation was to raise cattle and to market them as inexpensively as possible. With two railroads in the region perhaps competition would improve facilities on the San Antonio and Aransas Pass.

The ranchers in the region built enclosures to keep livestock in the proper pasture: partition fences, separating pastures on the ranch, and division fences, designating the boundaries of the property. When division fences needed repairing, range custom dictated that the owners of the adjacent lands each share equally in the expense. One such case was the entire rebuilding of the fence between the Coleman-Fulton Pasture Company and the T. P. McCampbell Ranch in February, 1893, when each paid one-half of the $471.99 repair bill.[109] To keep its enclosures intact, each firm employed persons to ride around the various fence lines, repairing gaps where they found them.

There were other men with specific functions; all together they made up a self-contained ranch. In November, 1893, George W. Fulton, Jr., estimated that the cost of labor required to conduct a purely livestock business upon the property of the Coleman-Fulton Pasture Company plus the wages paid each laborer was approximately $650 a month. The accompanying figures for ranch expenses were subject to variations in emergencies, but are in the main correct.[110]

[108] J. C. Fulton, Rockport, to A. Pfund, Canarvan, Iowa, December 12, 1891, CFPC, XII, 162. Report of G. W. Fulton to the Coleman-Fulton Pasture Company Stockholders, January 1, 1892, FC.

[109] Charles E. H. Glazbrook, Rincon Ranch, to Thomas P. McCampbell, Gregory, Texas, February 7, 1893, CFPC, XIV, 163.

[110] G. W. Fulton, Jr., to [unknown], November 23, 1893, CFPC, XIV, 371–372.

FOUNDERS AND DEVELOPERS OF THE FAMOUS TAFT PROPERTIES

TAFT FARMS

San Patricio County, Texas

"THE subdividing of a limited area of these world-famous farm lands, and the sale of these tracts upon a Ten Year plan, is without question, the greatest opportunity that has been offered to farmers and live stock raisers during the present generation—"

—*Coleman-Fulton Pasture Co.*

Where Permanent Prosperity Rewards Honest Effort

The Taft Ranch is a Two-Hundred-And-Fifty Thousand Acre Monument to Nature's Riches and Man's Honest Toil.

There is no room or welcome at Taft for the drone or for the "Get-Rich-Quick" prospector. The honest, clean-living, industrious toiler who seeks happiness, health and prosperity in return for his investment of dollars and energy will find them at Taft.

Courtesy Edward N. Tutt, Taft

Taft Ranch brochure, issued by the J. H. Kirkpatrick Company, San Antonio, which was commissioned to conduct the sale of farm lands and town lots in Taft, Texas, June 1, 1921.

Courtesy Mrs. May Mathis Green Watson, Corpus Christi

Cattle roundup at Rincon Ranch. Note the flat prairie land in the background.

Courtesy Mrs. May Mathis Green Watson, Corpus Christi

One of the several dipping vats used by the Taft Ranch in its fight against the mange mite and the fever tick.

Photo by Burton & Danforth, Courtesy Mrs. Dalton Green, Taft

Dipping vat at Rincon Ranch. President William Howard Taft and Joseph French Green are standing inside the fence, to the right.

Photo by Burton & Danforth, Courtesy Mrs. Dalton Green, Taft

Inspection of lands on Rincon Ranch by President Taft, 1909. Charles Phelps Taft, wearing a white suit, sits in the buggy. President Taft, on horseback, wears a Panama hat. Joseph French Green is to the President's left. From here the President joined the Taft Ranch cowboys in a roundup.

Photos by Burton & Danforth, Courtesy Mrs. Dalton Green, Taft

Two views of President Taft admiring the Taft Ranch prize bulls. The animals are tied to the fence so that the President may carefully inspect them individually.

Photo by Burton & Danforth, Courtesy Mrs. Dalton Green, Taft

Three ladies, who put on a riding exhibition for President Taft, pose in front of Rincon Ranch headquarters. Reading from left to right the three young ladies are Mary Oliver (later Mrs. Mary Williams), unidentified woman who was a member of a rodeo team, and Minnie Oliver (later Mrs. D. W. Buckley).

Photo by Burton & Danforth, Courtesy Mrs. Dalton Green, Taft

President Taft and party at Rincon Ranch headquarters. The bearded Charles Phelps Taft, wearing a white suit, stands slightly to the left. President Taft stands in the middle. Manager William Oliver, holding his hat, stands at the extreme left in white shirt.

Courtesy Ernest Guedin, Taft

Giant Hart-Parr tractor pulling a breaking plow, 1912.

Courtesy Mrs. May Mathis Green Watson, Corpus Christi

Farm workers picking cotton on one of the company farms. Note the productive yield from the fertile soil.

Courtesy Mrs. May Mathis Green Watson, Corpus Christi

Industrial site at Taft, Texas, around 1920.

Courtesy E. W. Sandars, Taft

Main Street in Gregory, Texas, 1914, showing Pasture Company garage, the Green Hotel, two-story brick building used as a bank, mercantile store, offices, and gathering place for public meetings.

Courtesy Jack L. Baughman, Rockport

Fulton Mansion, Fulton, Texas.

Courtesy Mrs. Maurice W. Cochran, Fulton

Coleman Mansion, Coleman Ranch, on Chiltipin Creek.

Courtesy Mrs. May Mathis Green Watson, Corpus Christi

La Quinta, home of Joseph French Green, Taft Ranch superintendent, 1907–1926. This impressive structure, on Corpus Christi Bay, was completed in 1907. President Taft stayed at

Photos Courtesy Mrs. May Mathis Green Watson, Corpus Christi

Wedding pictures of Mr. and Mrs. Joseph French Green, 1907.

From *Taft Farms* Brochure, *Courtesy Edward N. Tutt, Taft*

Charles Phelps Taft, half-brother of William Howard Taft, became a dominant policy maker in Coleman-Fulton Pasture Company affairs in 1885 and served as president from 1894 until shortly before his death in 1929.

From Daniell's "Personnel of the Texas State Government"
Courtesy University of Texas Library

Colonel George Ware Fulton, a founder of the original Coleman, Mathis, and Fulton firm, and president of the Coleman-Fulton Pasture Company from 1881 until his death in 1893.

Courtesy Philosophical and Historical Society of Ohio

David Sinton, Cincinnati financier who was the majority stockholder of the Coleman-Fulton Pasture Company from 1885 until his death in 1900.

From Daniell's, "Personnel of the Texas State Government," courtesy University of Texas Library

Thomas Henry Mathis, member of the original Coleman, Mathis, and Fulton firm.

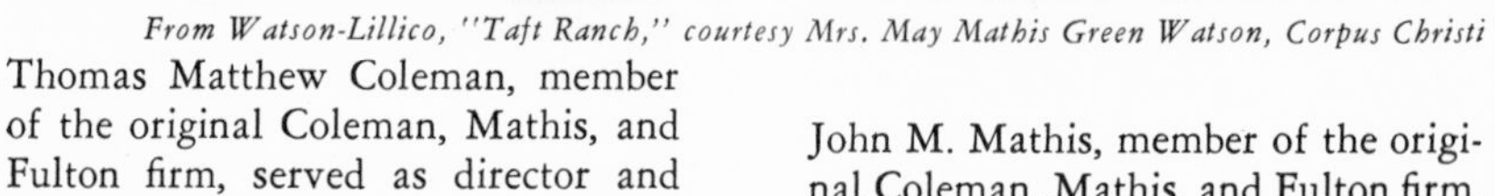

From Watson-Lillico, "Taft Ranch," courtesy Mrs. May Mathis Green Watson, Corpus Christi

Thomas Matthew Coleman, member of the original Coleman, Mathis, and Fulton firm, served as director and superintendent of the Coleman-Fulton Pasture Company from 1881 until he resigned in 1885.

John M. Mathis, member of the original Coleman, Mathis, and Fulton firm.

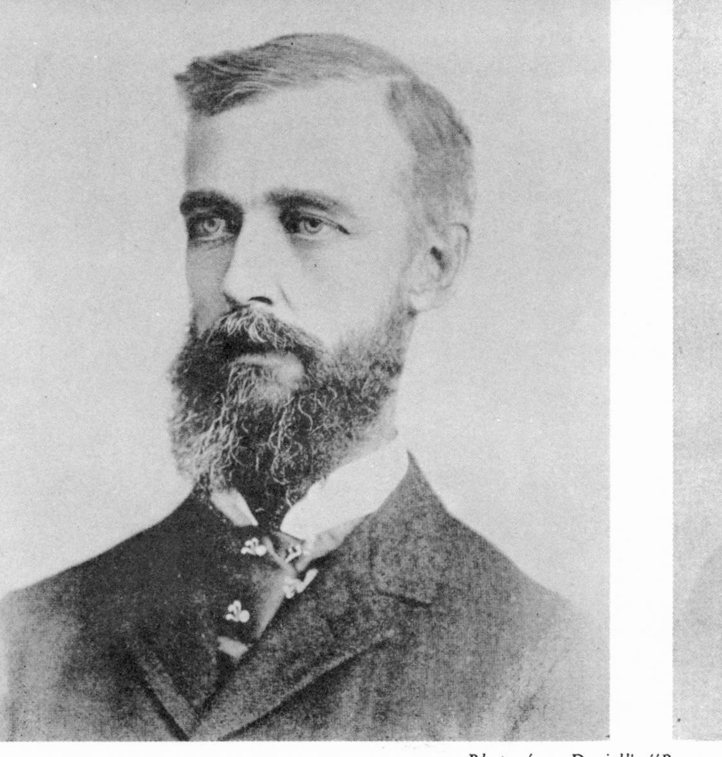

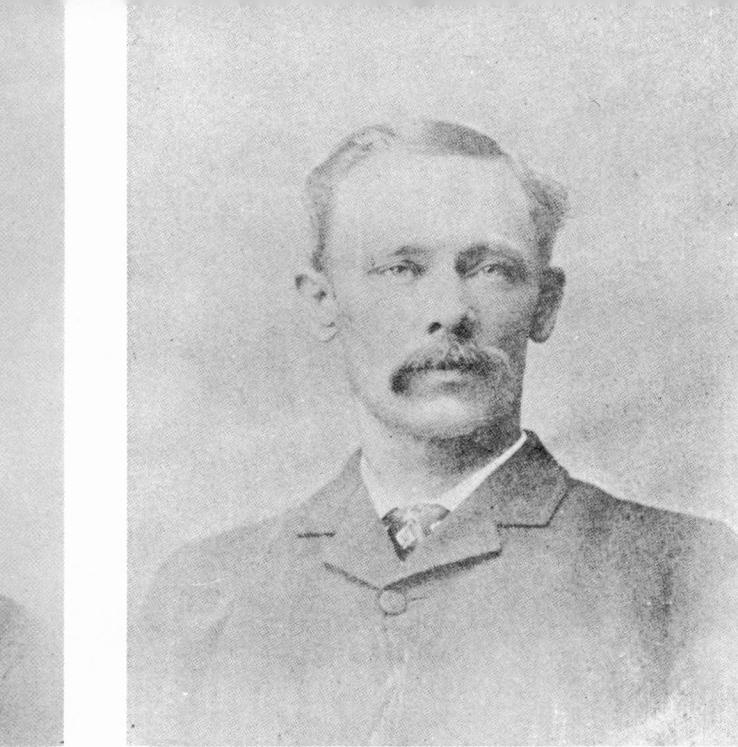

Photos from Daniell's "Personnel of the Texas State Government," courtesy University of Texas Library

George Ware Fulton, Jr., served as vice president, secretary, and superintendent of the Coleman-Fulton Pasture Company.

James C. Fulton, secretary of the Coleman-Fulton Pasture Company for several years.

Courtesy Edward N. Tutt, Taft

Coleman-Fulton Pasture Company stock certificate.

Rincon Ranch

1 Blacksmith	$2.00 per day	
1 Windmill Tender		$40.00 per month
1 Gardener	1.00 " "	
1 Cook (Ranch)	.50 " "	
1 Cook (Residence)		18.00 " "
1 Hostler	.50 " "	
1 Milkman &c	.50 " "	
1 Laundress & Housemaid	.50 " "	

Gregory Ranch

1 Foreman	30.00 " "
1 Laborer, teamster &c	15.00 " "
1 Cook	11.00 " "

Picacho Ranch

1 Foreman	37.50 " "
1 Helper	15.00 " "
1 Cook	12.00 " "

Stockley Ranch

1 Foreman (This man furnishes his own provisions)	50.00 " "
1 Helper (We pay his board @ 10.00 per mo.)	

Consado Ranch

1 Fence Rider (Tibunio Deanda)	1 yr.	12.00 per month
	1 "	16.00 per month

Note. [John J.] Welder keeps up our division fence one year, we the next and pay our fence rider $4.00 per mo. for increased work. We do not furnish this man with provisions except rations amounting to about 4.00 per mo.

Pocket Farm

1 Horse-breaker who also has charge of Stallions	@	30.00 per month
1 or 2 Helpers when occasions demand each	@	15.00 " "

Cow Crowd

1 Foreman	@	50.00 per month
1 S'Boss	@	25.00 " "
6 to 10 Riders	@ each .50 per day	

The "cow crowd" migrated to various divisions of the Coleman-Fulton Pasture Company for roundups; such areas other than those mentioned in this ledger were Doyle Water Hole, Cruz, Puentez, Mud Flats, and Beef Pastures.[111]

It was the practice of Colonel Fulton to prepare an official report to stockholders from time to time. In printed form he summarized recent events and included a "Statement of Total Receipts and Disbursements by Coleman-Fulton Pasture Company" and a "General Statement of Assets and Liabilities of Coleman-Fulton Pasture Company" for the reporting period.

The account of July 1, 1893, was attacked by two of the firm's larger stockholders. Lieutenant Colonel Samuel M. Mansfield of the United States Army Corps of Engineers was a long-time friend of Fulton's, but he did not mince his words when he noticed on the report that the company was financially supporting the work on a deep-water harbor and spending a large sum to bore artesian wells. All such money was wasted, he felt, and should be given to stockholders as dividends.

I see nothing bright in this statement of the Company and I must express my disapproval of the policy which fails so entirely to consider the interests of the present generation of stockholders and looks *only* to benefit posterity.[112]

David Sinton also had some comments about the 1893 statement. Believing that all ranges in Texas had the same capacity for carrying cattle, he became confused when Fulton gave the number of cattle on hand as 46,242 head and the number of horses and mules as 2,025 head on the 164,031 acres. Sinton wondered why his land in Dimmit County, purchased in 1891, could not do as well; ". . . on two hundred thousand acres of land only twenty five thousand head of cattle were pastured for two years, and the land was overstocked. This great difference seems strange."[113] Sinton did not understand that the brush-covered rocky area near Catarina and Encinal had little grass and that it did not receive as much average annual precipitation as did the Coleman-Fulton Pasture Company on the level, rich coastal plains.

Mansfield's accurate comment concerning the Fultons' management of the company's business was a truthful evaluation. The Fultons

[111] G. W. Fulton, Jr., Rincon Ranch, to G. W. Fulton, Sr., Rockport, July 1, 1890, CFPC, X, 75–76.

[112] Mansfield, Boston, to J. C. Fulton, Rockport, August 23, 1893, FC .

[113] Sinton, Cincinnati, to G. W. Fulton, Sr., Rockport, August 24, 1893, FC.

were interested in benefiting posterity by making the corporation a strong institution on the Coastal Bend.

Other callings, such as politics, were secondary for the Fultons. When the firm of Coleman, Mathis, and Fulton was at its height, its partners held high prestige in the community. At the time Colonel Fulton was asked to place his name in nomination at the 1878 Republican and Fusion convention for the South Texas congressional seat.[114] Fulton refused to consider the opportunity because he supported the incumbent and saw no reason to change. Although he was of a Republican background and had a brother who was high in the Republican hierarchy, Charles C. Fulton, editor of the Baltimore *American,* the Colonel claimed to be independent of political parties. Although he did not give the classic statement: "I will not run if nominated and will not serve if elected," Colonel Fulton came close to it when he wrote:

> . . . the only conditions upon which I would consent to go to Congress, would be the unanimous desire of every voter in the District, they having first convinced me that I was the *only man* that could '*save the country*' Then I should go with the feelings of one, who from a sense of duty, enters a home stricken with yellow fever—only that of the two I should prefer yellow jack.[115]

Although Fulton's sons did not share their father's aversion to politics, their political activities were restricted to the local scene. George Ware Fulton, Jr., served as county attorney for Aransas County in the early eighties when he first came to Rockport, but gave up that position when he moved to the Rincon Ranch in San Patricio County to become the Coleman-Fulton Pasture Company superintendent.[116] From 1891 to 1893 he represented the Eighty-fifth District in the House of Representatives of the Twenty-second Legislature, and then became a county commissioner of San Patricio County.[117] During the

[114] W. G. Holden, Corpus Christi, to G. W. Fulton, Sr., Rockport, August 27, 1878, FC.

[115] G. W. Fulton, Sr., to Holden, Corpus Christi, August 31, 1878, FC.

[116] G. W. Fulton, Jr., Rockport, to E. R. Rachal [n.p.], May 26, 1881, CFPC, II, 51.

[117] Daniell, *Personnel of the Texas State Government,* pp. 250–252. Glazbrook, Rincon Ranch, to Taft, Cincinnati, December 24, 1895, CFPC, XVII, 7.

1880's James C. Fulton was also an Aransas County official, filling the position of county commissioner.[118]

George Ware Fulton, for almost three decades a staunch supporter of the Coastal Bend and a promoter of the cattle industry, became so ill in the fall of 1892 that he was unable to resume his duties as president of the Coleman-Fulton Pasture Company. He remained in a weakened condition until October 31, 1893, when he died at the age of eighty-three. His concise obituary in the Corpus Christi *Caller* could easily serve as a eulogy: "Col. George W. Fulton, of Rockport, is dead. His was a long and useful life, and when he passed away that section of the state lost one of its most influential and progressive citizens."[119]

Colonel Fulton had been the dominant stockholder since the company was organized, even though Sinton had held a majority of the stock during most of the period. Under Fulton's leadership the firm made outstanding contributions to the development of the South Texas Plains—improving cattle with better breeds, fencing extensively, feeding livestock for an early spring market, assisting in the deep-water project, and increasing the population and the commercial value of the region by selling land to farmers. The bubble of hope for the Coastal Bend was pricked about the time of Fulton's death, when the harbor-construction firm failed to complete a passable channel. Faced with the reality of being denied a deep-water port, the newly arrived farmers became disillusioned and began to leave South Texas.

The ranch was again faced with the problem of low income and high expenses, being that land payments would not continue coming into its treasury till. The Panic of 1893 further injured economy in South Texas as Eastern capital became increasingly difficult to obtain. The era of the land boom with its resulting promise of new opportunities was fading from sight for the Fultons as the patriarch died.

The death of Colonel Fulton ended a period when Texans held the management reins of this vast spread of real estate. Control passed to the major stockholder, David Sinton, who looked upon this event as his opportunity to exercise a dominant hand in ranch affairs. Under Sinton's guidance the Pasture Company practiced strict economy as it embarked on a road that led the ranch to agricultural leadership.

[118] Daniell, *Personnel of the Texas State Government,* pp. 19–20.
[119] Corpus Christi *Caller,* November 10, 1893.

VII. PROGRESS UNDER ADMINISTRATIVE REORGANIZATION

THE POWER VACUUM following the death of George Ware Fulton was filled by persons completely nonconversant with agriculture. Rather than promoting the vice president-superintendent to the office of president and thereby taking advantage of his knowledge and his long association with the company's affairs, David Sinton chose to use this opportunity to rid himself of Fulton leadership. For years Sinton had disagreed with many of the acts done in the name of improvement, but had allowed the Colonel a large degree of freedom in carrying out plans. Now he had a chance to gain complete control without creating a power struggle. The program of agricultural progress led by Sinton during the immediately succeeding years attests to his genuine interest in the welfare of his investment.

Sinton named Charles Phelps Taft, the husband of Sinton's only daughter, Anna, to the dual position of president-treasurer; Sinton himself became a director, serving with Taft and George Fulton, Jr.[1] As the corporation's By-Laws provided that at least two of the three directors must be present at a meeting in order to have a quorum, Sinton was getting added assurance that decisions regarding financial matters or company policy would not be made by anyone except him-

[1] Minutes of the Coleman-Fulton Pasture Company Board of Directors' Meeting (hereafter cited as Minutes of Directors' Meeting), January 10, 1894, Coleman-Fulton Pasture Company Records (hereafter cited as CFPC).

self. This arrangement becomes understandable when one learns that Sinton agreed to underwrite all operating expenses for five years. After Sinton took charge of the company's affairs, the office of vice president was eliminated. George Fulton, Jr., resigned during the meeting on January 10, 1894, but remained with the ranch as superintendent; his brother, James C. Fulton, kept the secretaryship.[2]

At the January, 1894, meeting another change was effected, this one in banking. Since the inception of Coleman, Mathis, and Fulton, the Whitney National Bank of New Orleans had been the main depository, although when San Antonio became a South Texas trade center part of the Coleman-Fulton Pasture Company funds had been placed in the Lockwood National Bank there. From time to time local banks were used for small checking accounts, but the lack of operating capital in Corpus Christi or Rockport prevented completion of large business transactions in these towns. In 1893 the company changed its banking correspondent from New Orleans and San Antonio to Saint Louis and Chicago as a matter of convenience, because its cattle shipments to New Orleans had long since ceased. But, more important, as G. W. Fulton, Jr., stated, the move was made "with a view of reducing our interest upon such amounts as we may find it necessary to borrow from time to time."[3] The Corpus Christi National Bank was named the depository of the Coleman-Fulton Pasture Company in January, 1894. Two accounts were opened: one in the company's name and the other in the name of George Ware Fulton, Jr., Superintendent.[4]

Within a short time tragedy again struck at the ranch. While attending the funeral of Mifflin Kenedy in March, 1895, George Fulton, Jr., contracted a severe cold.[5] Upon seeking treatment at San Antonio, he was advised to take a deep-sea trip. On the cruise from Galveston to New York the superintendent partially recovered, but became worse in New York. At the Clifton Springs, New York, Sanitarium, Fulton's

[2] *Ibid.*

[3] George Ware Fulton, Jr., Rockport, Texas, to T. A. Stoddart, Saint Louis, Missouri, January 28, 1893, CFPC, XIV, 145.

[4] Minutes of Directors' Meeting, January 10, 1894, CFPC.

[5] James C. Fulton, Rockport, Texas, to Charles Phelps Taft, Cincinnati, Ohio, April 13, 1895, CFPC, XVI, 300.

condition was rediagnosed as anemia, and he was sent home for a complete rest.[6] Failing to respond to treatment, the forty-two-year-old rancher went for medical care to San Antonio, where he died on September 11, 1895.[7] Charles E. H. Glazbrook, appointed to the vacant position of superintendent, was given the title of general manager, and later was elected to the Board of Directors.[8]

When Sinton took charge of the company's affairs in January, 1894, it had a debt of $171,093.83, caused more by hard times and bad luck than by mismanagement. To consolidate the total indebtedness and to arrange for operating expenses, the corporation obtained a loan for four and one-half years from Sinton on January 10, 1894, for $185,000 at 8 per cent per annum.[9] As security, Sinton received a mortgage on the entire ranch, estimated at 183,805 acres, including land sold to farmers and to promoters, but not yet paid in full.[10] To reduce the huge liability as rapidly as possible, the Cincinnati financier began a policy of strict economy, or, as James C. Fulton defined it, "one of rigid retrenchment."[11] Notable exceptions to this financially austere program were improving ranch roads and drilling water wells. To improve transportation on the ranch and to prevent excessive damage to vehicles by rough trails, the company built a road from the railroad station at Gregory six miles north to the Rincon Ranch. Counting grubbing, grading, and finishing, the cost was $2,173.56.[12] To provide

[6] *Ibid.*, May 22, 1895, CFPC, XVI, 338; August 6, 1895, CFPC, XVI, 403–404; August 30, 1895, CFPC, XVI, 407.

[7] *Ibid.*, September 14, 1895, CFPC, XVI, 415–416.

[8] Charles E. H. Glazbrook, Rincon Ranch, to Taft, Cincinnati, January 28, 1896, CFPC, XVII, 57–58. Minutes of the Coleman-Fulton Pasture Company Stockholders' Meeting (hereafter cited as Minutes of Stockholders' Meeting), May 5, 1897, CFPC.

[9] Minutes of Stockholders' Meeting, January 10, 1894, CFPC. Deed of Trust Records, Aransas County, January 10, 1894, Vol. G, pp. 530–537. Deed of Trust Records, San Patricio County, January 10, 1894, Vol. C, pp. 179–187.

[10] *Ibid.* The metes and bounds of the range, described in the deed of trust filed in the county courthouse at Sinton in 1894, are included in an appendix following the text.

[11] J. C. Fulton, Rockport, to Samuel M. Mansfield, Boston, Massachusetts, April 30, 1894, CFPC, XVI, 129–130.

[12] Fulton, Rockport, to J. S. M. McKamey, Marble Falls, Texas, June 18, 1895, CFPC, XVI, 366.

water for livestock, James C. Fulton was allowed to finish the well at the Rincon Ranch. His effort was rewarded by striking an artesian pressure of thirty-five pounds to the square inch at 1,388 feet deep, but no more tests were made.[13]

One of the problems that plagued Southwest Texas ranchers, and the Coleman-Fulton Pasture Company in particular, was their inability to market fat steers at all seasons of the year. Cattle fed on spring grass did not become marketable until the summer or early fall when the price declined. A winter-feeding plan so long advocated by Colonel Fulton came within the reach of reality when it was discovered that cottonseed products and other feed stuff such as sorghum ensilage produced rapid gains. By the mid-1890's the Coleman-Fulton Pasture Company was using, on a limited scale, these commodities, which grew abundantly and cheaply in Texas.[14]

Distance from markets posed another problem for Texas ranchers. They were in communication with the commission houses in Saint Louis and Chicago, but at least six days elapsed from the time the men decided to ship until the cattle arrived at the destination. During this brief time the market could fluctuate drastically, making the whole matter appear to be a lottery. As a case in point, J. M. Chittim, a cattle buyer, purchased 1,400 steers from the Coleman-Fulton Pasture Company and sent 322 of them to Saint Louis. At the time of shipment the market was $3.30 a hundredweight, but by the time the stock arrived the price had slipped to $2.90.[15]

While the ranch hands were gathering cattle for the company's sales, it became evident that the number on hand was far short of the estimated 37,806 head as shown in the Cattle Register for January 1, 1896. Although the company allowed neighboring persons to take a cow from the range for milking purposes, provided the calf was turned back to the pasture when it was weaned, the number of animals borrowed by farmers in the vicinity did not account for the large reduction of the herd.[16] Rustling was not a problem because of the protection afforded by the Cattle Raisers' Association of Texas, whose

[13] Fulton, Rockport, to Taft, Cincinnati, August 6, 1895, CFPC, XVI, 404.

[14] *Ibid.*, June 19, 1895, CFPC, XVI, 371.

[15] *Ibid.*

[16] Glazbrook, Rincon Ranch, to James W. Dunlap, Sinton, Texas, March 23, 1896, CFPC, XVII, 148.

inspectors checked the brands of all livestock shipped from the area;[17] therefore, the reason for having fewer cattle on hand than were shown on the book lay elsewhere.

The Taft and Sinton element had pressed for a long time to count every cow to determine exactly the number present on the range. Colonel Fulton resisted this move while he was president because he believed that any handling of the cattle except that necessary for shipping them to market was economically unsound. When placed in close confinement for counting, the livestock became nervous and lost weight or injured themselves trying to escape. But after the Ohio group gained control it ordered a count. Beginning on May 1, 1896, the cowboys were mobilized into two independent drives, one in the top pastures, the other in the lower pastures.[18] In order to have an absolutely correct count, the ranch passed every animal through chutes at the Cruz Lake and Mud Flats corrals, where their tails were bobbed so that brush cattle could be counted later. The count was quite revealing: only 17,557 head were found on the entire range, less than half the previously estimated number.[19]

How would one account for such a great discrepancy? Glazbrook gave this story: "In the first place I have been told our former Foreman Matt McWhorter did report falsely in his branding—this was about ten years ago, then again during the die up in '93 '94 half were not found that actually died."[20] At a later date the superintendent elaborated further on the subject:

> . . . the former book keeper, Mr. Seymour, never to my knowledge as shown on our old books made any estimate for loss of cattle except in one year, when we had a large die up, and then only deducted 2–½ per cent on the whole Stock, instead of about 30 to 35 per cent. An entry made by Mr. Seymour June 30, 1893 shows an estimate branding of 7000 head, there were only branded in this year something over 4,000 head, this 7000 head

[17] Glazbrook, Rincon Ranch, to Taft, Cincinnati, December 2, 1896, CFPC, XVII, 593. The Coleman-Fulton Pasture Company paid $500 a year for this protection.

[18] *Ibid.,* May 1, 1896, CFPC, XVII, 207–208.

[19] *Ibid.,* January 1, 1897, CFPC, XVII, 644–645. Cattle Stock Register, 1893–1922, CFPC.

[20] Glazbrook, Rincon Ranch, to Taft, Cincinnati, July 13, 1896, CFPC, XVII, 369.

have been carried on in the inventories to the present date, this will account for a part of the shortage.[21]

James C. Fulton resented Taft's overt disapproval of the Fulton management of the corporation and bided his time for revenge. The opportunity came when Taft sold some beeves to be transferred to Sinton's Dimmit County ranch. Although the cattle were bargained for in May, the Coleman-Fulton Pasture Company was required to keep them on hand and at its own risk in the Beef Pasture until September; thus these extra animals deprived company livestock of grass.[22] Another occasion for protest was Taft's deal with John Welder, a neighboring San Patricio County rancher, for the sale of three-year-old steers for $21.50 a head, when in only three months the animals would have been rated as four-year-olds and would have brought more. Besides that, a conservative estimate for the same type of cattle that Taft sold, Fulton explained, was from $25.00 to $27.50 and, when fattened, $32.50.[23] Also, Taft had transferred horses from a good part of the ranch to a pasture along Nueces Bay with inferior grass and subject to overflow. Fulton summed up his feelings by stating to Taft that these decisions "are not those of which you should feel self congratulation."[24] Taft paid no attention to Fulton's vehement protests.

At the extensive roundup in 1896 ranch officials saw that a program for upgrading the herd was necessary if they were to have better calves to market. The improved stock introduced by the Coleman, Mathis, and Fulton firm and by the Coleman-Fulton Pasture Company in its early days did well; by 1896 nearly all of the animals on hand were crossed between Hereford, Durham, and Devon, having solid-colored bodies and white faces.[25] To guard against inbreeding, the ranch began buying new herd sires. In the fall of 1896 Glazbrook traded 250 old

[21] *Ibid.*, December 2, 1896, CFPC, XVII, 593–594.

[22] Fulton, Rockport, to Taft, Cincinnati, September 8, 1897, Fulton Collection (hereafter cited as FC).

[23] *Ibid.*, September 17, 1897, FC.

[24] *Ibid.*, September 8, 1897, FC.

[25] Glazbrook, Rincon Ranch, to E. A. Paffrath, Fort Worth, March 16, 1896, CFPC, XVII, 138.

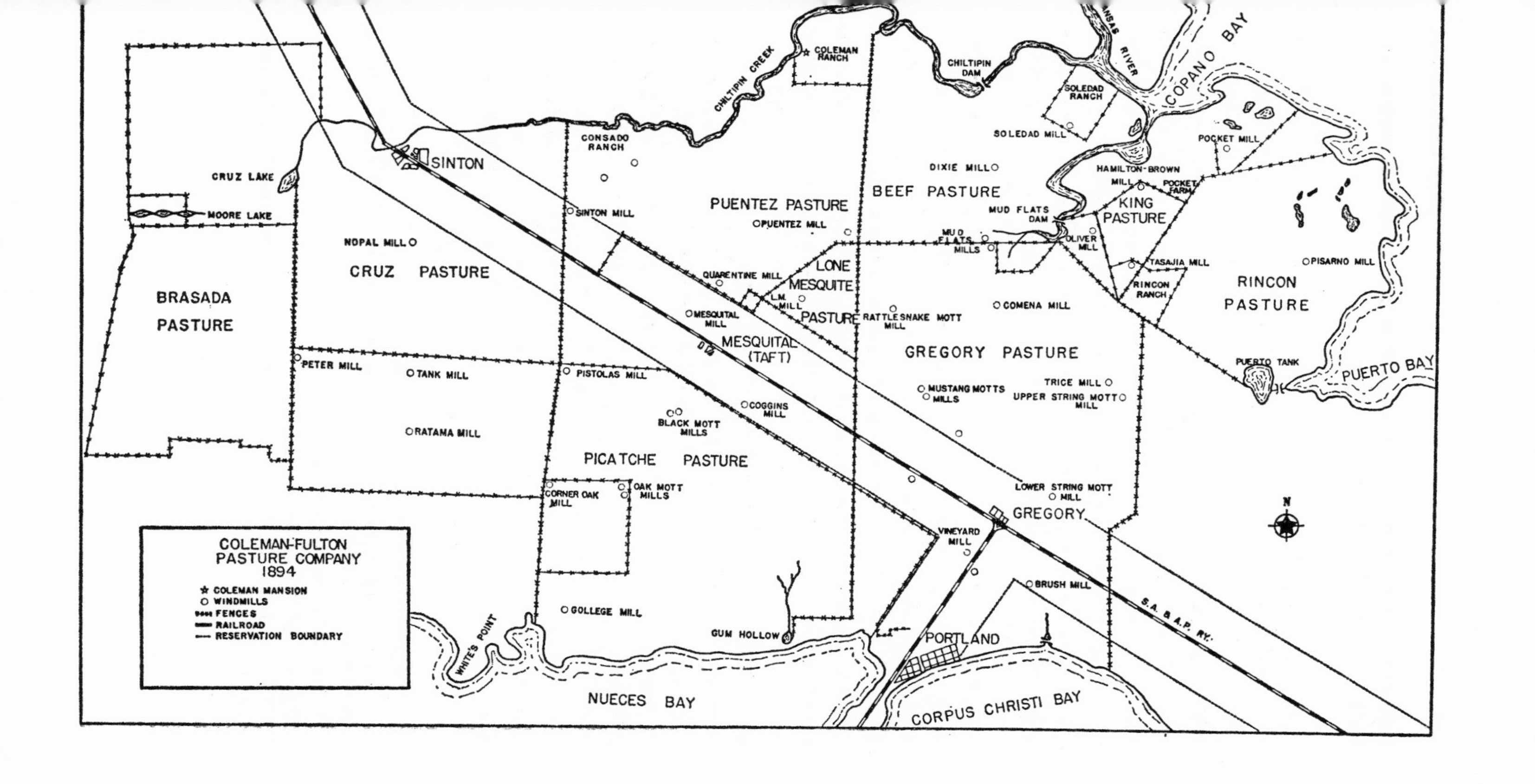
COLEMAN-FULTON
PASTURE COMPANY
1894
COLEMAN MANSION
WINDMILLS
FENCES
RAILROAD
RESERVATION BOUNDARY
BRASADA PASTURE
CRUZ LAKE
MOORE LAKE
CRUZ PASTURE
NOPAL MILL
SINTON
PETER MILL
TANK MILL
RATAMA MILL
CONSADO RANCH
SINTON MILL
CHILTIPIN CREEK
COLEMAN RANCH
PUENTEZ PASTURE
PUENTEZ MILL
QUARENTINE MILL
MESQUITAL MILL
MESQUITAL (TAFT)
LONE MESQUITE PASTURE
L.M. MILL
PISTOLAS MILL
COGGINS MILL
BLACK MOTT MILLS
PICATCHE PASTURE
CORNER OAK MILL
OAK MOTT MILLS
COLLEGE MILL
WHITE'S POINT
GUM HOLLOW
NUECES BAY
CHILTIPIN DAM
DIXIE MILL
BEEF PASTURE
SOLEDAD RANCH
SOLEDAD MILL
MUD FLATS DAM
MUD FLATS MILLS
COMENA MILL
RATTLESNAKE MOTT MILL
GREGORY PASTURE
MUSTANG MOTTS MILLS
TRICE MILL
UPPER STRING MOTT MILL
LOWER STRING MOTT MILL
GREGORY
VINEYARD MILL
BRUSH MILL
PORTLAND
CORPUS CHRISTI BAY
S.A. & A.P. RY.
COPANO BAY
HAMILTON-BROWN MILL
POCKET FARM
POCKET MILL
KING PASTURE
OLIVER MILL
TASAJIA MILL
RINCON RANCH
RINCON PASTURE
PISARNO MILL
PUERTO TANK
PUERTO BAY
N

bulls for 125 highly graded young Devons and sold the remaining old males for $13 a head.[26]

To interest a cattle buyer was one thing; to gather the bulls to a shipping pen was something else. The brushpoppers went to work running down the animals in the brush, where each must be roped, brought out, and its horns sawed off before the cowboys could get them to the pens.[27] After selling the old males the Coleman-Fulton Pasture Company found itself to be short of sires and likely to have a light calf crop in 1897 if more were not purchased immediately. Plenty of younger Hereford, Devon, and Durham bulls were on the range, but not many three- and four-year-olds. To remedy the situation the ranch advertised in the *Texas Stockman and Farmer* in San Antonio:

> WANTED
>
> At once from 50 to 75 head of graded bulls from 3 to 4 years old, Durham, Devon, or Hereford, cash payment, apply for further particulars to
>
> C. E. H. Glazbrook, Supt.
> Coleman-Fulton Pasture Co.
> Gregory, Texas.[28]

Most of the animals purchased as a result of this advertisement were from Sinton's ranch in Dimmit County.[29]

Gradually the old ways of raising cattle were slipping away. The open range gave way to barbed-wire fences; cattle began selling by the pound instead of by the head; and winter feeding necessitated changes from ranching to stock farming. In 1897 the Coleman-Fulton Pasture Company began to upgrade its herd in order to get better calves that would mature in three years rather than in four.[30] This policy meant a grass savings for one year, which could be used to start another calf on its way to maturity. No longer could a person place any type of cow on

[26] Glazbrook, Rockport, to Taft, Cincinnati, October 8, 1896, CFPC, XVII, 503; to N. R. Powell, Pettus, Texas, September 13, 1896, CFPC, XVII, 454.

[27] Glazbrook, Rincon Ranch, to Taft, Cincinnati, November 28, 1896, CFPC, XVII, 586–587.

[28] Glazbrook, Gregory, to the Editor, *Texas Stockman and Farmer,* February 18, 1897, CFPC, XVII, 764.

[29] Glazbrook, Gregory, to Taft, Cincinnati, March 20, 1897, CFPC, XVII, 811; April 9, 1897, CFPC, XVII, 821.

[30] *Ibid.,* June 1, 1897, CFPC, XVII, 882–885.

the range and make a profit. The aged and undesirable females must be culled, and those remaining mated with highly pedigreed males.

The Coleman-Fulton Pasture Company also reduced the size of its horse stock. Five hundred saddle horses, fourteen to fifteen hands high, were advertised at $30 a head if taken singly, $25 each for a railroad carload.[31] Seventy *potros,* wild or unbroken horses, were sold to the Mexican cavalry for $10 each.[32] Of the 1,800 head of draft animals owned by the ranch, 400 mares of Clydesdale and Percheron Norman stock, averaging fifteen hands high, were offered for sale at $16 each in lots, or by selection, at $20.[33] One of the parties that purchased mares from the company intentionally neglected to pay for them. Glazbrook wrote to him several times, but never received a reply. When the superintendent learned that the debtor was campaigning for county judge he wrote: ". . . it would be well for you to settle this matter before seeking office."[34] The implication was that, because the Coleman-Fulton Pasture Company owned approximately one-half of the county and because its land surrounded the county seat, it could control many votes. Unfortunately, there is no indication whether this display of power politics had any effect.

The ranch also offered mules for sale in 1897 at $32.50 a head in carload lots.[35] A good-neighbor policy was practiced whereby mules were loaned to farmers with the understanding that they would return the animals immediately when called upon to do so.[36] As most of the mules not in use were unbroken, the ranch was receiving a service because the borrowers were breaking its stock to the plow free of charge.

[31] Glazbrook, Rincon Ranch, to M. McFountain, Kempsville, Alabama, February 14, 1896, CFPC, XVII, 68; to Morin Brothers, San Antonio, February 24, 1896, CFPC, XVII, 107.

[32] Glazbrook, Gregory, to Taft, Cincinnati, May 15, 23, 1897, CFPC, XVII, 859, 870.

[33] Glazbrook, Rincon Ranch, to Charles Brothers, Uvalde, Texas, February 17, 1896, CFPC, XVII, 96; to J. E. Price, San Antonio, December 24, 1896, CFPC, XVII, 625.

[34] Glazbrook, Rincon Ranch, to Major [William?] Dunlap, Portland, Texas, September 7, 1896, CFPC, XVII, 441.

[35] Glazbrook, Rincon Ranch, to M. McFountain, Kempsville, Alabama, February 14, 1896, CFPC, XVII, 68.

[36] Glazbrook, Rincon Ranch, to John G. Willacy, Portland, Texas, September 27, 1896, CFPC, XVII, 475.

The reorganization initiated by Taft was extended to include the ranch's employees. The superintendent's office was changed from Rincon Ranch to Gregory in January, 1897.[37] Reasons for moving the ranch headquarters to the railroad were to place the superintendent nearer the center of the range, to eliminate the expense of transporting supplies to Rincon Ranch, and to make Glazbrook more accessible to visitors. The hotel, or Immigrants' Home, at Gregory would reduce the superintendent's heavy expenses in entertaining the company's guests at his own table and in his own house, for which he received no reimbursement.[38]

Taft's plan called for replacing white cowboys with Mexicans, who would undoubtedly work for less, and for reducing the work year to nine months.[39] Glazbrook complained that he would be left shorthanded on skilled help to care for the cattle, which he considered the company's main business. Three of the most valued employees were released during the reorganization: J. L. Quinn, R. K. Reed, and Chris Thompson, who were responsible for the fences, cattle, and water in separate divisions of the range. They guarded against encroachment on company property by residents of Gregory, Portland, and Sinton, while keeping stray livestock from the pastures.[40] It was a difficult task for Glazbrook to notify Reed, Quinn, and Thompson to leave, but out of courtesy for their fifteen years of service to the company he gave them thirty days' notice.[41]

One of the reasons for Taft's strict economy program was to meet the increased taxation on the Coleman-Fulton Pasture Company by San Patricio County. When the cotton crops of 1893 and 1894, excessively dry years, produced so well, county officials raised the assessment value on all land including pastures.[42] Additional revenue was needed to erect a courthouse and a jail at the new county seat at Sinton. The increase doubled the company's taxes for 1895, compared with the previous year.[43] The increased taxation imposed by county officials

[37] Glazbrook, Gregory, to Taft, Cincinnati, February 25, 1897, CFPC, XVII, 779.

[38] *Ibid.*, January 8, 1897, CFPC, XVII, 659–662.

[39] *Ibid.* [40] *Ibid.* [41] *Ibid.*

[42] J. C. Fulton, Rockport, to Mansfield, Boston, April 30, 1894, CFPC, XVI, 130–131.

[43] Glazbrook, Rincon Ranch, to Taft, Cincinnati, February 1, 1896, CFPC,

served as the impetus for the changes in ranch policy to realize the maximum yield from available resources. In order to save money the Coleman-Fulton Pasture Company bought scrip from San Patricio and Aransas Counties, usually at less than par, to pay its taxes. On one occasion Glazbrook purchased the scrip for eighty-five cents on the dollar.[44]

Collecting money owed the company was necessary in order to pay debts. James C. Fulton, chief stockholder and virtual owner of the Aransas Lumber Company in Rockport and Sinton, mortgaged his firm's machinery and planing mill to the Coleman-Fulton Pasture Company when he started that business in 1890. In April, 1896, his Sinton yard was taken from him for debt, followed by a foreclosure on the Rockport plant.[45] Fulton was in trouble; with the two lumber yards and the planing mill gone, he had no income except that received as secretary of the Coleman-Fulton Pasture Company, and his stipend would not pay his large debts. The Pasture Company held claims against J. C. Fulton and his Aransas Lumber Company totaling $15,000. In order to meet Sinton's demand that these obligations be absolved immediately, Fulton sold to Sinton $30,000 worth of the corporation's capital stock for fifty cents on the dollar.[46] Although this requirement appears harsh, it left Fulton with no alternative; so he complied. At this time the George Ware Fulton estate sold 254 shares at the same ratio to settle its debt with the ranch.[47] Mrs. George Ware Fulton, Jr., discharged the $2,259.74 indebtedness against her husband's estate by transferring to the Coleman-Fulton Pasture Company forty-one shares for one-half of par value.[48]

Taft's frugality and tightfistedness in the ranch's economic affairs paid handsome rewards. In his report on the corporation's condition

XVII, 69; to Corpus Christi National Bank, January 31, 1896, CFPC, XVII, 63.

[44] Glazbrook, Gregory, to Taft, Cincinnati, May 23, 1897, CFPC, XVII, 870.

[45] Glazbrook, Rincon Ranch, to Fulton, Rockport, July 10, 1896, CFPC, XVII, 360; to Taft, Cincinnati, June 12, 1896, CFPC, XVII, 303. Fulton, Rockport, to J. W. Dunlap, Sinton, April 18, 1896, FC; to Burrows Hardware Company, Beeville, April 6, 1903, FC.

[46] Taft, Cincinnati, to Fulton, Rockport, May 14, 1897, FC.

[47] Fulton, Rockport, to Mrs. Hattie Fulton Holden, Farmington, Delaware, June 11, 1899, FC. Taft, Cincinnati, to Fulton, Rockport, May 29, 1897, FC.

[48] Taft, Cincinnati, to Fulton, Rockport, July 12, 1897, FC.

at the May 2, 1898, stockholders' meeting, he emphasized that the $185,000 note to Sinton had been reduced to $38,239.51 with interest at 8 per cent.[49] The only sums owed, in addition to Sinton's mortgage, were $17,712 for the San Patricio County school lands, which were purchased in 1877 but not paid for, and miscellaneous accounts amounting to $2,553.65.[50] Taft felt proud of the company's achievement during the past four years, but he correctly shared credit with Glazbrook for making the ranch a profitable concern again.[51]

In matters other than ranching Glazbrook was also a dominant figure. He replaced George W. Fulton, Jr., as director and trustee in the Sinton Town Company in February, 1896. In order to become a director Glazbrook had to own stock in the Town Company; therefore, to fill that requirement, he bought one share from the other directors, Sidney G. Borden, D. C. Rachal, and John J. Welder. The Coleman-Fulton Pasture Company owned ten and one-fourth shares at $100 each in the Sinton Town Company, which were signed over to Glazbrook as trustee for the ranch. The superintendent was chosen over James C. Fulton for this post because of his residence in San Patricio County and his nearness to the town of Sinton.[52]

Largely through Glazbrook's influence a county school was started at the Rincon Ranch in 1896. School was held there in the 1880's, but evidently was not kept active. The scholastic census in the spring of 1896 reported sixteen to eighteen children of the proper age nearer Rincon than Gregory. As the Coleman-Fulton Pasture Company paid one-half of the county's tax revenue, Glazbrook asked the trustees to establish a school at Rincon and to allot twenty dollars a month for a teacher's salary.[53] The request was approved, a teacher, Miss E. Evans, was appointed, and on Monday, October 5, 1896, the five months' term began with seven scholars in attendance.[54]

[49] Minutes of Stockholders' Meeting, May 2, 1898, CFPC.

[50] *Ibid.*

[51] *Ibid.*

[52] Glazbrook, Rincon Ranch, to Taft, Cincinnati, February 5, 1896, CFPC, XVII, 73–75.

[53] Glazbrook, Gregory, to J. G. Willacy, Portland, Texas, June 19, 1897, CFPC, XVII, 319.

[54] *Ibid.,* September 27, 1896, CFPC, XVII, 475; October 5, 1896, CFPC, XVII, 485; October 10, 1896, CFPC, XVII, 507.

Sporting guests at the ranch looked forward to pleasurable moments because of the abundance of game and fish. They could hunt fox, wild cats, panthers, and wolves the year around; and in season they could find countless snipe, quail, geese, brant, ducks in many varieties, deer, turkey, and prairie chicken within one day's travel.[55] For a person interested in fishing there were many varieties and great quantities to catch: tarpon, red snapper, red fish, trout, sheep head, June fish, pike, saw fish, oysters, clams, and shrimp.[56]

The sporting event that attracted the most visitors was duck shooting at Gum Hollow. A gully approximately three miles west of Portland on Nueces Bay was dammed up to form a lake for watering cattle in that part of the range. Its large water-surface area and nearby grain fields became a magnet for wildfowl, so that each winter thousands of birds would stay at Gum Hollow. In some localities persons go duck *hunting,* because an actual searching is necessary to find game; but at Gum Hollow sportsmen went duck *shooting,* a quite descriptive term as no hunting was necessary. A fence rider allowed no one to enter the area except on written permission of the Coleman-Fulton Pasture Company superintendent. Permits were issued to friends and neighbors who requested them, but those persons had to agree to certain conditions: no market or commercial hunters were allowed in the enclosure, and sportsmen receiving permits were asked to consider the safety of livestock watering at the lake.[57]

James C. Fulton escorted his visitors, a number of influential guests, to "your most excellent 'Duck Patch'," as one satisfied hunter described Gum Hollow. Local youngsters earned nickels and dimes by carrying dead ducks back to Portland, where the ducks were iced and then shipped all over the United States, depending on the location of the visitor's home. A few of the visitors are listed to show how far the fame of this sportsman's paradise spread: F. P. Holland, editor of the *Texas Farm and Ranch,* Dallas; Colonel I. L. Ellwood, "possibly the wealthiest man outside of Chicago, Illinois";[58] Charles H. Thorne, secretary

[55] J. C. Fulton, Rockport, to John E. Ennis, Chicago, February 24, 1893, CFPC, XV, 15.

[56] *Ibid.*

[57] Glazbrook, Rincon Ranch, to George F. Obee, Portland, Texas, September 29, 1896, CFPC, XVII, 477.

[58] F. P. Holland, Dallas, to Fulton, Rockport, September 26, 1898, FC.

and general manager of Montgomery Ward and Company, Chicago; W. B. Liffingwell, advertising manager of Montgomery Ward and Company, Chicago; Arthur Stephens, general manager of the Moline [Illinois] Plow Company; James Barker, general passenger and ticket agent for Missouri, Kansas and Texas Railway Company, Saint Louis; J. A. L. Waddell, consulting engineer, Kansas City; E. H. R. Green, chairman of the Texas Republican State Executive Committee and son of the "witch of Wall Street," Hetty Green, Terrell, Texas; L. J. Polk, general manager of the Gulf, Colorado and Santa Fe Railway Company, Galveston; Bishop George H. Kinsolving, of the Middle Diocese of the Episcopal Church of Texas; Reverend C. M. Beckwith, Rector of Trinity Church in Galveston; and others from over the United States.[59]

As a testimony to the excellent hunting on the property of the Coleman-Fulton Pasture Company many of those persons who came once usually made it a point to return the following year. The fame of the hunting reserve became widespread in the early 1890's, when the Coastal Bend was advertised as the place for a deep-water harbor. After the luster was off the boom, Gum Hollow was still popular.

The excitement that prevailed earlier in the Aransas Pass area quieted down in the mid-1890's, when the channel was not deepened as rapidly as anticipated. The Aransas Pass Harbor Company ran short of funds and saw other parts of its assets disappear. The Coleman-Fulton Pasture Company's conditional warranty deed for 10,000 acres in its Brasada Pasture, if twenty feet of water over the bar was obtained, expired in December, 1894. As the Harbor Company needed this $100,000 asset to get money by mortgaging, its officials persuaded Charles P. Taft to convey the land to them without restrictions.[60] Work continued on the channel without appreciable results until 1896, when the deep-water enterprise appeared to be a failure.[61] The

[59] *Ibid.* L. J. Polk, Galveston, to Fulton, Rockport, January 14, 1897; E. H. R. Green, Terrell, Texas, to W. C. Connor, Dallas, January 14, 1897; J. A. L. Waddell, Kansas City, Missouri, to Fulton, Rockport, December 21, 1897; James Barker, Saint Louis, Missouri, to Fulton, Rockport, December 23, 1897; J. A. Edson, Tyler, to Fulton, Rockport, January 1, 1897; all in FC.

[60] Deed Records, San Patricio County, April 20, 1895, Vol. L, pp. 448–450.

[61] Glazbrook, Rincon Ranch, to Taft, Cincinnati, September 6, 1896, CFPC, XVII, 438.

Coleman-Fulton Pasture Company's lawyers, McCampbell and Welch of Corpus Christi, a firm composed of John L. McCampbell, E. A. McCampbell, and Stanley Welch, were instructed to enter suit for recovery of the land given to the Harbor Company as a bonus.[62]

A survey by the Army Engineers in 1897 revealed that improvements made by the deep-water company were of no value whatever; rather, they did positive damage to navigation at that point.[63] The Chief of Engineers suggested to the Rivers and Harbors Committee of Congress that the Aransas Pass harbor was sufficiently important for federal government support and recommended that the uncompleted two-jetty plan started in 1887 be adopted.[64] Under authority of the act of Congress of March 3, 1899, the Aransas Pass Harbor Company relinquished its franchise of channel improvement to the United States on the following March 27.[65] The federal government carried on a program of construction at the pass, employing a plan that called for two jetties to prevent sand from shifting into the inlet and a dredging machine to remove the present sand from the gap. Financed through appropriation by the Congress, the work continued for a quarter of a century before the aim was achieved.

The demise of the Aransas Pass Harbor Company was not the only fatality of the deflated boom. The Aransas Harbor *Herald,* the official organ of the deep-water project, was forced to stop its press in 1897 for lack of paying subscribers.[66] The region was so destitute that the publisher, S. P. Panton, could not collect enough from subscriptions to leave the area and was forced to borrow the money.[67]

Deserted portions of the land sold by the Coleman-Fulton Pasture Company during the boom were later confiscated by the county for back taxes or reconveyed to the ranch. In one case, when P. C. Mays, a farmer, abandoned his tract, purchased in 1890, the sheriff claimed

[62] *Ibid.,* September 13, 1896, CFPC, XVII, 453.

[63] Brewster Cameron, Philadelphia, to Fulton, Rockport, September 27, 1897, FC.

[64] *House Documents,* 55th Congress, Third Session, Serial No. 3747, Doc. No. 2, p. 1542.

[65] *House Documents,* 56th Congress, Second Session, Serial No. 4089, Doc. No. 2, pp. 392–393.

[66] S. P. Panton, Aransas Harbor, to Fulton, Rockport, November 18, 1897, FC.

[67] *Ibid.*

the property for the county and sold it to the Pasture Company in 1898 for a fraction of the original price.[68] Persons leaving the region after the harbor project failed and after dry weather discouraged cultivation must have felt disillusioned, for the value of their property, $3-an-acre land bought at the inflated $10 price, declined before it was paid in full. The J. N. Thompson family was one tragically affected by the changing conditions.

South Arm Charlevaire Co. Michigan
June 2 [1896]

Mr. G. W. Fulton

Dear Sir

I write to ask a favor My husband J. N. Thompson bought land of you several years ago investing all he had. We were ruined by the transaction when the boom went down We were obliged to sell for what we could get which was enough to get away with Mr. T worried himself into a fever from which he never recovered he lived about 2 years and died leaving us in poverty my health is very poor I cannot labor physically I have 2 little children to support and ask help. A very little would be much to us I would not ask for help but it is hard for a mother to hear her children cry for bread. The times are so close, and no work, every job has a dozen applicants If I had 2 or 3 cows I could keep from starving (I mean cows of this country) Can you help me I am yours respectfully

Mrs. Laura Thompson[69]

Existing records do not reveal any action taken by the company on this letter. Colonel Fulton was no longer living, and the current president, Charles Phelps Taft, felt no particular obligation toward pleas from persons whose business with the company was transacted before he took charge.

As a result of his strict management Taft was able to report to the stockholders on May 1, 1899, that all the company's obligations to Sinton were paid and that the mortgage on the ranch was lifted.[70] This was welcome news, indeed, for the long-suffering stockholders

[68] Deed Records, San Patricio County, April 5, 1898, Vol. P, pp. 55–56.

[69] Mrs. Laura Thompson, South Arm, Charlevaire County, Michigan, to George Ware Fulton, Rockport, June 2 [1896], FC.

[70] Minutes of Stockholders' Meeting, May 1, 1899, CFPC. Deed Records, San Patricio County, May 9, 1899, Vol. P, pp. 189–191. Deed Records, Aransas County, May 9, 1899, Vol. H, pp. 315–317.

who had received no return on their investment since 1884. When the bookkeeper used black ink again, it was apparent that there would be a profit: on May 20, 1899, a 5-per-cent dividend was paid, the first in fifteen years.[71] At last the ranch was back on its feet. The reorganization under Sinton and Taft had led toward marked progress.

When the Coleman-Fulton Pasture Company emerged from its large indebtedness, it attracted a new stockholder who became an employee of the ranch and who guided its destiny for the next quarter of a century. Joseph French Green, Sinton's foreman at the Dimmit County ranch, obtained a list of the Coleman-Fulton Pasture Company stockholders and sent letters to them, offering to purchase their shares at 40 per cent of par.[72] Some of the stockholders became curious and asked Fulton what Green was planning. It soon became clear what the scheme was. Green wrote that he wanted to buy all the company's stock outside the immediate families of James C. Fulton and David Sinton. The idea was to concentrate the stock among those two and himself.[73] By the time of the annual stockholders' meeting at Rockport on June 4, 1900, Green held 58 shares; to these were added 101 more within six months.[74] For some time Glazbrook feared that Green had a better access to Taft's ear than he; in 1900 it became clear that he was right.

Taft and Sinton did not attend the 1900 stockholders' meeting. They gave their proxy to Green, who had Fulton, Taft, and himself elected as directors and who named Taft president and treasurer. Green substituted for Glazbrook, who resigned and moved to San Antonio, as superintendent and general manager, and Fulton remained as secretary.[75] Everything went off as planned and a new era of leadership began for the ranch.[76]

[71] Minutes of Directors' Meeting, May 1, 1899, CFPC. Taft, Cincinnati, to Fulton, Rockport, May 19, 1899, FC.

[72] Mansfield, San Francisco, to Fulton, Rockport, May 28, 1900, FC. J. F. Green [n.p.] to Mrs. Annie B. Mansfield, San Francisco, May 9, 1900, FC.

[73] J. F. Green [n.p.] to Fulton, Rockport, May 18, 1900, FC.

[74] Clamp and Harris, Attorneys at Law, San Antonio, to Fulton, Rockport, May 18, 1900; J. F. Green [n.p.] to Fulton, Rockport, May 18, 1900; Taft, Cincinnati, to Fulton, Rockport, May 25, June 18, November 15, 1900; all in FC.

[75] Taft, Cincinnati, to Fulton, Rockport, May 25, 1900, FC.

[76] Minutes of Stockholders' Meeting, June 4, 1900, CFPC. Minutes of Directors' Meeting, June 4, 1900, CFPC.

VIII. FROM BRANDING IRONS TO PLOWSHARES

JOSEPH FRENCH GREEN was born in Troy, Ohio, on April 5, 1856, attended normal school at Lebanon, Ohio, married Jennie Saucer, the librarian at the institution, and taught school in Illinois for two years. In connection with his wife and his brother, Zelora Green, Joseph F. Green owned and operated a tile factory for several years, then left his wife and brother in charge of the plant, and entered law school at Valparaiso, Indiana.[1] Upon graduation he went to Oakland, Illinois, to practice. During the course of his activities in the law profession, Green was retained as counsel in a case against David Sinton. Sinton, impressed with Green's ability, employed him in 1888 to oversee his large farming, mining, and legal interests in the Oakland, Illinois, vicinity.[2] Green remained in this capacity until a physician advised him to change climates to seek relief for his rheumatism.[3]

In May, 1896, Green arrived at Carrizo Springs, Dimmit County, Texas, to assume duties as foreman of the sprawling 224,000-acre

[1] Interview with Mrs. Fay Green Hunt, Gregory, August 7, 1961. Mrs. Hunt is a daughter of Joseph F. and Jennie Saucer Green.

[2] Mrs. May Mathis Green Watson (compiler), "Josiah Mathis and His Descendants: A Genealogical Record of the Mathis Family in the United States," unpublished booklet, in possession of Mrs. May Mathis Green Watson.

[3] Taft *Tribune*, May 8, 1925, November 25, 1926.

Catarina Ranch, which he later leased.[4] He performed his trust so well that four years later he was given the additional responsibility of the general managership of the Coleman-Fulton Pasture Company. With his wife, Jennie, and two daughters, Anna and Fay, Green moved to Gregory, San Patricio County, on July 23, 1900.[5]

At once he and his foreman, Robert E. Miller, began an intense tour of the ranch. At the directors' meeting on August 16, 1900, the new superintendent made an extensive and sweeping report with recommendations for improving the efficiency and the profit-making ability of the Coleman-Fulton Pasture Company, which led to its international recognition. "Having made a careful examination of the Fences, Buildings, Windmills, and Tanks . . . I . . . recommend, that steps be taken at an Early day, to fence the Company's Pastures!"[6]

The primary fault found with existing ranch conditions was the badly deteriorated fences, which neither kept company cattle at home nor excluded neighbors' livestock. The three line riders employed during the 1890's to check enclosures for security and to keep trespassing animals out were dismissed when Charles P. Taft reorganized the ranch in 1897; subsequently, rotted posts and broken wires were not repaired. Approximately 500 to 1,200 head of livestock belonging to persons living nearby roamed at will over the company's pastures.[7] Green recommended that those animals be removed immediately and that all fences be made strong in order to keep the poachers away. *Senderos,* roads, were cut through the brush, providing a path for line riders—who strung wire fences and who inspected them periodically—and for cattle moving between pastures.[8] After estrayed ani-

[4] Charles E. H. Glazbrook, Rincon Ranch, to Joseph F. Green, Catarina Ranch, May 11, 1896, Coleman-Fulton Pasture Company Records (hereafter cited as CFPC), XVII, 233; to John J. Welder, Victoria, Texas, May 12, 1896, CFPC, XVII, 235.

[5] Green, Gregory, Texas, to James C. Fulton, Rockport, Texas, July 24, 1900, Fulton Collection (hereafter cited as FC). All of Green's correspondence originated at Gregory, Texas, unless specified otherwise.

[6] Minutes of the Coleman-Fulton Pasture Company Board of Directors' Meeting (hereafter cited as Minutes of Directors' Meeting), August 16, 1900, CFPC.

[7] *Ibid.* Green to Samuel M. Mansfield, San Francisco, June 25, 1901, CFPC, XVIII, 150.

[8] Minutes of Directors' Meeting, August 16, 1900, CFPC.

mals were trapped, their owners were notified to claim them at once.[9]

When Green took command of the 161,337-acre ranch, 500 acres were in cultivation, primarily in corn and grain sorghums for cattle feed.[10] The company had a large number of horses and mules on hand, but only half the amount of machinery necessary to till the soil; rather than purchase additional equipment, the superintendent disposed of the surplus stock. After advertising unsuccessfully in local news media, he sold them to Joseph F. Green and Company of Encinal, Texas.[11]

In partnership with John M. Green of Encinal, no relation, and Thomas Atlee Coleman of San Antonio, Coleman-Fulton Pasture Company superintendent Joseph F. Green leased the 224,000-acre Catarina Ranch from David Sinton. The mammoth cattle spread covered parts of Dimmit, La Salle, and Webb Counties, approximately one hundred miles southwest of San Antonio, and included the area around the towns of Carrizo Springs, Catarina, Encinal, Cotulla, Artesia Wells, and Asherton.[12] To provide workers on the Catarina Ranch with supplies, Joseph F. Green and Thomas Atlee Coleman owned a large store in Encinal: the Green, Coleman and Company.[13]

The brand of the Coleman-Fulton Pasture Company, a *T* on the right hip, must have been a popular design, because at the time Green became general manager several basically similar brands were used in the community.[14] Slight alteration by the dishonest could change the symbol; therefore, to make thievery more difficult and to improve the means of recognizing its own livestock, the company conducted a re-branding program in 1900 and 1901. In addition to the *T* on the right

[9] Green to Dennis McBride, Corpus Christi, January 24, 1903, CFPC, XX, 83.

[10] Report of Charles P. Taft, president, to the Coleman-Fulton Pasture Company Stockholders, December 31, 1899, FC. Minutes of the Directors' Meeting, August 16, 1900, CFPC.

[11] Green to Fulton, Rockport, December 24, 1900, XVIII, 51–52; to Schwartz Brothers, Schulenburg, Texas, November 25, 1900, XVIII, 44–45; to R. G. Blake, Shiner, Texas, July 8, 1903, XXI, 244; all in CFPC.

[12] Green to Ira H. Evans, Austin, December 17, 1902, CFPC, XX, 52; to Thomas Atlee Coleman, Encinal, Texas, May 10, 1904, CFPC, XXI, 350.

[13] Green to Staacke Brothers, San Antonio [November, 1900], CFPC, XVIII, 45; January 1, 1901, CFPC, XVIII, 57.

[14] Minutes of the Coleman-Fulton Pasture Company Stockholders' Meeting (hereafter cited as Minutes of Stockholders' Meeting), January 5, 1881, CFPC. Minutes of Directors' Meeting, August 16, 1900, CFPC. Marks and Brands Book, San Patricio County, Vol. 1, p. 17, filed August 14, 1899.

hip of the older cattle, a *T* was placed on either the left hip or the left side. On the younger animals only the left side and the left hip were imprinted.[15] When the branding was completed the herd count turned up approximately 5,000 head short of the 14,416 head on the company's Cattle Stock Register.[16]

Green continued the policy of replacing bulls of poor quality with highly graded registered males by purchasing 250 head from the King Ranch in 1901.[17] He wanted to establish a breeding herd so that the company could raise sires necessary for the cattle-improvement program; thus, he purchased forty-six head of registered Shorthorn heifers and four double-standard Polled Durham bulls.[18] Green was impressed with the beef-producing qualities of the Shorthorn in South Texas, favoring that breed over all others, although he did regard the Hereford highly. After trying Angus for five years at Catarina Ranch, Green became discouraged with their performance, stating that they were not suitable to the Southern climate. For many years the Fultons favored Durhams and stocked the ranch with that type, although they had also brought some Herefords to it.

In December, 1901, Green began a program to shift the emphasis from Durhams to Shorthorns by arranging to sell the entire registered Red Polled herd at the Fort Worth Fat Stock Show in March, 1902. Although he had written to other Durham breeders in Texas, the superintendent was unable to interest enough persons in the sale to be given a part on the program by the show's manager.[19] Undaunted by this failure, Green fed cottonseed-oil cake ordered from Kansas City to get the bovines as fat as possible before taking them to the Fort Worth

[15] Marks and Brands Book, San Patricio County, September 4, 1900, Vol. 1, p. 22; September 18, 1900, Vol. 1, p. 27; December 4, 1900, Vol. 1, p. 27. Cattle Stock Register, 1893–1922, CFPC.

[16] Green to Mansfield, San Francisco, June 25, 1901, CFPC, XVIII, 150; to Mrs. Hattie Fulton Holden, Farmington, Delaware, March 27, 1901, CFPC, XVIII, 90.

[17] Fulton, Rockport, to Charles D. Kinney, Cincinnati, February 6, 1901, FC.

[18] Minutes of Directors' Meeting, August 16, 1900, CFPC. The term "double standard" implies an animal with both beef and dairy qualities.

[19] Green to J. F. Hovenkamp, Fort Worth, December 27, 1901, XVIII, 190, 195; to W. R. Clifton, Waco, January 10, 1902, XVIII, 207; to J. H. Jennings, Martindale, Texas, January 10, February 12, 1902, XVIII, 208, 256–257; all in CFPC.

affair, where he sold them privately. One of the cows was a champion at the Dallas Fair in October, 1901, and one of the bulls won a prize ribbon at the Chicago International Fair. For these animals the price asked was $300 and $500 respectively, a sizeable figure, as range cattle were worth less than $20 a head.[20]

Persons laying the foundation for a show herd paid particular attention to pedigrees, and often the cost of these animals was great. Joseph F. Green, John Kenedy of Alice, and R. J. Kleberg of the King Ranch commissioned John Miller of Markham, Ontario, Canada, to buy approximately one hundred head of the best Scottish-imported registered Shorthorns that could be found in Canada and to ship them to Texas.[21] Green, interested in exhibiting them all over the United States to advertise the ranch, wanted six heifers and two bulls of the best strain, regardless of cost. He was becoming well known as a Shorthorn breeder and had many customers who wanted sires from the herd of the Coleman-Fulton Pasture Company and from that of his own Joseph F. Green and Company. The strong interest Green displayed in boosting the red Scottish breed netted him the presidency of the Texas Shorthorn Association in 1903.[22]

After the tally of the Coleman-Fulton Pasture Company cattle and the subsequent discovery that approximately one-third of the number in the Cattle Register were unaccounted for, the ranch allowed natural increase to bolster the count to a correct animal-acre ratio by reducing livestock sales during 1900 and 1901. On January 1, 1900, the herd numbered 14,416 head, reached 21,466 by January 1, 1902, and then decreased during the following years as marketing increased; by 1910 there were only 10,899 head in the pastures.[23]

[20] Green to A. J. Peavy, Lufkin, Texas, February 27, 1902, XXI, 45; to J. W. Johnson, Haskell, February 27, 1902, XXI, 46; to J. H. Jennings, Martindale, Texas, February 12, 1902, XVIII, 256–257; to American Linseed Company, Kansas City, Missouri, December 26, 1901, XVIII, 187; all in CFPC.

[21] Green to John Miller, Markham, Ontario, April 9, 1902, CFPC, XXI, 83–84; to John Kenedy, Alice, Texas, August 30, 1902, CFPC, XXI, 161.

[22] Green to S. F. Lookridge, Green Castle, Indiana, August 31, 1903, CFPC, XX, 688.

[23] Stock Report, January 1, 1902, in "Statements sent to General Office, 1894–1902," p. 296, CFPC. Cattle Stock Register, 1893–1922, CFPC.

In the early years of the twentieth century the price of cattle was quite deflated as compared to a decade before. Although most of the Coleman-Fulton Pasture Company's steers were 75- to 90-per-cent Shorthorn or Hereford by 1903, the firm sold 2,000 head for an average of $13 each.[24] This low market was rumored to be caused by a price-fixing scheme of the larger meat-packing houses in the Midwest and the Northeast. The federal government investigated the beef-packing industry in 1904 without proving that a beef trust actually existed.[25] In testimony taken for the Bureau of Corporations of the Department of Commerce and Labor, Joseph F. Green stated that the butcher shop in Corpus Christi belonging to the Coleman-Fulton Pasture Company competed with Armour and Company; but he added that he could not say with certainty that the Chicago and Saint Louis markets were manipulated by a conspiracy of packing houses.[26]

Home markets were limited in their ability to exchange livestock for cash. In addition to sending loads to Saint Louis and New Orleans, the Coleman-Fulton Pasture Company shipped cattle steadily to Fort Worth by 1904. Local butcher shops in Gregory, Sinton, and Corpus Christi were excellent places to sell fat cows at top-notch prices and at a greater profit than could be realized by shipping them away. When Green asked the ranch president, Taft, for permission to establish a butcher shop in Corpus Christi, he pointed out in his argument that the small Gregory shop had made a profit of more than $4,000 the previous year.[27] Taft quickly consented to the plan when he heard that this firm would be another outlet for company cattle at no extra labor expense, since the same personnel would do the slaughtering for all shops. By 1904 the Pasture Company was handling sheep as well as cattle and

[24] Green to Allen Gray, Evansville, Texas, February 23, 1903, CFPC, XX, 109.

[25] *House Documents*, 58th Congress, Third Session, Serial No. 4833, Doc. No. 382, pp. 1–315.

[26] Report of Special Agent T. A. Carroll to Commissioner of Corporations, August 30, 1904, concerning an interview with Joseph F. Green, Report Number 172, United States Department of Commerce and Labor, Bureau of Corporations.

[27] Green to Charles Phelps Taft, Cincinnati, June 14, 1904, CFPC, XX, 581; December 6, 1904, CFPC, XXII, 188–190. Green to Roy Willis, Sinton, October 6, 1904, CFPC, XXII, 120.

horses, but its only purpose was to supply its own meat markets, not to profit from grazing or shearing.[28]

As the best time for marketing livestock in the Midwest was from January 1 to July 1, when few regions had fat cattle to sell, the Coleman-Fulton Pasture Company sought to take advantage of that season and to practice winter feeding. In addition to buying cottonseed ginned at Gregory and the feed products from local farmers, the ranch ordered linseed-oil cake and cottonseed-oil cake from Kansas City and San Antonio and cottonseed hulls from Beeville.[29] The need for supplementing the rations of weak cattle to help them through a grass-scarce winter was another reason for purchasing feed. It soon became evident to Green that Midwestern ways of feed-lot stock farming were not practical in Texas. Green followed the example set by the older ranches in the area, particularly the King and Kenedy spreads, in selling steers while they were yet yearlings and before they became mature beeves. "This is considered a good breeding country but not good for maturing cattle," the Coleman-Fulton Pasture Company superintendent wrote to Taft explaining the action.[30] Sales during 1903 and 1904 permitted the Pasture Company to declare a 2-per-cent dividend on May 2, 1904, in addition to paying the $17,771 vendor's lien note held by San Patricio County for the four leagues of school land purchased in 1877.[31]

A severe winter plus outbreaks of two new animal diseases in 1904–1905 caused a slight reduction in the Coleman-Fulton Pasture Company herd. Blackleg, an infectious disease, especially fatal among young animals from the time they are weaned until they are approximately two years old, is so named because the only organic disorders found on postmortem examination are dark and soft muscular tissues with bloody

[28] Green to Taft, Cincinnati, December 6, 1904, CFPC, XXII, 188–190.

[29] Green to Charles Schmalstig, Cincinnati, August 5, 1904, XXII, 31; to American Linseed Company, Kansas City, Missouri, December 26, 1901, XVIII, 187; to Western Cotton Oil Company, San Antonio, February 11, 1902, XVIII, 255; to G. C. Street and Company, Houston, December 19, 1902, XX, 57; to Campbell and Verquhart, San Antonio, February 6, 1903, XX, 91; to Beeville Cotton Seed Oil Mill Company, Beeville, November 29, 1903, XX, 371; all in CFPC.

[30] Green to Taft, Cincinnati, April 14, 1905, CFPC, XXII, 404.

[31] Minutes of Stockholders' Meeting, May 2, 1904, CFPC. Deed Records, San Patricio County, October 4, 1904, Vol. R, p. 273.

fluid beneath the animals' swollen limbs.[32] The company started an inoculation program in April, 1903, and completed it in February, 1905, but not before it suffered heavy losses from the disease in the harsh winter of 1904–1905.[33] A hard snow and sleet storm in February, 1905, ruined the budding orange and lemon trees in the area in addition to delaying the arrival of spring grass. The superintendent estimated that the weather would detain the date for market by at least two months.[34]

The second disease affecting the South Texas animal industry was the mange, a skin disease caused by a parasite. In June, 1904, Green built a dipping vat on the ranch; and with a mixture of Beaumont oil and Chloral Naphtha lime, in which the cattle were dipped twice, the mange mite was destroyed. By burning pastures and by moving livestock to fresh ranges when dipped, the ranch eliminated all evidence of scabby cattle by June 1, 1905.[35] The vat continued to be used in the long struggle against the fever tick.

During the early years of the twentieth century at least 90 per cent of the cattle were highly graded Shorthorn or Hereford.[36] A small number of Longhorns still lived in the brushy part of the pastures, and occasionally the ranch attempted to remove them completely, but without success. It was difficult to drive the animals from the brush, and, if taken to pens, they were so wild that no enclosure could prevent their escaping. Out of necessity a new technique was devised.

Watering places, usually around windmills, were fenced off, and a gate was placed beside a windmill. A man stationed in the tower pulled a rope that closed the gate when several head of cattle entered; in the words of a man who was a cowboy and farmer for the Coleman-

[32] United States Department of Agriculture, "Tick Fever," *Farmers' Bulletin No. 1625*, p. 22.

[33] Green to Taft, Cincinnati, April 10, 1903, CFPC, XIX, 135–138; March 1, 1905, CFPC, XXII, 325.

[34] *Ibid.*, April 7, 1905, CFPC, XXII, 393. Green to W. S. Jones, Estherville, Iowa, February 25, 1905, CFPC, XXII, 310–312.

[35] Green to Taft, Cincinnati, June 8, 1904, XX, 577; to West Disinfectant Company, New York, New York, February 25, 1905, XXII, 319; to Dr. Joseph W. Parker, San Antonio, August 28, 1905, XXII, 470; all in CFPC.

[36] Green to A. Gray, Evansville, Texas, February 23, 1903, CFPC, XX, 109.

Fulton Pasture Company at the time, "then the fun taken place."[37] The wild beasts tried to climb the eleven-strand, heavy, smooth-wire fence, sometimes tearing it down and escaping. The Longhorns had to be roped right then, even though it was dusk, or they would gore each other in their frenzied charging around the enclosure. Each was roped, tied to a tree, and secured to a corn-fed, tame steer wearing a large leather collar around its neck; the steer then escorted a wild bovine on each side to a corral.[38]

A second method used to capture and to gentle the wild animals was to leave them tied to a tree after they were roped. A short, seven-foot rope, carried by the cowboys for this purpose, was looped and tied in a knot around the Longhorn's neck to prevent choking—the horns could not be used because the animal would pull them off trying to escape. The steer then circled the tree until he became exhausted. At times the cattle crippled themselves, and the ranch employees butchered them on the spot. The meat was given to cowboys assisting in the drive or to neighbors who would come for it; then, if any were left, it would be carried in a wagon to the local butcher shop and sold.[39]

Changes were made in the Pasture Company's personnel as well as in its livestock. When David Sinton died in 1900, his daughter, Mrs. Anna Sinton Taft, inherited the 5,225 shares of capital stock owned by her father.[40] Charles Phelps Taft became the chief policy maker for the corporation in reality, as he had been in fact for several years. While Taft and his wife were on a European tour in 1901–1902, they gave Green authority to vote their majority capital stock at the stockholders' meetings. With their stock, plus his own 230 shares, the superintendent was able to bring about further changes in company officials.

Rather than naming James C. Fulton, the secretary, to the Board of Directors to replace Sinton, Green chose one of his Joseph F. Green and Company partners, Thomas Atlee Coleman.[41] Purchasing ten shares of capital stock in order to qualify for an official position, Coleman was subsequently named a director and the temporary president

[37] Interview with S. Frank Hunt, Sinton, August 8, 1961.
[38] *Ibid.*
[39] *Ibid.*
[40] J. C. Fulton, Rockport, to Taft, Cincinnati, November 10, 1900, FC.
[41] Minutes of Stockholders' Meeting, May 6, 1901, CFPC.

of the corporation until Taft returned from Europe.[42] Green asked Fulton to resign as secretary, stating that this was an order from Taft, although Fulton did not believe him:

My own impression is, that Mr. Taft had nothing to do with this change. . . . The fact is, Mr. Green has persistantly [*sic*] endeavored to depreciate the value of the company's stock: for the sole purpose of enabling him to buy it up at low figures.[43]

At any rate, Fulton was replaced by J. W. Hoopes of Rockport as secretary on May 6, 1901.[44] Hoopes was the son of J. M. Hoopes, Rockport banker, and the son-in-law of the late George W. Fulton, Jr.

Within a year the secretaryship again changed when Hoopes found employment outside the Rockport area that paid more than the annual stipend of $300 allowed him by the Coleman-Fulton Pasture Company.[45] His successor, Mrs. Joseph F. Green, held the post until she was replaced by her husband in 1903, who added the position of secretary to his titles of superintendent and of general manager. Taft, who had returned from Europe by this time, was again named president and treasurer; together Taft and Green were the principal officers for many subsequent years.[46]

Green continued his acquisition of Coleman-Fulton Pasture Company capital stock, sometimes purchasing shares at 60 per cent of par value,[47] perhaps as a result of his letters to stockholders describing a gloomy future for the ranch, as Fulton had insinuated. Green's stockholding increased to 374 shares in 1902, 967 in 1903, 1,718 in 1906, and 1,881 in 1909, when together with the 6,069 shares of the Tafts, which he voted by proxy in the stockholders' meeting, Green controlled approximately 93 per cent of the corporation's capital stock.[48] As the Articles of Organization stated that at least two directors must

[42] J. W. Hoopes, Rockport, to Fulton, Beaumont, June 3, 1901, FC.

[43] Fulton, Beaumont, to C. D. Kinney, York Cliffs, Maine, August 13, 1901, FC.

[44] Minutes of Directors' Meeting, May 6, 1901, CFPC.

[45] *Ibid.*, May 5, 1902, CFPC.

[46] *Ibid.*, May 4, 1903, CFPC.

[47] Fulton, Rockport, to Mrs. Annie W. Holden [n.p.] September 12, 1902, FC; to Mrs. Hattie F. Holden, Farmington, Delaware, September 11, 1902, FC.

[48] Minutes of Stockholders' Meeting, May 5, 1902; May 4, 1903; October 22, 1906; January 4, 1909; all in CFPC.

be present at a meeting to conduct business, Green appointed another Joseph F. Green and Company partner, John M. Green, to replace Thomas Atlee Coleman, who resigned in 1907.[49] To comply with the requirement that officers must also be stockholders, John M. Green bought one share. In 1908 John M. Green filled the position of vice president, vacant since George W. Fulton, Jr., resigned in 1894, to assist Joseph F. Green with the administration of the ranch at the time increased land sales made the job too large for one person.[50]

When Joseph F. Green became superintendent of the ranch its primary business was cattle raising. Only a few farmers remained on the land sold during the boom. These cultivators raised cotton in the region on a limited scale, but with "worn out cow ponies, poor implements and untrained Mexican labor."[51] Nevertheless, the yield was good. The San Patricio County Board of Equalization invited Green to appear before it and to express his future plans for the ranch. Knowing of the reason for the requested conference and hoping to discourage the assessment of additional taxes, the superintendent emphatically stated that his only concern was raising cattle. In fact he voiced a doubt that row-crop farming on a large scale was feasible. Undaunted by this statement of singleness of purpose for land use in the county, the Board, seeking to encourage diversified farming, advised Green that the ranch's land valuation for taxes would be raised so high that he could not afford to pasture it. Therefore, he should investigate the possibility of having the ranch cultivate the soil.[52] The county officials were interested also in bringing in new families who would develop the region, and thereby increase the county's revenue potential. Green was not convinced that the Coastal Bend was suited to farming; but to satisfy himself and the Board of Equalization he took steps to put a small acreage in cotton.

A swale two miles northwest of Mesquital along the San Antonio and Aransas Pass railroad right-of-way was selected as the place for the experiment. Water stood in the low place after rains, thus stunting the growth of good grass, while fostering vegetation that was harmful

[49] *Ibid.*, May 9, 1907, CFPC.

[50] Minutes of Directors' Meeting, May 4, 1908, CFPC.

[51] Joseph F. Green, *Farm Experience on Taft Ranch* (booklet published for the Union National Bank, Houston, Texas), pp. 3–4.

[52] *Ibid.*

to cattle. In 1903 the ranch hired a force of Latin Americans to grub trees and roots from the designated area and purchased a machine to dig drainage ditches to prevent inundation. Carpenters began to construct houses and buildings necessary for farming purposes; shortly afterwards four farmers signed contracts to cultivate fifty acres of cotton each.[53] Despite the beautiful, growing crop and the excellent prospects for a good yield in 1904, Green reflected his greater interest in following cows rather than plows when he wrote Taft that the cotton fields were a sight to see, "but I would so much prefer to have you see these cattle in their improved condition, especially in the feeding, and the ranch with all the improvements we have made."[54]

Ranch officials were surprised when the worthless swale land produced one-half bale of cotton to the acre. The company's rent from one-fourth of the crop was over $8 an acre.[55] The ranch received an extra benefit when good grass came back on the drained land not yet in cultivation. To improve pasture facilities and to increase the number of farms, Green hired forty grubbers, cut more drainage ditches, and set his carpenters to work during the last half of 1904—at an expense of $4,000 a month.[56] The original 200 acres, a portion of a 10,000-acre tract where water stood for an extended period after each sizeable rain, was the site of the new farms. As the San Antonio and Aransas Pass railroad ran adjacent to the farms, Superintendent Green, who was something of a showman, spent "a little necessary money . . . for the reason they were in a conspicuous place and I desired to make them as advertisement to the ranch."[57] The cost of grubbing, draining, breaking sod, drilling wells, erecting fences, homes, and barns, and building roads was estimated at $2,000 for each of the farms or $40 an acre.[58] For the 1905 crop 200 additional acres were put into cultivation, followed by 400 in 1906, 600 in 1907, 900 in 1908, and 1,050

[53] Green to Taft, Cincinnati, August 22, 1904, XXII, 53; December 6, 1904, XXII, 188, 190; December 16, 1904, XXII, 233; all in CFPC. Minutes of Stockholders' Meeting, May 4, 1903, CFPC.

[54] Green to Taft, Cincinnati, July 27, 1904, CFPC, XXII, 28–29.

[55] Green, *Farm Experience on Taft Ranch*, p. 5.

[56] Green to Taft, Cincinnati, December 6, 16, 1904, CFPC, XXII, 188–190, 233; to Schmalstig, Cincinnati, August 30, 1904, CFPC, XXII, 49–50.

[57] Green to Taft, Cincinnati, December 16, 1904, CFPC, XXII, 231–232.

[58] *Ibid.*

in 1909, making a total of 2,300 acres planted in row-crop commodities at the end of the 1909 season.[59]

The pattern set for locating houses for tenants and for Latin American laborers on the farms was followed for the next two decades. Roads connected each farm with nearby settlements; along the lanes on each side, scattered one mile apart, were the buildings. With the residences placed near the corner, where the various tracts met at the road, four farms could be watered from one well; only one road would join all the farms with a village. The local name for the series of houses, four in a group, separated at one-mile intervals, became "spiderville" because of the resemblance to a spider's appendages connected at regular distances on the body.

When grubbing first began in January, 1903, the Coleman-Fulton Pasture Company established a store at Mesquital to serve the itinerant laborers, ranch employees, and families that would move to the farms. The entire stock of staples amounted to only $1,000, half in clothing and the remainder in groceries.[60] A warehouse was built in which to keep ranch supplies as well as goods for sale. Well-built houses in the Aransas Pass-Rockport region were constructed in abundance during the boom, but were later abandoned. As it was less expensive to buy a house and to move it a long distance than to build one of equal size, the ranch purchased a large, two-story dwelling in Rockport and moved it to Mesquital in August, 1904, to be used as the company store and as the residence of the storekeeper. Green paid only $150 for a structure valued at $1,600 when new.[61]

In the spring of 1904 the company added a post office, and that summer enlarged the house purchased in Rockport. The settlement expanded further when the ranch built three small houses for Latin American laborers, established a blacksmith shop, and dug two wells for the residents of the village.[62] As the railroad station gained popu-

[59] H. V. Fetick, Secretary of the Coleman-Fulton Pasture Company, Taft, Texas, to the Commissioner of Internal Revenue, Washington, D.C., November 7, 1923, Income Tax Information Folder (hereafter cited as Fetick to Commissioner of Internal Revenue), CFPC.

[60] Green to Norman W. Swink, Encinal, Texas, January 18, 1903, CFPC, XX, 77.

[61] Green to Taft, Cincinnati, August 22, 1904, CFPC, XXII, 53.

[62] Green to Oliver Chilled Plow Works, Dallas, January 28, 1904, CFPC, XX, 440; to Schmalstig, Cincinnati, August 30, 1904, CFPC, XXII, 49–50.

lation, Green changed the name of Mesquital to "Taft" in honor of the corporation's leading stockholders, Mr. and Mrs. Charles Phelps Taft.[63]

With more acreage now set aside for cultivation, additional families moved to the Taft vicinity. In order to provide for the education of scholastic-age children, the Coleman-Fulton Pasture Company's stockholders in 1906 authorized construction of a community building in the town for school, church, or public meetings.[64]

Other services brought to Taft in 1906 were a railroad depot and communication lines. For $10 the ranch sold eight acres in the town for a depot warehouse, platform, and sidings to accommodate the business of the community.[65] The Southwestern Telegraph and Telephone Company, a New York corporation with its main Texas office in Dallas, was given permission to construct, operate, and maintain communication lines along the San Antonio and Aransas Pass right-of-way through the entire ranch, including the towns of Taft, Gregory, and Portland. The Coleman-Fulton Pasture Company, or as it became popularly known, the Taft Ranch, was given the right to use the telephone company's poles to string two wires from Gregory, Portland, Taft, and Sinton, connecting its offices in those towns, but at its own expense and for its exclusive use.[66] The ranch further indicated its willingness to assist in the development of the community when it installed the first cotton gin in Taft in 1907 in order that tenants would not be required to haul cotton to Gregory, eight miles away.[67]

At the time the cotton fields were developed around Taft, ranch officials saw the value of the western range increase when the Saint Louis, Brownsville, and Mexico Railway Company extended its tracks from Sinton to the Nueces River in 1905. Railroad officials informed Superintendent Green that all other ranchers had granted free rights-of-

[63] Green to Oliver Chilled Plow Works, Dallas, September 19, 1904, CFPC, XXII, 84.

[64] Minutes of Stockholders' Meeting, July 2, 1906, CFPC.

[65] *Ibid.* Deed Records, San Patricio County, October 29, 1906, Vol. S, pp. 448–451.

[66] Minutes of Stockholders' Meeting, July 2, 1906, CFPC. Deed Records, San Patricio County, July 7, 1906, Vol. T, pp. 501–506.

[67] May M. Green Watson and Alex Lillico, *Taft Ranch: A History of the Fifty Years of Development sponsored by Coleman-Fulton Pasture Company with sketches of Gregory and Taft, the two towns it created*, pp. 15–16.

way and had paid a bonus of $1,000 a mile where the road crossed their property. The Coleman-Fulton Pasture Company agreed to this proposition if the route were placed where Green selected, but his offer was refused. The outcome was that the Saint Louis, Brownsville, and Mexico Railway Company received a deed for a 100-foot-wide strip of land 7.4 miles in length across the Brasada Pasture, containing ninety acres in all, for the legal minimum consideration of $1.00.[68]

The right-of-way was through land given to the Aransas Pass Harbor Company by a warranty deed in 1895. The ranch sought to regain title to the approximately 10,000 acres in 1896, as it was evident that the Harbor Company would not complete a navigable channel; but when new contracts were let later that year ranch officials decided to wait for results. After the Harbor Company released its franchise in 1899, the ranch's attorneys, McCampbell and Stayton of Corpus Christi, introduced a law suit into the San Patricio District Court in Sinton.[69] On September 17, 1906, the court allowed the Coleman-Fulton Pasture Company to recover 3,971.55 acres of the tract, which was the area east and south of the Saint Louis, Brownsville, and Mexico railroad.[70]

The 5,957.46 acres awarded to the Aransas Pass Harbor Company, valued at $10 an acre in 1895, sold in 1907 to the Texas Channel and Dock Company for $50,000; John J. Welder and Dave Odem purchased this land for $80,000 in 1908.[71] The Welder and Odem Subdivision of San Patricio County was created from 4,903 acres of this tract west and north of the Saint Louis, Brownsville, and Mexico railroad, and the town of Odem was established there.

Having made improvements in the expanding town of Taft and elsewhere on the ranch to accommodate its employees and tenants, the

[68] Green to Taft, Cincinnati, July 23, 1904, CFPC, XXII, 24; to Schmalstig, Cincinnati, July 18, 1904, CFPC, XXII, 18, 20. Minutes of Stockholders' Meeting, May 2, 1904, July 2, 1906, CFPC. Deed Records, San Patricio County, July 14, 1906, Vol. S, pp. 316–318.

[69] Fulton, Rockport, to McCampbell and Stayton, Corpus Christi, September 18, 1902, FC.

[70] *Coleman-Fulton Pasture Company, Plaintiff* vs. *Aransas Pass Harbor Company*, ET AL., Defendants, Case No. 1313, San Patricio County, District Court Judgments in Civil Cases, September 17, 1906, Vol. 1. Deed Records, San Patricio County, September 18, 1906, Vol. T, p. 383.

[71] Deed Records, San Patricio County, February 5, 1907, Vol. U, p. 29; May 19, 1908, Vol. V, p. 109.

superintendent believed that a larger residence was necessary for the convenience and comfort of ranch officials. Whenever Mr. and Mrs. Charles P. Taft came to South Texas they stayed at Green's modest-sized home in Gregory. To provide more suitable quarters for the Tafts, for the superintendent, for visiting stockholders, and for guests of the ranch, the corporation in 1906 authorized Joseph F. Green to erect, equip, and furnish a building of modern style.[72] The site selected was along Corpus Christi Bay three miles south of Gregory. The forty feet of elevation, described by one newspaper reporter as the highest spot on the Gulf Coast between Corpus Christi and the Atlantic Ocean, afforded some protection when storms and high tides threatened in subsequent years.[73]

Although construction began in 1906 inclement weather hampered the progress on the house and the necessary out-buildings, such as a carriage house, barns, and servants' quarters. In May, 1907, Green estimated that approximately $38,000 would be required to conclude the improvements, including the placement of shell on the road connecting the residence with Gregory.[74] When completed in December, 1907, the home faced the bay over a bluff approximately one hundred yards away.

An impressive sight greeted visitors traveling through the mesquite trees and the bramble bushes when they suddenly came upon the clearing with a three-story mansion in the midst of carefully landscaped grounds. Long verandas encircled the house on the north and east sides, where persons sat shaded in the afternoon and enjoyed the luxury of such extraordinary quarters. Inside the home were a living room and a dining room at each end of the ground floor, accommodating one hundred persons each. A large hall connected the two rooms; when all doors were open one could see the entire length of the house ninety feet away. The upper floors contained twelve bedrooms and six baths, with a gallery on the second level and an observation platform on the third.[75] The place became well noted for its friendliness and hospitality.

[72] Minutes of Stockholders' Meeting, July 2, 1906, CFPC.

[73] Taft (Texas) *Tribune*, February 23, 1928.

[74] Minutes of Stockholders' Meeting, May 9, 1907, CFPC.

[75] T. N. Blackwell (compiler), *Taft Ranch, San Patricio County, Texas: The Land of perpetual Sunshine, Sea Breezes, Fat Cattle, Hogs, Dairy Cows, Cotton,*

Amusements provided for guests were boating, fishing, hunting, bathing, tennis, and golf.[76] Superintendent Green kept a large kennel of greyhounds for the sporting convenience of visitors as well as for his own entertainment.

In the fall of 1907 Joseph F. Green, a divorcee at the time, married Miss May Mathis of Rockport, the daughter of Thomas Henry Mathis, one of the partners in the Coleman, Mathis, and Fulton firm. For two months they lived in Gregory until December 24, when their home became the large house on the bay. The following day, Christmas, a housewarming was held for the superintendent and his bride, the first of the annual open-house occasions held on Christmas or New Year's Day for two decades. Everyone was invited—friends, neighbors, tenants, employees—and usually as many as 450 persons came to celebrate the holiday season.[77] The residence became known as "La Quinta," Spanish for "countryhouse." The name originated with Mrs. Green's mother, Mrs. Thomas Henry Mathis, who, hearing the term applied to an elaborate structure while on a tour to Mexico, interpreted it to mean "a baron's villa," thought it was fitting for this occasion, and suggested it to her daughter.[78]

A region of the ranch more densely infested with brush than the La Quinta grounds was that part of the range south and west of the San Antonio and Aransas Pass railroad, and south and east of the Saint Louis, Brownsville, and Mexico railroad. For a long time the Brasada had been useless for grazing, and by 1908 much of the Picatche Pasture was so thoroughly covered with mesquite and chaparral that cattle could not be raised profitably there. It would not be feasible to clear the land for grazing purposes; therefore, its best use after reclamation was for cultivable crops.

Feed, Prosperity and Happiness, p. 10. William Howard Taft, Gregory, to Mrs. William Howard Taft, Washington, D.C., October 22, 1909, William Howard Taft Papers, Presidential Letter Book No. 7 (hereafter cited as William H. Taft to Mrs. Taft). Taft *Tribune*, June 12, 1924.

[76] Taft *Tribune*, February 23, 1928.

[77] Mrs. May Mathis Green Watson (compiler), "Josiah Mathis and His Descendants," unpublished booklet in possession of Mrs. May Mathis Green Watson.

[78] Interview with Mrs. May Mathis Green Watson, Corpus Christi, March 2, 1961.

When the corporation officials saw the success of farming in the vicinity of Taft, they resolved to put more land to the plow, not for themselves alone, but for individual farms. To promote the development of the company's property and the country surrounding it, the stockholders authorized the president in 1906 to sell a maximum of 10,000 acres in one tract at a location he might select, keeping in mind the company's purpose of increasing the value of its land.[79] The number of acres for sale was increased to 50,000 the following year, in one or more tracts, including town lots.[80] Permission to sell in several blocks allowed the ranch to dispose of farming land in San Patricio County and of the Little or Shipping Pasture on Live Oak Peninsula, which was sold in June, 1907, for $30,293.30, a rate of $8.28 an acre.[81]

The Coleman-Fulton Pasture Company included in the sale price the preparation of a land title or an abstract to the purchaser. To accomplish this work, it engaged the services of F. Stevens of Rockport and H. M. Holden of Sinton, attorneys, to make the abstracts in Aransas and San Patricio Counties, respectively.[82]

The company sold no land from 1897 to 1903, and made only a few sales for three years following. In 1907 activity increased as the ranch's productive soil became known; buyers persuaded Green to sell them several hundred acres at prices ranging from $16 to $30, depending on the location.[83] From 1908 to 1913 the Gregory office sold scattered tracts without a significant increase in price. Since the ranch chose not to engage in land promotion on a large scale, it selected a firm of Washington, Iowa, the George H. Paul Company, which at that time was successfully selling part of the Driscoll Ranch near Robstown in Nueces County.[84]

George H. Paul, the guiding genius behind the George H. Paul Company, was only thirty-one years old in 1908, but had gained experience in land promotion through his association with the Luse Land

[79] Minutes of Stockholders' Meeting, July 2, 1906, CFPC.

[80] *Ibid.*, May 9, 1907, CFPC.

[81] Deed Records, Aransas County, June 28, 1907, Vol. V, p. 309.

[82] Minutes of Stockholders' Meeting, May 9, 1907, CFPC.

[83] Account Land Sales Book, 1890–1909, CFPC. Land Sales Book No. 1, 1906–1923, Taft Ranch, Charles Phelps Taft and Anna Sinton Taft Collection.

[84] George H. Paul, Omaha, to author, October 6, 1961.

Company of Carroll, Iowa, for whom he sold Canadian land to Midwestern farmers. Organizing his own firm, Paul came to Corpus Christi in 1907, contracted with Robert Driscoll to sell a part of the Driscoll Ranch in Nueces County, and was so successful that he attracted attention to his work from all over South Texas.[85]

In order to raise money for improvement and development of the remainder of its real estate, the Taft Ranch decided to sell the brushy area unfit for grazing south and west of Taft and south of Sinton, except for a mile reserve parallel to the railroad tracks.[86] With this revenue the ranch later brought in industry to utilize their own surplus commodities and those of neighboring farmers. On February 13, 1908, the Coleman-Fulton Pasture Company sold the George H. Paul Company 2,000 acres between Portland and Sinton at $16 each.[87]

Paul had effective means to get "homeseekers" to come to Texas with him and to buy his land. Approximately 1,100 agents at one time covered the United States from West Virginia to Colorado, and from North Texas to Canada, recruiting prospective buyers to ride the excursion trains to South Texas.[88] The railroad companies realized that with more settlers in a region the greater their potential revenue would be in transporting goods; thus, they gave landmen excellent cooperation by arranging special trains and rates. Although Paul paid $45-a-day rental on Pullman cars, he and those who came with him paid the regular homeseekers railroad fare of $23 for a round-trip ticket from all points outside Texas, plus $1.50 a day for berth and meals.[89] Even if a person were not interested in land he could sight-see; but in spite of joyriders the Paul Company sold property to 85 per cent of the persons making the trips, a commendation to the effectiveness of the salesmen.[90]

State agents were paid a 15-per-cent commission; in turn, they

[85] *Ibid.*

[86] Fetick to Commissioner of Internal Revenue, CFPC.

[87] *Ibid.* George H. Paul recalls the date as *March* 13, 1908 (Paul, Omaha, to author, October 6, 1961).

[88] Howard A. Burrell, "George H. Paul," *History of Washington County, Iowa: Also Biographical Sketches of Some Prominent Citizens of the County,* pp. 72 ff. Paul, Omaha, to Mrs. Lyra Haisley Sparks, Taft, October 23, 1961; to author, October 16, 1961. Corpus Christi *Caller*, November 6, 1908.

[89] Paul, Omaha, to author, October 16, 31, 1961.

[90] *Ibid.*, October 16, 1961.

remunerated subagents according to the amount of land purchased by the persons they sponsored.[91] On one occasion the Paul homeseeker train had ten Pullmans and two hotel cars, in addition to dining and baggage cars, altogether forming a train of fourteen units and 350 homeseekers. One Pullman each came from Pittsburgh, Pennsylvania; Chicago, Illinois; Muscatine and Des Moines, Iowa; Omaha and Lincoln, Nebraska; and four from Kansas City, Missouri.[92]

Around 1908 the Coleman-Fulton Pasture Company became popularly known as the Taft Ranch. The George H. Paul Company helped to bring about the change. When William Howard Taft, half-brother of Charles Phelps Taft, received the Republican nomination for the presidency in 1908, George H. Paul capitalized on the family name. His agents distributed thousands of printed circulars on which appeared the word *Taft* in large letters and a description of real estate for sale in smaller print. A person attracted to the sign for information on the political candidate soon discovered that he was reading an advertisement concerning land in Texas. In Paul Company literature the term "Taft Ranch" was deliberately associated with property owned by the Coleman-Fulton Pasture Company because it had more eye-catching appeal to Midwesterners than did the corporation's correct styling. Gradually, the new designation became accepted and eventually became used entirely except on legal documents. Paul estimated that several hundred additional homeseekers were recruited for his trains because of this clever employment of the Taft name.[93]

The Paul Company sold the first tract so rapidly that on April 20, 1908, it contracted to purchase an additional 24,000 acres at $18 each.[94] Originally, Paul received permission to sell approximately 50,000 acres of the ranch within two years, but the Pasture Company released blocks to him singly in order that the cattle could have access to this area until it was actually sold to farmers. The land company was so successful that the Coleman-Fulton Pasture Company's stockholders in a meeting on July 6, 1908, authorized the president to sell Paul

[91] *Ibid.*, October 16, 31, 1961.

[92] Burrell, "George H. Paul," *History of Washington County, Iowa*, pp. 91–92. Paul, Omaha, to Sparks, Taft, October 23, 1961.

[93] Interview with George H. Paul, Omaha, Nebraska, May 3, 1963.

[94] Fetick to Commissioner of Internal Revenue, CFPC. Corpus Christi *Caller*, May 1, 1908.

30,000 acres more, which he did on July 17 at $20 an acre.[95] Within a year the Paul Company had sold all the property, at prices ranging from $25.00 to $42.50 an acre direct to prospective settlers, with an average of $35.00 for the 56,000 acres.

George H. Paul—not a real-estate agent for the Taft Ranch—had purchased the land outright. An arrangement was made, however, whereby the Paul Company did not pay for the land under contract until a settler purchased, at which time the ranch was paid $5 an acre in cash with the balance divided in five annual vendor's lien notes, at 6-per-cent interest.[96] Fred M. Percival of Rockport, under contract to the ranch, surveyed and subdivided the land into plots ranging from eighty acres to a section, cut to suit the buyer. Waldo E. Haisley of Sinton, an Indiana attorney who had recently migrated to Texas on a Paul homeseeker train, did the abstract work on the huge subdivision, and later performed the same service for the Pasture Company.[97]

To compensate the ranch superintendent for his time and effort in guiding the sale of land to promoters and cultivators, in drawing up deeds and filing them, and in making abstracts, the corporation's stockholders on July 6, 1908, followed the recommendation of Charles P. Taft and voted to pay Joseph F. Green a commission on land sales, retroactive to June 1, 1907, in addition to his annual salary of $7,000.[98] They allowed 2 per cent on sales of undivided tracts, with 5 per cent on subdivided land.

The trip to Texas on the excursion or homeseeker trains became an eventful ride for many persons who were persuaded to break away from their homes and to make new roots in South Texas. The following excerpt from a letter written by a traveler describes her trip to the Coastal Bend and what she saw upon arrival.

> Thinking perhaps you would be interested in hearing from us, we will attempt to tell you something of the sights and the scenes that have come under our observation since leaving home. We joined the George H. Paul

[95] Minutes of Stockholders' Meeting, July 6, 1908, CFPC. Fetick to Commissioner of Internal Revenue, CFPC.

[96] Fetick to Commissioner of Internal Revenue, CFPC. Paul, Omaha, to author, October 31, 1961; to Sparks, Taft, October 27, 1961, January 3, 1962.

[97] Paul, Omaha, to Sparks, Taft, August 12, 1961; to author, October 31, 1961. Corpus Christi *Caller*, July 24, 1908.

[98] Minutes of Stockholders' Meeting, July 6, 1908, CFPC.

company's special car at Kansas City. From here on our trip was made without any farther change, as the engine, sleepers and diner are under control of the company. There were about 160 passengers on the train. The evenings were spent in entertainment, consisting of music and speeches; the days of becoming better acquainted and seeing new countries. We became so well acquainted that before the journey was over we felt almost as members of one big family.

On reaching Sinton, we found brother Waldo Haisley and family [who rode a homeseeker train from Indiana to Texas in October, 1908] well and enjoying their new home. We took a short drive in the morning, passing a most beautiful grove of live-oak with hanging moss, which is being considered as a suitable place for a park. Winding around, we came to a magnificent home owned by a wealthy rancher which is certainly all that could be desired in the way of a country home, having all the conveniences of the city with the freedom of the country.

In the afternoon we went to Taft, seven miles east of here; the country there having been under cultivation longer than here; we thought we might get a better idea of the methods and general characteristics of this country. Field after field of rich, black soil plowed and harrowed, waiting for cotton seed which is to be planted next month, so pleased Henry that I began to fear that I was going to have to call out some of the ranchers to lasso him to keep him from buying a team of mules, donning his blue overalls, and going to work at once. It was a very interesting afternoon spent there. We met and talked with some of the farmers, who seemed very prosperous and contented.[99]

The homeseeker mentioned that the group saw the Taft farms. This trip was an essential element in Paul's plan to convince travelers to buy a farm. To demonstrate the region, the land firm either used his leased train engine to pull the excursion cars along the San Antonio and Aransas Pass to Gregory and Portland or utilized buggies to carry prospective settlers over the productive soil where farmers had abundant crops growing.[100] From there the group was carried to the land currently for sale and told that the same crops could be grown just as

[99] Etta Doherty, Sinton, to the Editor, Fairmount (Indiana) *News*, February 5, 1909, clipping in possession of Mrs. Lyra Haisley Sparks, Taft.

[100] *San Patricio County News* (Sinton, Texas), June 9, 1910. Paul, Omaha, to author, October 12, 1961. Interview with E. I. Crow, Taft, November 21, 1961: as a youth, Mr. Crow drove a buggy in San Patricio County for the George H. Paul Company.

well as on the property they just saw. At times the land was sold at first sight. Paul wrote that frequently every member of his hack spoke for a certain farm location before the sight-seeing tour was completed.[101]

High-pressure salesmanship on persons looking at real estate was forbidden by the land-company director. The method Paul himself used to get the signature on the dotted line, with the least amount of mental anguish for the homeseeker in deciding to buy or not, was to sign the contract first and then to offer the pen to the buyer.

> You see he was not sure he was buying, even though I was, so if I had handed him the contract and pen, it would just have opened the door for a lot of questions, but when he saw me sign it and then turn it around for his signature, he knew he was buying land and just signed. Now remember I always had my men tell people they would never be high pressured, and that Mr. Paul would never ask them to buy, and while that was absolutely true at all times, can you imagine anything in the way of *high pressure,* or asking them to buy, that would have worked any better.[102]

Why would a person leave a region he was adjusted to and go to a strange climate with different agricultural techniques? A newspaper reporter in 1908 was interested in the reason for this voluntary uprooting and questioned the migrants. The answers he received then are echoed by George H. Paul, who, reflecting on his experiences half a century ago, recalls that the less expensive land in Texas was the prime motive for emigration.[103] Property prices had climbed so high in North Texas and in the Midwestern United States that a young person could not afford the capital necessary to enter farming there.

By the end of 1908 the Coleman-Fulton Pasture Company had reduced its land holdings to 85,796 acres, aside from the 56,000 acres sold to Paul. To the original purchase in 1880, 164,145 acres, was added 2,575 between 1880 and 1908, but during this time 80,924 acres were sold.[104] Following its successful, if not spectacular, sale

[101] Paul, Omaha, to author, October 12, 1961.

[102] Paul, Omaha, to Sparks, Taft, August 9, 1961.

[103] Corpus Christi *Caller*, January 31, 1908. Paul, Omaha, to author, October 16, 1961.

[104] Anna Sinton Taft, Cincinnati, to United States Internal Revenue Agent, Dallas, November 30, 1928, Income Tax Information Folder, CFPC.

of the Taft land, the George H. Paul Company contracted for 85,000 acres in Nueces County from Robert Driscoll in 1909[105] and closed a deal with John J. Welder on May 3, 1910, for 69,000 acres adjoining the town of Sinton and extending several miles northward on the west side of the San Antonio and Aransas Pass tracks.[106]

Other land-development schemes in progress during this period on the Coastal Bend were the operations of F. Z. Bishop, who opened for settlement more than 80,000 acres in southern Nueces County near the town of Bishop, and the Welder and Odem Subdivision of approximately 5,000 acres in western San Patricio County.[107] Officials of the Taft Ranch could not resist the colonization desire, although they restricted it mainly to three acres of town lots in Portland. In June, 1910, Joseph F. Green, Charles P. Taft, and Anna S. Taft purchased for $300 three acres in what was known as the New England tract, which the Coleman-Fulton Pasture Company had repurchased after the New England Land Company and the New England Real Estate Company had discontinued their Texas business on April 21, 1900.[108]

After the Little or Shipping Pasture was sold, the remaining Aransas County tracts owned by the ranch were the Rincon Pasture and the Pocket Farm in the northeastern part of the range adjacent to Copano and Puerto Bays. As it was no longer practical to maintain a Rockport office, the company changed its official place of business. The Texas Secretary of State would not agree to an amendment to the corporation's charter making Sinton the domicile, but did approve Gregory for that purpose in 1908.[109] At the same time the maximum capital

[105] H. B. Baldwin, "The Development of Agriculture in San Patricio and Nueces counties," Taft *Tribune,* May 15, 1924.

[106] *San Patricio County News,* May 5, 1910.

[107] Baldwin, "The Development of Agriculture in San Patricio and Nueces counties," Taft *Tribune,* May 15, 1924. [Anonymous], "Developer of Bishop Opened 80,000 Acres," Corpus Christi *Caller-Times,* January 18, 1959. C. C. Wentz and F. Z. Bishop (compilers), *Bishop, Texas, and Surrounding Country,* pp. 1–32.

[108] Deed Records, San Patricio County, June 23, 1910, Vol. 34, pp. 212–214. New England Real Estate Company, Charter No. 591, Certificate of Dissolution, April 21, 1900; New England Land Company, Charter No. 426, Certificate of Dissolution, April 21, 1900; both in the Office of the Texas Secretary of State.

[109] Minutes of Stockholders' Meeting, July 3, 1905, July 2, 1906, May 4,

stock was established at $849,700 in shares with par value at $100.[110]

The prominence of the Taft Ranch gained through its practice of progressive agricultural techniques and through the vast advertising of the George H. Paul Company was extended to a national scale when President William Howard Taft was a guest at La Quinta in October, 1909. Soon after the President's inauguration in March, 1909, Charles extended him an invitation to visit the ranch to rest after the strenuous campaign. When the President answered, "It would do me good to visit Texas with you, and I hope it is possible that we may go,"[111] the ranch owner immediately laid plans for the trip. To accommodate the large numbers of government officials and the press that accompany such tours, Charles instructed the superintendent to erect a building to take care of the expected crowds, which was so ordered by the stockholders at a meeting on May 3, 1909.[112]

Beginning in September, 1909, President Taft began an excursion that carried him from his summer home in Beverly, Massachusetts, to thirty states in five sections of the nation.[113] When the party reached Texas, it went to the Taft Ranch for four days of relaxation before continuing the tour.

On October 18, 1909, the presidential train arrived at the Gregory station, where President Taft was greeted by his brother and by ranch officials, who escorted him to La Quinta. Among the members of the official group, besides the President, were military aide Major Archibald Butt, Secretary of War Jacob M. Dickinson, and Cecil Andren Lyon of Sherman, Republican national committeeman for Texas.[114] The arched gate to the La Quinta grounds was directly across from the

1908, CFPC. Coleman-Fulton Pasture Company, Charter No. 1206, Amendment, May 5, 1908, Office of the Texas Secretary of State.

[110] *Ibid.*

[111] William Howard Taft, Washington, D.C., to Charles Phelps Taft, Cincinnati, April 17, 1909, William Howard Taft Papers, Presidential Letter Book No. 2.

[112] Minutes of Stockholders' Meeting, May 3, 1909, CFPC.

[113] The number of states was determined by the headings of letters President Taft wrote to his wife while on his excursion (William Howard Taft Papers, Presidential Letter Book No. 7).

[114] *San Patricio County News*, October 21, 1909. Taft *Tribune*, December 1, 1921. Corpus Christi *Caller-Times*, January 15, 1956. William H. Taft, Gregory, to Mrs. Taft, Washington, D.C., October 22, 1909.

depot, and, as the President was driven in an automobile down the shelled road lined with four hundred palm trees to the mansion on the bay, he commented to his brother: "Charley, old boy, you said 'Let's go to Texas and rough it.' I don't call this roughing it."[115]

Knowing the President's fondness for golf, Green hired J. P. Connelry, the golf champion of Texas, to lay out a course just for the occasion. Despite a heavy rain the day the party arrived, the Taft brothers spent Tuesday morning and all day Wednesday on the links. After defeating Charles in practically every round, the President played against Connelry, "who beat me six up, but who wanted to play with me because he had laid out the grounds, and I suppose he wanted to make a reputation. He was a good fellow, however, and I enjoyed the game."[116]

Secret-service men formed the presidential bodyguard, assisted by the San Patricio County sheriff and eleven deputies, most of whom were Taft Ranch cowboys.[117] Newspapermen were quartered in the newly completed Green Hotel in Gregory and were told to keep off the La Quinta grounds. When one press agent tried to get past the gate, a cowboy on guard stopped him; and, when he was told that the President said it would be okay for him to enter, the cowboy answered, "J. F. Green is the high power here and no one gets in without his written permission."[118] Green finally relented and allowed the newsmen to enter, but first made them promise to stay away from the President. They went to the bathing pier on the bay below La Quinta and watched the proceedings from that vantage point until the President joined them for a swim and a chat.[119]

Secretary Dickinson and Major Butt went hunting and bagged their limit of ducks, as well as a panther, a bobcat, and several javelinas, but the President chose not to participate in the outings.

[115] Interview with Mrs. May Mathis Green Watson, Corpus Christi, March 2, 1961.

[116] William H. Taft, Gregory, to Mrs. Taft, Washington, D.C., October 22, 1909. *San Patricio County News*, October 21, 1909.

[117] *Ibid.* Aransas Pass (Texas) *Progress*, October 22, 1909. Interview with Mrs. May Mathis Green Watson, Corpus Christi, March 2, 1961; with Mrs. Dalton Green, Taft, November 22, 1961.

[118] Interview with Mrs. May Mathis Green Watson, Corpus Christi, March 2, 1961.

[119] Aransas Pass *Progress*, October 22, 1909.

Annie was very regretful on the estate that neither Charley nor I was a sportsman enough to carry a gun and shoot birds. It has turned out in a singular way that the only member of our family that is a really good shot is Fanny [Mrs. William Edwards, the President's sister]. She hunts on their Mexican ranch, and Bill says that she is as good a shot as he knows. I hate to kill things anyhow, and I am content to be a tenderfoot.[120]

One event the President especially enjoyed was the roundup, or rodeo, held in his honor at Rincon Ranch. With the Chief Executive, his party, and a host of newspaper reporters in attendance, the Taft Ranch cowboys held roping, branding, and riding exhibitions, dipped cattle in a tick-killing solution at the Rincon vat, and invited President Taft to join them on a jackrabbit hunt on the prairie after he had inspected Superintendent Green's kennel of greyhounds.[121] Taft was presented a special twenty-two-inch saddle custom-tailored by Mrs. Henrietta King in the King Ranch leathershop. A spirited horse was selected to carry the President on the chase; when the 320-pound Taft mounted, Old Sam, the horse, groaned and moaned, but finally consented to carry the extra weight and eagerly joined the group of horses and riders for the event.[122] After watching several rabbits be caught, the President joined the cowboys in driving range cattle to the corral.

The Taft Ranch show herd of Shorthorns, of which many had been awarded prize ribbons, were well groomed for the President's inspection. When Taft was shown a large, fat bull of immense proportions, and advised that the animal fully measured up to the specifications of the Shorthorn Breeders' Association, Taft injected a bit of humor into the occasion by remarking that he believed he, too, would measure up to the standard.[123] After congratulating William Oliver, foreman in charge of the fine herd of show cattle, the President returned with the party to La Quinta for more golf.

After almost a week of relaxation in the Coastal Bend, including a reception in his honor at Corpus Christi, President Taft continued his

[120] William H. Taft, Gregory, to Mrs. Taft, Washington, D.C., October 24, 1909.

[121] *San Patricio County News*, October 21, 1909. Interviews with Mrs. May Mathis Green Watson, Corpus Christi, March 2, 1961; Mrs. Dalton Green, Taft, November 22, 1961.

[122] *Ibid*. Corpus Christi *Caller-Times*, January 15, 1956.

[123] *San Patricio County News*, October 21, 1909.

tour through the Southern states. An aftermath of the distinguished visit was the privilege extended to the horse Taft rode; it was given the best of care, but never ridden again. Old Sam became the symbol of endurance in Texas when the Dallas *Morning News* reported: "Speaking of your other troubles, how much would you have liked to be the cow pony that Mr. Taft rode to the roundup?"[124]

Hotel Green, which served during the visit as a residence for newspapermen, secretaries, and secret-service men, was used later to board and house ranch employees. Its facilities were open to visitors and the public in general; community receptions were held there, and for a long time its kitchen enjoyed a reputation of quality throughout the Coastal Bend.[125] When Mr. and Mrs. Joseph F. Green toured Europe in 1910, they were impressed with the management of the hotels they visited, and, in particular, one in London operated by Alfred Donovan. The visiting Taft Ranch general manager persuaded the Englishman and his complete staff to move to Gregory and to manage the Green Hotel.[126]

During the first decade of Green's management of the Pasture Company he instituted many basic changes in ranch policy. With vigorous action he continued the reorganization of the corporation toward a more efficient operation, increased the quality of the range cattle, introduced diversified agriculture, unwillingly at first but then enthusiastically, and supervised the transfer of large acreages to a land speculator who brought in hundreds of homeseekers. As the Taft Ranch shifted its objective from cattle to cotton its financial position improved. Row-crop commodities yielded more revenue per acre than did livestock, indicating the productivity of the soil when cultivated, and causing the value of real estate to rise. Green's chief contribution to his employer and to his adopted region was yet to come: with the introduction of agriculture-related industry and of corporate farming the full potential of the Taft Ranch was achieved.

[124] Dallas (Texas) *Morning News*, date unknown; clipping in Mrs. May Mathis Green Watson's scrapbook for 1909, Corpus Christi.

[125] Corpus Christi *Caller-Times*, March 11, 1955.

[126] *Ibid*., January 15, 1956. Interview with Mrs. May Mathis Green Watson, Corpus Christi, March 2, 1961; with E. W. (Ted) Sandars, Taft, August 9, 1961.

IX. NEW PHASE IN INDUSTRY

UNDER THE TUTORSHIP of Joseph French Green the Taft Ranch embarked upon a project that heightened its contributions to the economic life of the Coastal Bend. The incentive for the action was to tap the potential trade of newcomers to the community and to provide them needed services in their new environment. Innovations by the corporation during the next several years brought about a new phase in industry that attracted agricultural experimenters from around the nation and the world. The venture became so successful that it served as an example of what could be done under similar circumstances anywhere. The capitalistic motive of making a profit from business investments was, of course, foremost in the minds of those responsible for the changes that were made, but those persons in charge were concerned also with providing migrants a market for surplus commodities. Realizing that its most valuable asset was real estate, and that to obtain a maximum price on future land sales it must make its property attractive to purchasers, the ranch fostered manufacturing.

Beginning in 1909 the Pasture Company inaugurated a program of establishing industrial plants in and around the town of Taft at a cost of approximately $1,000,000. Each of these enterprises was kept absolutely distinct, and each was expected to show a profit. Departments were organized with a foreman who was in charge of each semiautonomous unit and who was responsible to Green.

The division heads held monthly meetings at Gregory and discussed problems or issues pertaining to the entire group. Occasional complaints of one subdivision against another were voiced, and then left to the summary decision of Superintendent Green, who served as the presiding officer. At these gatherings the foremen asked for repairs, equipment, or services by another company department. Ranch units broken down into various categories were (1) manufacturing: packing house and oil mill; (2) public service: banks, mercantile stores, drug store, hotels, hospital, garage, lumber yards, telephone exchange, and waterworks; (3) ranch service: shops for paint, carpentry, harnesses, and machinery; (4) livestock: dairies, hog ranch, range cattle, registered beef cattle, and registered dairy cattle; (5) company farms; and (6) administration.

The company's main interest for a long time was centered on Gregory, but that town was eclipsed by Taft soon after farming became successful there and after industry was established to absorb surplus farm commodities. The discovery of abundant water hastened Taft's ascendancy. After unsuccessful attempts at digging wells around Gregory and Portland, Julian and Rufus McNeill drilled near Taft in 1909 and struck a strong flow in artesian sand two hundred feet below the surface, thus assuring the accelerated growth of that settlement.[1]

In 1909 the corporation's stockholders authorized the superintendent to sell $500,000, face value, of vendor's lien notes obtained from the sale of land to the George H. Paul Company to finance a number of extensive development projects, both industrial and agricultural.[2] One of the first business enterprises started was the erection of a large packing house, commenced in May, 1909, and completed two years later. The Taft Ranch's decision to install an abattoir was based upon

[1] Taft *Tribune*, June 17, 1943. Corpus Christi *Caller-Times*, May 9, 1954. Coleman McCampbell, *Texas Seaport: The Story of the Growth of Corpus Christi and the Coastal Bend Area*, p. 175.

[2] Minutes of the Coleman-Fulton Pasture Company Stockholders' Meeting (hereafter cited as Minutes of Stockholders' Meeting), December 14, 1909, Coleman-Fulton Pasture Company Records (hereafter cited as CFPC).

multiple reasons: to have a place for disposing its own livestock, to provide a market for cattle and hogs owned by farmers renting or buying land from the company, and to have a means of supplying beef, pork, or mutton to local residents conveniently.[3] Another reason for establishing this plant as well as the other industries, perhaps the most basic reason, was to enable the Coleman-Fulton Pasture Company to set and secure a price for its land higher than that for property in adjoining counties without these advantages.[4]

Under the able direction of W. T. George of Liberty, Missouri, who was brought to Taft especially to construct and to manage the abattoir, the Taft Packing House rapidly became a mainstay to ranch economy. Although its initial capacity was less than one hundred head of cattle and hogs a week, the plant ultimately expanded until it handled one thousand head in a seven-day period.[5] In addition to the usual operations done by a packing house, this institution manufactured a vegetable compound that gained widespread sales under the trade name of Taft Crystal Shortening.

Besides supplying the company shops in Taft, Gregory, Sinton, and Corpus Christi, the ranch employed seven representatives to travel and take orders for packing-house products from merchants in a region bounded by Floresville, Victoria, Cuero, and Port Lavaca on the north and east, and by the lower Rio Grande Valley on the south and west.[6] Later a salesman was stationed in San Antonio to supply that city and the area north.[7]

Steam-powered generators produced electrical energy for the industries and residences of Taft.[8] An ice factory and a fertilizer plant

[3] Interview with Edward N. Tutt, Taft, November 27, 1961.

[4] H. V. Fetick, Secretary of the Coleman-Fulton Pasture Company, Taft, Texas, to the Commissioner of Internal Revenue, Washington, D.C., November 7, 1923, Income Tax Information Folder (hereafter cited as Fetick to Commissioner of Internal Revenue), CFPC.

[5] George Frederic Stratton, "Mr. Taft's Tenants: How They Earn Farms on His Big Texas Ranch," *Country Gentleman*, LXXXIV, No. 9 (March 1, 1919), 40.

[6] *Ibid.* Interviews with Edward N. Tutt, Taft, November 27, 1961; with C. J. Meyer, Taft, March 2, 1961. Taft *Tribune*, October 6, 1921.

[7] Taft *Tribune*, October 6, 1921.

[8] Interview with Edward N. Tutt, Taft, November 27, 1961.

were operated in conjunction with the packing house to supply the community with their respective products.[9]

Lumber yards established in the towns of Portland, Gregory, and Taft in 1910 served the ranch departments and the persons outside the corporation. Hundreds of farmers, recently moved to the region, bought materials for homes and barns to improve their investments, thus increasing the value of ranch real estate nearby. In addition, it was profitable for the company to be the retail merchant. Only $10,000 was allotted initially for the Portland yard, but the Gregory and Taft enterprises were started with $20,000 each.[10] Reinvested profits provided an increase in merchandise stock, thus enabling the businesses to expand.

At the Portland yard in 1913 the ratio of purchases by company departments and by individuals was almost even. Of the $24,920.73 total sales, outsiders accounted for 51 per cent.[11] Half a dozen years later, when the Portland boom deflated and the corporation directed its attention on Taft, the Portland Lumber Yard registered only $14,644.24 in receipts, of which 20 per cent was signed by the Taft Ranch.[12] Gregory, boosted as the company's main town, sold a large part of its lumber-yard commodities to various divisions of the ranch in 1912 and 1913, the only years that figures are available for this lumber yard. The ranch purchased 75 per cent of the $76,970.11 sales of the Gregory company in 1912 and 71 per cent of the $61,190 sold in 1913.[13]

The great amount of construction done at Taft from 1910 to 1920 insured a large turnover of merchandise in the Taft Lumber Yard, in fact, much more than that at the Gregory and Portland yards combined. The $81,982.80 total sales in 1913 increased to $82,625.46 in 1919, to $108,549.03 in 1920, and to $197,255.10 in 1921. The com-

[9] Minutes of the Coleman-Fulton Pasture Company Heads of Departments Meeting (hereafter cited as Minutes of Departmental Meeting), June 19, 1921, CFPC. Taft *Tribune,* November 24, 1921.

[10] Statements for the Portland, Gregory, and Taft Lumber Yards, 1913, CFPC.

[11] Statement for the Portland Lumber Yard, 1913, CFPC.

[12] *Ibid.*, 1919, CFPC.

[13] Statements for the Gregory Lumber Yard, 1912 and 1913, CFPC.

pany departments purchased 57 per cent of the amount vended in 1913, but, as the ranch disposed of more land, outsiders eclipsed the departments, taking 68 per cent in 1919, 64 per cent in 1920, and 52 per cent in 1921.[14]

Industry was centered at Taft because of an abundant supply of fresh water available from wells. Tests made near Gregory and Portland failed to yield domestic water in large quantity. To provide a sufficient supply for the residents the corporation's stockholders in 1911 had a ten-inch tube laid from Taft to Gregory and Portland, with lateral six-inch lines to houses and farms along the way.[15] Service was extended to outside customers as well as to company departments, but at a higher price. For each 1,000 gallons of water consumed by the ranch, the waterworks department charged $0.4206, but it billed individuals $0.7500 for the same quantity.[16] In addition to providing water for its employees and for community residents, the ranch also sold food and farming implements in two large company-owned stores.

The small merchandise shop at Taft begun in 1903 had become an emporium less than a decade later. The ranch kept this establishment for the convenience of company departments and of outside individuals, and raised the stock, initially valued at from $15,000 to $20,000, to $40,000.[17] In 1908 a shop of equal size was organized at Gregory, but this establishment never reached the Taft Store's volume in trade.[18] Principal sources of supply for merchandise were wholesale houses in the larger Texas cities and drummers representing mercantile firms from all over the nation. When the ranch put in large cotton farms, it opened commissaries at each farm headquarters, but limited the commodities to staple food items. Implements, clothing, feed and seed, in addition to groceries, were handled in the Taft and Gregory Stores.

[14] Statements for the Taft Lumber Yard for 1913, 1919, 1920, and 1921, CFPC.

[15] Minutes of Stockholders' Meeting, May 1, 1911, CFPC. Interview with Edward N. Tutt, Taft, November 27, 1961.

[16] Statement of the Water Works Department, 1914–1915, CFPC.

[17] Testimony of Joseph F. Green before the Committee on Industrial Relations, Dallas, March, 1915, *Senate Documents*, 64th Congress, First Session, Serial No. 6938, Doc. No. 415, pp. 9214–9228.

[18] Fetick to Commissioner of Internal Revenue, CFPC.

Credit was extended to ranch employees or to outside individuals from payday to payday, or until the harvest season, but, with the large numbers of persons hired as employees in the industries, as seasonal agricultural workers, and as grubbers, installment buying of small purchases presented an administrative problem. The head storekeeper, A. M. Brooks, was faced with the dilemma of ending credit altogether or of employing a force of bookkeepers to record the nickel and dime sales. Years before he had come to Taft, Brooks had worked for a large store in Kansas that used a coupon system, and in 1914 he introduced that method on the Taft Ranch to reduce the accounting expenses.[19]

The foreman of each farm or department issued coupon books in denominations of $1, $2, $5, or $10 to an employee, who signed a chit acknowledging receipt, then the auditor at the company office deducted the amount from the person's wages. The coupons, sometimes referred to as "Taft Legal Tender," were accepted anywhere in the community, including for train fares, as if they were cash.[20] Local farmers also used this credit system, then settled their accounts each fall after harvest.[21]

The stores were operated as a service to local residents and employees, and by no means did the company force its people to trade only with it. Other mercantile enterprises in the region were open to the trade of ranch people, as far as Superintendent Green was concerned.[22] The markup on goods was 10 per cent above cost on implements to farmers and 20 per cent above cost to company departments; freight cost was additional.[23] The company did not take advantage of its virtual monopoly on mercantile items by charging exorbitant prices as oftentimes occurred in stores owned by large corporations or plantations.

[19] Testimony of Joseph F. Green before the Committee on Industrial Relations, Dallas, March, 1915, *Senate Documents*, 64th Congress, First Session, Serial No. 6938, Doc. No. 415, pp. 9214–9228.

[20] Testimony of Charles H. Alvord before the Committee on Industrial Relations, Dallas, March, 1915, *Senate Documents*, 64th Congress, First Session, Serial No. 6938, Doc. No. 415, pp. 9214–9228. Interview with E. W. Sandars, Taft, August 9, 1961; with C. J. Meyer, Taft, March 2, 1961.

[21] Interview with E. W. Sandars, Taft, August 9, 1961.

[22] Testimony of Joseph F. Green before the Committee on Industrial Relations, Dallas, March, 1915, *Senate Documents*, 64th Congress, First Session, Serial No. 6938, Doc. No. 415, pp. 9214–9228.

[23] Interview with Mr. and Mrs. Dalton Green, Taft, November 22, 1961.

Volume of trade for the Gregory Store in 1912 hit $71,872.88, rose to $80,521.25 in 1913, but dropped to $55,748.30 in 1915, the year after World War I started, a period of austerity in South Texas.[24] Amount of sales in the Taft Store was much larger for the same period, ranging from $139,635.56 in 1912, to $182,377.88 in 1913, and down to $135,149.35 in 1915. At Taft sales hit $249,255.23 in 1919 and an all-time record during the excellent cotton-yield year of 1920—$335,798.27.[25]

In order to supply markets with dairy supplies the ranch established a dairy in 1909, stocked it with Jerseys and Holsteins, then started a creamery in 1912 to manufacture butter and ice cream.[26] Commercial outlets, known as ice-cream parlors, sold the frozen dairy product at the Green Hotel in Gregory and later at the Taft Hotel in Taft.[27]

The corporation opened restaurants at the hotels in Gregory and Taft as a service to its employees and its visitors. When possible, the management served food produced on the ranch only. The firm advertised its wares in the company-operated eating establishments, as a menu of one of the meals indicates.

Taft Hotel, Taft, Texas

MENU

Choice Taft Packing House Chops
Taft "Little Pig" Sausage
Taft Ranch Cold Boiled Ham
Taft Ranch "Wienie" Sausage
Taft Special Baby Beef Roast
Taft Ranch Lunch Sausage
Taft Ranch Special Bacon

Baken Dressing	Green Onions
Potatoe Chips	Head Lettuce
Turnip Greens	Devilled Eggs
Homemade Relish	Celery Tips

[24] Statements of the Gregory Store for 1912, 1913, and 1915, CFPC.

[25] Statements of the Taft Store for 1912, 1913, 1915, 1919, and 1920, CFPC.

[26] Statement of the Taft Dairy, 1912, CFPC. Minutes of the Coleman-Fulton Pasture Company Board of Directors' Meeting (hereafter cited as Minutes of Directors' Meeting), August 24, 1912, CFPC.

[27] *San Patricio County Press* (Gregory and Taft, Texas), May 29, 1913.

Assorted Homemade Jellies
Taft Fig Preserves
Hot Biscuits
Taft Creamery Butter

Milk Coffee

Taft Ranch Custards with Whipped Cream and Homemade Cookies
(Biscuits made with "Taft Crystal Shortening.")

This Dinner Consists of Food Produced on the Ranch. We go out into our gardens, gather the vegetables, then go to our Packing House and get the Choicest Meats, Milk, Cream and Butter.

Taft is a good place to live, we believe in it.[28]

As the company's business expanded with the introduction of industry and with the increase of cotton acreage, the old frame office building in Gregory proved inadequate. In 1912 a two-story brick building was constructed in Gregory at a cost of $46,809.22 to serve as an office, store, and bank building, as well as a place for company and community meetings.[29]

A concern closely connected with the Coleman-Fulton Pasture Company was the Taft Oil and Gin Company, established in 1910 as a partnership between Charles P. Taft, Anna S. Taft, and Joseph F. Green.[30] These three persons saw the definite need for an oil mill in the ranch region to provide a market for the abundance of cottonseed grown there. J. W. Roberts, who had experience in gin and mill operation, built the plant and operated it until 1915, when he was succeeded by R. F. Isbell, who managed the mill and gins until 1920.[31] H. V. Fetick, the Coleman-Fulton Pasture Company secretary from 1917 to 1919 and again from 1920 to 1925, handled the plant's af-

[28] Menu, Taft Hotel, Taft, Texas, in possession of Mrs. May Mathis Green Watson.

[29] Fetick to Commissioner of Internal Revenue, CFPC. Minutes of Stockholders' Meeting, May 1, August 7, 1911, CFPC.

[30] Interview with Walter Roberts, Taft, November 22, 1961. Taft *Tribune*, May 22, 1924. Minutes of Stockholders' Meeting, June 4, 1910, CFPC. May M. Green Watson and Alex Lillico, *Taft Ranch: A history of the Fifty Years of Development sponsored by Coleman-Fulton Pasture Company with sketches of Gregory and Taft, the two towns it created*, p. 22.

[31] Interview with Walter Roberts, Taft, November 22, 1961. Watson and Lillico, *Taft Ranch*, p. 22.

fairs during an interim while the partnership searched for a manager. On March 15, 1921, W. Leroy Weber, who had served in similar positions in San Antonio, Beeville, and Terrell, Texas, began a tenure that lasted for three decades.[32]

At that time the Taft Oil and Gin Company owned an oil mill, eight gins located in Taft, Gregory, Sinton, Saint Paul, Odem, and Portland, a machine shop, a grain elevator, a mixed-feed plant, and a cottonseed-oil refinery. Cottonseed kernels were pressed at a capacity of seventy tons a day, and the oil was extracted and refined to a fine quality for food purposes. Part of the processed oil was sold to the Taft Packing House as the principal ingredient of Taft Crystal Shortening. By-products made from the seed remains were cottonseed cake, cottonseed meal, cottonseed hulls, roughage for livestock feed, and lintage for upholstery stuffings.[33] At the mixed-feed mill, where farmers sold their surplus grain, livestock rations were manufactured under the trade names of Taft Ranch Dairy Feed, Taft Ranch Mule and Horse Feed, Taft Ranch Chicken Feed, and Taft Ranch Steer Fattener.[34]

The ranch imported labor for the oil mill as well as for the other industries and especially encouraged Negroes to immigrate to Taft. For members of this ethnic group who had recently moved to the Taft region the ranch furnished houses near the plant site practically rent-free, with no charge for wood and water.[35]

The industrial plants were located together on a tract approximately twenty-five acres in size. In such an arrangement of buildings a fire was of particular danger, for once out of control it could jeopardize the entire group of structures. To guard against a potential destructive blaze the Taft Ranch organized a volunteer fire department in 1912

[32] Interview with W. Leroy Weber, Taft, November 17, 1961. Watson and Lillico, *Taft Ranch*, p. 23.

[33] Interview with W. Leroy Weber, Taft, November 17, 1961. Taft *Tribune*, July 14, 1921. Stratton, "Mr. Taft's Tenants," *Country Gentleman*, LXXXIV, No. 9 (March 1, 1919), p. 40.

[34] T. N. Blackwell (compiler), *Taft Ranch, San Patricio County, Texas: The Land of perpetual Sunshine, Sea Breezes, Fat Cattle, Hogs, Dairy Cows, Cotton, Feed, Prosperity and Happiness*, p. 8.

[35] Interview with Edward N. Tutt, Taft, November 27, 1961; with W. Leroy Weber, Taft, November 17, 1961; with Walter Roberts, Taft, November 22, 1961.

equipped with a La France Chemical Engine and a hose cart.[36] A water main laid around the industries with fireplugs scattered at effective intervals provided water when needed to extinguish blazes. The chemical engine was used until it was replaced in 1922 by a fire truck, the chassis of which was ordered from the Ford Motor Company and the body of which was designed, constructed, and painted in the Taft Machine Shop.[37]

In 1921 fuel oil used in the Taft Ranch industries was replaced by natural gas piped from White Point, twelve miles south of Taft on Nueces Bay. Several companies drilled for oil and gas along Nueces Bay during the early years of the twentieth century, particularly on land owned by the Coleman-Fulton Pasture Company. State Senator John G. Willacy, long-time promoter of the town of Portland, formed a company in 1910 and leased the area near Portland known as Doyle Water Hole, which was the site of James C. Fulton's gas strike in 1893.[38] Willacy was unsuccessful in discovering any hydrocarbons, but in 1913 a company not far away from ranch property on Nueces Bay struck natural gas with a force so enormous that it was uncontrollable. The pressure of the gas, combined with a geyser of water that erupted frequently, made a crater approximately 200 feet in diameter and 150 feet deep before it choked itself out. A second shaft started close by in 1914 proved to be the spectacle of South Texas when it caught fire and burned uncontrolled for months with a terrific velocity before it finally extinguished itself. Not until the fourth attempt at the White Point location were the drillers successful in capping a productive well.[39]

Although the Coleman-Fulton Pasture Company continued leasing to prospectors, neither oil nor gas was struck on its property. By 1920 the manufacturing facilities of the ranch had grown to the point that around one hundred barrels of oil a day were being consumed under

[36] Minutes of Departmental Meeting, December [no day given], 1912, April 16, 1913, CFPC. Interview with Mr. and Mrs. Dalton Green, Taft, November 22, 1961; with C. J. Meyer, Taft, November 26, 1961.

[37] Taft *Tribune*, January 25, 1923.

[38] Minutes of Stockholders' Meeting, May 2, 1910, CFPC.

[39] Taft *Tribune*, June 14, 1923.

the boilers,[40] a considerable expense initially, to say nothing of the high freight costs in transporting the fuel to Taft. At that time a contract was made with the White Point Development Company of Corpus Christi to supply gas to Taft industries and to the townspeople. By April, 1921, the Coleman-Fulton Pasture Company had spent $65,000.00 for equipment to separate water from the natural gas and $46,057.80 to lay a pipeline the twelve miles to Taft.[41] During the first month that natural gas was used, the fuel bill for the industries was reduced two-thirds.[42] Needless to say, the abundance of inexpensive natural gas in the area and its availability to residents of Taft were drawing cards to farmers and merchants in the early 1920's.

To provide available capital for the growing community the Pasture Company and other firms established banks. Before 1909 the ranch superintendent had allowed local residents to deposit money in the company safe in Gregory, withdrawing it as needed, but in the year the industrial phase began, Green received authorization from the corporation's stockholders to organize a formal banking institution, which became known as the Taft Ranch Bank.[43] Another depository in the county in which Pasture Company stockholders had an interest was the Sinton State Bank, founded in 1906 by the Sinton Town Company. For over a decade Joseph F. Green was its president, and together with Mrs. Anna Sinton Taft he owned a large portion of the capital stock.[44] By 1909 Gregory had two banks, the other having been opened in 1900 by J. S. M. McKamey, local businessman and farmer.[45] A limited amount of cash was kept on hand by the company, $2,000 in Gregory and $1,000 in Taft, but the ranch's main funds were deposited in the National Bank of Commerce, San Antonio; the Corpus Christi National Bank; the First National Bank of Rockport; and the Sinton State Bank.[46]

Other institutions in the field of finance opened. By 1910 the Taft

[40] *Ibid.*

[41] *Ibid.* Minutes of Directors' Meeting, May 2, 1921, CFPC.

[42] Taft *Tribune*, May 12, 1921.

[43] Interview with Edward N. Tutt, Taft, November 27, 1961. Minutes of Stockholders' Meeting, May 1, 1911, May 5, 1913, CFPC.

[44] Interview with Edward N. Tutt, Taft, November 27, 1961.

[45] Minutes of Stockholders' Meeting, May 5, July 7, 1913, CFPC.

[46] Tax Statement for 1912, CFPC.

Bank, Unincorporated, was established in Taft to assist in the expansion of the ranch's trade territory.[47] At this time Gregory citizens organized the Farmer's Bank, Unincorporated. In 1912 the Taft Ranch Bank assumed the name of the First National Bank of Gregory. The Coleman-Fulton Pasture Company owned none of the above banks although officers and stockholders of the ranch controlled the Taft Bank, Unincorporated, and the First National Bank of Gregory.[48]

With the establishment of formal financial institutions on the Pasture Company property, the stockholders in 1910 changed the firm's depositories to the Taft Ranch Bank, the Taft Bank, Unincorporated, and the Sinton State Bank.[49] When the Taft Ranch Bank became the First National Bank of Gregory, it remained as a keeper of company funds. In 1912 the Corpus Christi National Bank was added to the list, followed later by the First State Bank and the City National Bank, both of Corpus Christi.[50]

During the second decade of the twentieth century the Coleman-Fulton Pasture Company made a significant humanitarian contribution to the Coastal Bend when it founded a hospital on the ranch, particularly for its employees, but open to anyone who cared to use it. Conditions for the health care of persons on the ranch were quite inadequate before 1910. Residents in Taft, for example, could seek treatment in Sinton, eight miles away, or in Corpus Christi, a distance of eighteen miles. For serious ailments one was required to go to San Antonio.

Realizing the need of resident medical facilities, Joseph F. Green called a meeting of department foremen on March 26, 1910, to discuss the subject; at this time a committee was appointed to lay the groundwork for a hospital.[51] A beneficiary plan for maintaining the institution was agreed upon with assessments amounting to 1 per cent withheld from the paycheck of volunteers for the program. Deficits, if any,

[47] Taft *Tribune*, July 31, 1941. *San Patricio County Press*, February 6, 1914.

[48] *Senate Documents*, 64th Congress, First Session, Serial No. 6938, Doc. No. 415, pp. 9214–9228.

[49] Minutes of Stockholders' Meeting, June 4, 1910, CFPC.

[50] Minutes of Directors' Meeting, May 5, 1912, June 7, 1919, CFPC.

[51] Miss Effie Miller, Kelowna, British Columbia, to author, February 23, 1962. Minutes of the Coleman-Fulton Pasture Company Hospital Department Meeting (hereafter cited as Minutes of Hospital Department Meeting), March 26, April 30, 1910, CFPC.

were to be assumed by the Coleman-Fulton Pasture Company.[52] Dependents of those who paid fees received deductions of one-third the regular cost for medical treatment, but outsiders paid three dollars a day while in the hospital. Benefits were extended to the one-half–share tenants on the ranch in return for their paying dues of one dollar a month.[53] Employee contributions increased in 1915 to a straight 3 per cent for those with a monthly salary over $50; persons with wages under that amount paid fifty cents a month.[54]

Founded at a time when the ranch brought in scores of migrant workers to clear the land, the hospital provided medical attention for them also. As more soil was devoted to row crops and as additional laborers were hired, the policy of extending hospital benefits to new employees was changed. Before a person could apply for membership in the medical association, he received a physical examination within thirty days after he began work. The purpose of this practice was to protect the company against giving free medical care to persons who contracted a chronic disease before joining the ranch.[55]

A building on the south outskirts of Taft across the road from Farm 20 was designated as the hospital in 1910; but only Latin American and Negro patients were cared for there by a Latin American male nurse, who divided his time with the Taft Dairy. Miss Elsa Trepton serving as nurse supervised a room at the Green Hotel in Gregory for the use of Anglo-Americans.[56] In May, 1910, the ranch erected two additional houses in Taft next to the hospital, providing a separate structure for each of the three ethnic groups. When the Taft Ranch Hospital was functioning in one locality, Joseph F. Green secured the services of two daughters of John Miller of Toronto, Ontario, his Canadian Shorthorn cattle buyer, to manage the institution. On July 1, 1910, Miss Effie Miller, a recent graduate of a nursing school, became

[52] Interview with C. J. Meyer, Taft, March 2, 1961. Minutes of Hospital Department Meeting, March 26, June 22, 1910, CFPC.

[53] *Senate Documents,* 64th Congress, First Session, Serial No. 6938, Doc. No. 415, pp. 9214–9228. Minutes of Departmental Meeting, January 16, May 23, 1912; Minutes of Hospital Department Meeting, January 9, 1911; all in CFPC.

[54] Minutes of Departmental Meeting, May 5, 1915, CFPC.

[55] *Ibid.*

[56] Minutes of Hospital Department Meeting, April 30, 1910, CFPC.

head nurse at Taft, and her sister, Miss Kate Miller, served as housekeeper; each received a monthly salary of $100.[57]

The first physician, Dr. Edgar G. Mathis, brother of Mrs. Joseph F. Green, maintained an office in Taft and came to the hospital only to see patients, to put on casts, or to perform surgery. Mathis was paid $75 a month by the hospital association, which collected dues from company employees; in addition, he received fees for professional services to persons in the community not connected with the ranch.[58] Among the physicians employed by the company during the next two decades were L. E. Devendorf, Frank Schmidt, S. D. Stone, and Lucian Penrod. Nurses who succeeded Miss Effie Miller were Mrs. Florence McDougal, Mrs. Daisy Freeman, and Mrs. Alice Wolf.[59]

Joseph F. Green, representing the Coleman-Fulton Pasture Company, lavished attention on the medical institution and obtained every piece of modern equipment available at the request of the attending physician and nurse.[60] Within a short time the hospital grounds covered five acres, upon which were three large cottages that housed an X-ray machine, quarters for patients, rooms for surgery, for sterilizing, and for storing supplies, and a home for nurses. Nearby were four smaller cottages: a washhouse, an apartment for colored domestic help, a three-room residence for Latin American patients, and one of equal size for Negroes. To prevent the spreading of communicable diseases, a special cabin known as the pesthouse was placed five hundred feet from the other units. Each building had hot and cold running water, electricity, and natural gas, and was near a central sewerage disposal plant.[61] Although the infirmary was built and equipped for ranch em-

[57] *Ibid.*, June 4, 22, 1910, CFPC. Miss Effie Miller to author, February 23, 1962.

[58] Minutes of Hospital Department Meeting, April 30, June 22, 1910, CFPC.

[59] Interview with C. J. Meyer, Taft, March 2, 1961; with Mrs. Alice Wolf, Taft, November 3, 1961. Taft *Tribune*, August 2, 1923; June 4, 1925; July 29, 1926; November 9, 1939; March 11, 1959.

[60] Miss Effie Miller, Kelowna, British Columbia, to author, February 23, 1962. *Senate Documents*, 64th Congress, First Session, Serial No. 6938, Doc. No. 415, pp. 9214–9228. Minutes of Stockholders' Meeting, May 1, 1911, CFPC.

[61] Minutes of Departmental Meeting, May 23, 1912, CFPC. Taft *Tribune*, June 5, 1924, November 9, 1939. Interview with Mrs. Alice Wolf, Taft, November 3, 1961.

ployees, no one was ever turned away nor was any surgeon refused use of the facilities.

Prescriptions were filled at the Taft Drug Store, which was founded by the Pasture Company in 1909 and operated by Dr. Edgar G. Mathis for ten years. When the drug stock was sold in 1919 to Dr. L. E. Devendorf, the company physician, and to Jimmie N. Stone of Gonzales, the Taft Drug Store became the first independent enterprise in the otherwise solid company town.[62] Stone became the sole owner of the dispensary in 1923 and expanded his business with the growing Taft community for a score of years.[63]

Cases treated at the Taft Hospital ran the gamut of illnesses. In the hospital record book, kept from 1910 until the ranch disposed of the sanitarium in 1928, the most prevalent disease was "la grippe," the majority of those cases happening in 1918–1919. Second in occurrence was typhoid, a result of impure water and unsatisfactory sanitation conditions that frequently plagued new communities.[64] Among other complaints attended at the clinic were pneumonia, dysentery, spinal meningitis, rattlesnake bites, measles, lumbago and rheumatism, anthrax and carbuncle, pleurisy, tonsilitis, lead poisoning, tumors, tuberculosis, malaria, and housemaid's knee.[65] The hospital cared also for many victims of industrial accidents, but for few injured by farm mishaps.

Childbirth was a common event at the ranch hospital. One must keep in mind that the country was just developing and was filled with young couples. Most births in the community occurred in the hospital rather than in homes, something of a social revolution and a departure from the frontier tradition. A physician was always present for deliveries in obstetric cases; no midwifery was practiced at all.[66]

Transportation was a problem on the Taft Ranch when the development of industries and large farms started. The only routes were trails

[62] Taft *Tribune*, July 31, 1941. Watson and Lillico, *Taft Ranch*, p. 31.

[63] Corpus Christi *Caller-Times*, September 29, 1940.

[64] Hospital Register, Coleman-Fulton Pasture Company Hospital Department, CFPC.

[65] *Ibid.* Miss Effie Miller, Kelowna, British Columbia, to author, February 23, 1962. Interview with Mrs. Alice Wolf, Taft, November 3, 1961.

[66] Hospital Register, Coleman-Fulton Pasture Company Hospital Department, CFPC. Interview with Mrs. Alice Wolf, Taft, November 3, 1961.

along the railroad between towns and *senderos,* or paths, cut through the brush to windmills. With the introduction of automobiles in South Texas, it became necessary to construct highways; this work was done on the ranch under Green's guidance and with Taft's money. By 1913 over sixty miles were graded and improved with shell.[67] The company owned water-sprinkler units to care for the town streets of Taft and Gregory.[68] Rural thoroughfares designated as county roads were maintained by area residents, who donated labor, teams, wagons, slips, or money, by obligatory work under the direction of a road commissioner.[69]

For cross-country traveling one followed unmarked trails using as a guide a book explaining which fork in the road to take or when to turn left after passing a particular large red barn on the east side of a knoll. An interstate highway, labeled the Tex-O-Kan, linking Corpus Christi with Dodge City, Kansas, was routed through the Taft Ranch in 1917, but its name was changed the following year to the King of Trails when it was extended northward to Winnipeg, Canada. The route was marked by yellow-chrome bands on fence posts or on public-utility poles, at all crossroads, turns, and forks, and also at four places in each mile of road. The designation to let one know he was on the correct course was a yellow band with the initials "K. T." in black.[70]

A causeway linking Corpus Christi with San Patricio County was constructed by Nueces County in 1914–1915 across Nueces Bay to Portland; the Taft Ranch and San Patricio County built the approaches on the east end. Before that time the only way one could cross Nueces Bay was to travel by railroad or to follow the oyster reefs which provided a shallow-water crossing. The bridge and approaches were damaged in the 1916 hurricane, destroyed in the 1919 storm, but rebuilt

[67] Unlabeled, July, 1913, newspaper clipping in possession of Mrs. May Mathis Green Watson, Corpus Christi. Minutes of Departmental Meeting, May 1, 1911, CFPC.

[68] Minutes of Departmental Meeting, April 15, 1914, CFPC.

[69] Interview with Mr. and Mrs. J. D. Moore, Sinton, November 18, 1961. Petition for signers to work on roads of San Patricio County Road District No. 1, September 1, 1921, loose sheet inserted in Minutes of Departmental Meeting book, CFPC.

[70] *San Patricio County News* (Sinton, Texas), August 10, 1917, April 19, 1918. Interview with Mr. and Mrs. Walter C. Sparks, Jr., Taft, August 4, 1961; with Mr. and Mrs. Claud Boykin, Taft, August 4, 1961.

in 1921 by Nueces County, San Patricio County, and the Coleman-Fulton Pasture Company.[71]

The Taft Ranch operated a garage, the first in the county, and became the dealer for the Overland, Franklin, and Buick companies.[72] Automobiles were used by foremen on ranch business or rented to the public at a combined rate of ten cents a mile and fifty cents an hour.[73] By 1914 the corporation owned five cars and one truck, the latter being used to haul meat from the packing house to the railroad depot or to butcher shops in neighboring towns.[74]

While waiting for automobile business, the company's mechanics repaired the one-cylinder windmill motors that pumped water for cattle when the wind was not blowing, worked on the firm's giant tractors, chauffeured hunters from Hotel Green to the company-operated hunting lodges on Copano Bay, or overhauled the ranch's party boat.[75] The forty-eight-foot craft, the "Sacajawea," came from the Great Lakes area with a motor not designed for use in salt water, much to the sorrow of the Gregory Garage mechanics, and required a complete renovation after each trip on the bays. For approximately ten years this cruiser served as entertainment for visiting dignitaries before it was finally destroyed in the 1919 hurricane.[76] The Coleman-Fulton Pasture Company operated the repair shop until 1921, when E. W. Sandars, the garage foreman, purchased the building and moved it to Taft.[77]

The Taft Ranch served as a benefactor of social and cultural life for its employees, in fact, for that entire region of South Texas, during

[71] Donna Nalley, "Mrs. [Adele] Fisher Recalls Portland's Early Days," Corpus Christi *Caller-Times*, August 6, 1961. *San Patricio County News*, May 29, 1914; February 12, 1915; July 30, 1915; January 28, 1916. Taft *Tribune*, October 6, 1921. Mrs. Waldo E. Haisley, Sinton, to Mrs. Luella Mendenhall, Marshalltown, Iowa, August, 1913; letter in possession of Mrs. Lyra Haisley Sparks, Taft. Statement, Coleman-Fulton Pasture Company Real Estate Improvement, CFPC.

[72] Interview with E. W. Sandars, Taft, August 9, 1961; with Jack E. Dodson, Sinton, August 8, 1961.

[73] Minutes of Departmental Meeting, April 15, 1914, CFPC.

[74] Statement, Coleman-Fulton Pasture Company, December 31, 1914, CFPC. Interview with Jack E. Dodson, Sinton, August 8, 1961.

[75] Interview with E. W. Sandars, Taft, August 9, 1961; with Jack E. Dodson, Sinton, August 8, 1961.

[76] *Ibid.*

[77] Interview with E. W. Sandars, Taft, August 9, 1961.

these first years of community growth. Chautauqua assemblies and lyceum courses, offered in Taft as early as 1912, usually attracted a full house for traveling performers. Ranch employees, neighboring farmers, and townspeople from Gregory, Portland, Sinton, Aransas Pass, Rockport, and Corpus Christi met at the Assembly Hall for these events. Outstanding talent brought in by the Coleman-Fulton Pasture Company and by the Taft Parents-Teachers Association featured educational and musical programs. Examples of travelers of the lyceum circuit were a female orchestra named the University Girls; T. J. Kellam, baritone reader and singer, and Miss Lela Lowery, singer and pianist, together labeled as the Kellam Duo; and other persons unidentified by local newspapers but listed as the New York Players, Frank Church, Irene Bewley, The Scotts, and the Sheehan Company.[78] When the company's two-story brick building in Gregory was completed, lyceum courses were held there also.[79]

The New Year's Day open houses at La Quinta became an institution. On each January 1 company employees gathered at the big house on Corpus Christi Bay for food, fun, and fellowship to usher in the new year together; alcoholic beverages were never present. One of the unwritten codes of Superintendent Green was the immediate release of anyone caught drinking on the ranch premises. Christmas parties held in Taft around a giant mesquite tree featured presents for everyone; but as the ranch increased in population this practice became too expensive.[80] Thereafter, Christmas festivities were limited to the distribution of candy sacks to the Anglo-Americans, Latin Americans, and Negroes, each group meeting in separate places.[81] To round out the employees' celebrations, the Coleman-Fulton Pasture Company proclaimed holidays on the Fourth of July for everyone, furnishing the refreshments, music, transportation, and fireworks and sponsoring a baseball game; on June 24, Saint John the Baptist Day, for the Latin Americans; and on "June 'teenth" for the Negroes, commemorating June 19, 1865, the day of emancipation for Texas Negroes.[82]

[78] *San Patricio County News,* November 28, December 13, 1912. Taft *Tribune*, October 4, 1923.

[79] *San Patricio County Press,* February 6, 1914.

[80] Interview with Mr. and Mrs. Dalton Green, Taft, November 22, 1961.

[81] Minutes of Departmental Meeting, December 2, 1916, CFPC.

[82] *Ibid.*, May 23, June 19, 1912, CFPC.

On such occasions music was provided by the Taft Ranch Band, composed of male employees of the company who received free instruments, uniforms, and lessons. At times the band was the main attraction in the Taft Assembly Hall, in Gregory Auditorium, or at an open-air concert. The Dallas Fair, the Fort Worth Fat Stock Show, and almost all regional gatherings were on the itinerary of this select group, which gave its first performance on January 30, 1914.[83] Under the direction of Charles Weyland, the company gardner, the Taft Ranch Band served as entertainment for the homefolks, and as cheerful advertisement when away.

For adult males who qualified for membership the local Masonic Lodge afforded a place to work together benevolently and in friendship for the betterment of the entire community. Gregory Lodge No. 998, Ancient Free and Accepted Masons, was chartered by the Texas Grand Lodge in December, 1909, and held its first meeting on January 5, 1910.[84] After the Taft Ranch office building was erected, the lodge rented space in it, remaining there until the meeting place was changed to Taft in 1924. During the two decades the Coleman-Fulton Pasture Company and the Gregory Lodge coexisted, by far the majority of ranch employees were active members of the fraternal order.[85]

The Pasture Company was a benefactor to the local schools as it sought to provide the children with the best of education possible at that time. The older communities of Gregory and Portland had schools for many years, but Taft could not boast of one until 1907, when the Coleman-Fulton Pasture Company provided a building and paid part of the teacher's salary.[86]

When the Assembly Hall was built in 1909, it became the schoolhouse as well as a church and community gathering place. Subjects taught were the basic fundamentals for the elementary grades, and high-school courses similar to those now offered at that level. Agriculture as a subject was initiated in 1910 at the insistence of Joseph F.

[83] *San Patricio County News*, February 6, 1914.

[84] Charter No. 998 issued by the Grand Lodge of Texas, December, 1909, in the hall of Gregory Lodge No. 998, Taft. Minutes of initial meeting, Gregory Lodge No. 998, January 5, 1910, Lodge Records.

[85] From a cross-checking of names on the Coleman-Fulton Pasture Company payroll books and in the records of the Gregory Lodge No. 998.

[86] Interview with Mr. and Mrs. Dalton Green, Taft, November 22, 1961.

Green, who desired to interest children at an early age in techniques of tilling the soil. The Taft school had a six-acre garden near the classroom; each child had a certain number of rows to cultivate under the supervision of the teacher.[87]

Green was not the only patron of public schools on the ranch; Charles P. Taft also was interested in providing community children with every educational facility available. In a speech to department foremen in 1912 Taft stated that he wanted local systems to be the best in the state, and that if the county did not pay enough to attract good teachers the Coleman-Fulton Pasture Company would pay the difference; but quality educators must be induced to come.[88]

As the ranch population increased, the school expanded into a fairly large institution. To provide for the Spanish-speaking children, the ranch erected a separate building and hired educated Latin American teachers for a six-month term at no cost to the farm laborers.[89]

Five acres in Taft were donated for school purposes in 1917; to this area was added an entire block in the new addition of the town a month before the 1921 land sale.[90] Although the ranch did not provide the school building or pay part of the teachers' salaries in Gregory and Portland, it did award those districts free property for educational institutions. Superintendent Green conveyed to the Portland Board of Trustees one acre in 1910, and four acres to Gregory in 1916.[91]

The Coastal Bend region had also a state-accredited college, but the school's only connection with the Coleman-Fulton Pasture Company was its purchase of a ranch building, which was to be used as a dormitory. Bay View College at Portland, a home-boarding school, was established in September, 1894, by Thomas M. Clark of Thorp Spring, Hood County, Texas; its first class graduated in 1897.[92] The institution

[87] Interview with Mr. and Mrs. Henry R. Moore, Taft, November 24, 1961.

[88] Minutes of Departmental Meeting, March 20, 1912, CFPC.

[89] *Senate Documents,* 64th Congress, First Session, Serial No. 6938, Doc. No. 415, pp. 9214–9228.

[90] Minutes of Stockholders' Meeting, May 7, 1917, CFPC. Deed Records, San Patricio County, April 25, 1921, Vol. 71, pp. 237–239.

[91] Minutes of Directors' Meeting, May 1, 1916, CFPC. Deed Records, San Patricio County, May 3, 1910, Vol. 30, pp. 540–542.

[92] Wallace R. Clark, "Early Beginnings of Old Bay View College in Portland Brought Back to Life by Son of the Institution's Founder"; "Early Days at Bay View College See A Strong Start Made toward Founding Lasting In-

exerted a great deal of influence over South Texas for two decades until it was mortally injured in the 1916 hurricane.[93] By that time, however, the area had adequate public schools, which, to some limited degree, filled the vacuum left by the passing of the college.

Believing that the moral fiber of a community is strengthened by the existence of churches, the Coleman-Fulton Pasture Company fostered the growth of religious bodies by gratuitously providing land for buildings. Before edifices were raised the ranch allowed religious groups to meet in the Taft Assembly Hall and in the Gregory Auditorium. When the grubbing camps were in full operation the Pasture Company gave $200 to aid in the erection of a Roman Catholic church in Taft and also supplied the ground on which it was placed.[94]

This money gift to churches was the only one of its kind by the Taft Ranch; the remainder of its benevolences was in real estate. The Baptist organization in Gregory was awarded land in 1913, Portland's Disciples of Christ received two lots the same year, and the Presbyterian group in Portland became the owner of a small piece of company real estate in 1916.[95]

In 1904 a tract at Gregory was deeded to the public for use as a cemetery. When Taft became the industrial and agricultural center, the Pasture Company set aside property known as the Bellevue Cemetery and sold burial lots, using the proceeds for maintenance only.[96]

Taft Ranch citizens were also provided a local newspaper. In May, 1913, the *San Patricio County Press,* described as the "Official Paper of Gregory and Taft, Texas," began at Gregory on a printing press owned by the Pasture Company, but operated by Esther B. and Marguerite MacGugin.[97] The plant published two other weeklies, the Portland

stitution of Higher Learning," Taft *Tribune*, dates unknown, newspaper clippings in possession of Mrs. Fay Green Hunt.

[93] Wallace R. Clark, "Portland's Bay View College Destroyed by 1916 Hurricane," Taft *Tribune*, October 18, 1956.

[94] Minutes of Stockholders' Meeting, May 3, 1909, CFPC.

[95] *Ibid.*, May 5, 1913, January 1, 1917, CFPC. Deed Records, San Patricio County, May 12, 1913, Vol. 46, pp. 604–605; January 8, 1916, Vol. 59, pp. 536–538.

[96] Minutes of Stockholders' Meeting, May 2, 1904, November 27, 1911, CFPC.

[97] *San Patricio County Press*, May 29, 1913. Watson and Lillico, *Taft Ranch*, p. 27. Interview with E. I. Crow, Taft, November 8, 1961.

Herald, and the Saint Paul *Record,* but did not own them.[98] When the operation folded after approximately two years, the ranch retained the machinery to handle its printing needs, but sold it to W. S. Clark in 1921. Clark, recently of Pocahontas, Iowa, moved the Crandall Press to Taft, and on May 5, 1921, began publishing the Taft *Tribune* one month before the first big subdivision of company land.[99] During the 1920's the newspaper devoted a great deal of space to heralding the ranch and its activities.

While the Coleman-Fulton Pasture Company fostered the growth on only a portion of the Coastal Bend, it pointed the way to economic production heretofore unknown in the region and served as an example of what could be done through industrialization. New techniques for utilizing farm products were introduced, which led to a desired goal of diversified use of capital. While the progressive measures were being taken, the Taft Ranch did not overlook its people, providing well for them culturally, educationally, and medically. After surveying the ranch's activities during its first dozen years of industrial expansion, one surmises that nothing in the way of intense development of company property or in the way of public welfare was overlooked.

[98] O. C. Payne, "Corporation Farming in Texas," *Farm and Ranch,* Vol. 33, No. 22 (May 30, 1914), p. 3.

[99] Taft *Tribune,* June 17, 1943. Watson and Lillico, *Taft Ranch,* p. 27.

X. BIGNESS IN SOUTH TEXAS AGRICULTURE

ACROSS THE BROAD EXPANSE of fertile soil of the Coastal Plains a new sight greeted visitors who might suppose they were still in the cattle kingdom. Workers by the hundreds grubbed mesquite roots from the soil, tractor drivers followed immediately to break the sod, and other men came along to plant seed, thus completing a revolution which won additional land for the plow. This activity heralded in the age of bigness in agriculture for South Texas. A sense of excitement permeated the Taft Ranch employees and other Coastal Bend residents as the scientific and experimental farming sponsored by the Pasture Company demonstrated the possibility of high yields in exportable commodities. Although the corporation carved out vast fields from the pastures primarily to gain revenue, it wanted also to demonstrate the productivity of the soil in order to increase the value of its unsold real estate.

The Taft Ranch channeled a large amount of the proceeds from the sale of land to the George H. Paul Company to agricultural pursuits. The 2,300 acres in cultivation on January 1, 1909, were increased to 3,350 in 1910, to 4,500 in 1911, to 5,754 in 1912, to 8,451 in 1913, and to the maximum number of 10,006 in 1914.[1] The 1913 allotment

[1] H. V. Fetick, Secretary of the Coleman-Fulton Pasture Company, Taft, Texas, to the Commissioner of Internal Revenue, Washington, D.C., Novem-

was divided among five large demonstration farms engaging in experimental agriculture on 5,230 acres and twenty smaller farms leased to tenants on 3,221 acres. The total of 8,451 acres in cultivation were approximately one-fourth of the entire 34,668 acres being tilled in San Patricio County.[2]

Before each plot was ready for cultivation, it must be cleared of trees and brush. Hundreds of Latin American laborers used grubbing hoes and axes to cut the surface vegetation and to dislodge roots from the soil, and then carried the debris to a central location for burning. Only limbs large enough for fence posts were salvaged. Because of insufficient housing, the grubbers lived in tents issued to them for the time they were in the community. Various settlements sprang up near the center of operations, not only on the Taft Ranch, but over the entire Coastal Bend region, for other property owners also were clearing the land. Prevailing wages for Latin American laborers was seventy cents a day; although it was hard work, it was steady employment and paid more than they made on the Texas-Mexico border.[3] After the fields were cleared large tractors cut the turf.

In 1909 a department of the ranch known as the Rarig Plow Camp was organized to do the plowing with steam tractors stoked with mesquite wood until oil and gasoline vehicles were brought in.[4] W. C. Rarig, the foreman of the Plow Camp, invented a root plow to turn the soil efficiently after vegetation was cleared from the surface. The equipment designed by Rarig was forged in the Alamo Iron Works at San Antonio and assembled at the Taft Ranch Machine Shop. Giant three-bottom plowshares turned the sod, while workers followed them through the fields gathering loose roots thus upended.[5] Section harrows pulled by mules pulverized the soil to make the fields ready for plant-

ber 7, 1923, Income Tax Information Folder, Coleman-Fulton Pasture Company Records (hereafter cited as CFPC).

[2] *San Patricio County News* (Sinton, Texas), June 12, 1914.

[3] Interview with S. Frank Hunt, Sinton, Texas, August 8, 1961; with Ernest Guedin, Taft, Texas, November 17, 1961. Coleman-Fulton Pasture Company Pay Roll Book, CFPC.

[4] Interview with E. I. Crow, Taft, November 2, 1961; with Ernest Guedin, Taft, November 17, 1961.

[5] Interview with Ernest Guedin, Taft, November 17, 1961.

ing. Even though this process was expensive, it was necessary in order to realize the maximum value of the land.

During 1912, a representative year, 2,407 acres were put into cultivation at an average cost of $31.28 an acre.[6] Grubbing, costing $20.26 an acre, was more expensive than plowing.[7] At first the Taft Ranch utilized its Hart-Parr and Twin Cities tractors until a sufficient amount of land had been broken, but in 1913 it sold this equipment.[8]

The one-mile reservation on each side of the San Antonio and Aransas Pass railroad tracks was the area selected by Joseph F. Green for the company farms and the tenant farms. The units were numbered for administrative purposes, but some were given names by the persons working on them.

On July 26, 1911, Green as general manager of the entire ranch selected Charles H. Alvord, head of the agricultural department at the Agricultural and Mechanical College of Texas, to supervise the agricultural pursuits of the ranch.[9] Born in Michigan, Alvord attended school there, graduated from Michigan Agricultural College, and for several years farmed in that state. From 1899 to 1904, and again from 1908 to 1911, he taught in the Agricultural and Mechanical College of Texas.[10] Alvord selected seed, determined time of plantings, supervised the cultivation of the crops, and advised neighboring independent farmers in their operations without cost to them.

Only three company farms operated in 1912: Farm 21, also known as Terre Bonne, 1,425 acres; Farm 22, Terre Belle, 1,049 acres; and Farm 23, Portland, 1,064 acres.[11] Customary practice was to plant 20 per cent of each farm in feed for animals—usually oats, corn, kafir, milo, feterita, sorghum, and Sudan grass—and to devote the remainder of the acreage to cotton. From the approximately 2,800 acres in cotton in 1912, 1,559 bales were harvested for a gross income of $62.29 per

[6] Statement covering cost of grubbing and plowing virgin soil, 1912, CFPC.

[7] Statement covering cost of grubbing, 1912, CFPC.

[8] Interview with Ernest Guedin, Taft, November 17, 1961.

[9] Minutes of the Coleman-Fulton Pasture Company Stockholders' Meeting (hereafter cited as Minutes of Stockholders' Meeting), August 7, 1911, CFPC.

[10] *Senate Documents*, 64th Congress, First Session, Serial No. 6938, Doc. No. 415, p. 9214.

[11] Recapitulation, Company Farms Investment Statement, December 31, 1912, CFPC.

bale, out of which the expenses of production were deducted, leaving $10.32-a-bale profit.[12] Operating costs included labor, feed purchase, supervision expense, supplies and repairs, insect poisoning, seed for planting, fertilizer, and stock and equipment depreciation.[13]

Part of the expenses for the year was hiring the mechanical cotton picker owned by Theodore H. Price of New York City, who operated two machines in South Texas in 1912 at $500 a week as an experiment to interest cotton growers in his work. The Coleman-Fulton Pasture Company bought $1,250 in stock in the Price company to encourage the manufacture of the machine, joining with R. J. Kleberg of the King Ranch, Robert Driscoll of Nueces County, and the McFaddins of Victoria. Although neither the Pasture Company nor other large cotton growers on the Coastal Bend bought a mechanical picker that year, it was their consensus that the $500 a week was worth the expense, for the laborers worked faster and picked more when they could hear the sound of the machine that threatened to take their place.[14]

The tenant farmers also did well during 1912. From 2,722 acres in cotton, 1,175 bales were harvested to provide a net revenue of $6.31 for an acre.[15] Feed grown on the tenant farms yielded an average revenue of $6.39 an acre.[16] Under lease agreements signed with the Coleman-Fulton Pasture Company, the renters gave to the landowner one-third of the grain, delivered in bulk to the nearest silo on the ranch, and one-fourth of the cotton.

Silos in that part of South Texas were an innovation by Joseph F. Green, who initiated their construction in 1910 for storing livestock feed. By 1914 thirty-six silos averaging two hundred tons each were in use on the ranch. Cattle were fed ensilage mixed with cottonseed meal to carry them through a severe winter or to prepare them for slaughter.[17] Green constantly experimented to determine what would prove

[12] Company Farms, Gross Income, Cost of Production and Net Profit per bale, 1912, CFPC.

[13] Statement, Company Farms Investment, 1912, CFPC.

[14] Minutes of Stockholders' Meeting, May 5, 1913, CFPC.

[15] Statement, Tenant Farms, 1912, CFPC.

[16] Statement, Cotton and Feed Revenue from Farm Tenants, 1912, CFPC.

[17] O. C. Payne, "Corporation Farming in Texas," *Farm and Ranch* (Dallas), Vol. 33, No. 22 (May 30, 1914), p. 2; May M. Green Watson and Alex Lillico, *Taft Ranch: A history of the Fifty Years of Development sponsored*

suitable to agrarians on the Coastal Bend in an effort to fulfill his dream of diversified farming.

An even greater return was realized the following year when the company farms netted $11.43, and the tenant farms $14.34 an acre.[18] The good crop of 1913 over the entire county was not, in the main, owing to the extremely good soil. According to J. W. Benson of Sinton, the demonstration agent for San Patricio County, the reason for such a profitable year was that the farmers were progressive and recognized the advantages of practicing scientific agriculture.[19] Benson gave credit to the Taft Ranch for these new measures when he stated: "The efficient manner in which the big Taft Ranch has been conducted has served as a good object lesson for the farmers in San Patricio County."[20] Credit for the company's assistance in the development of the Coastal Bend came also from the director of an experimental station of Texas Agricultural and Mechanical College, who was present at a meeting of the Taft Ranch department heads in June, 1913.

> Not only to the few but to the world this is a most successful enterprise, it is unique in Texas because of its organization. You know it was thought a long time ago that farming on such a large scale could not be done with any profit. This farm is doing a great amount of good to this country, it may run on as it is for a hundred or even a thousand years, but it has opened up and developed this country and shown what it can do in a big way. I made a visit to this ranch quite a long time ago and did not think it would amount to much if you struck it in a dry year. We know now that this is one of the greatest cotton growing sections in the world especially in the state of Texas. I am anxious and pleased to see the development of this country.[21]

By 1913 five company farms were in operation with approximately 1,000 acres each, developing procedures that lasted while the Taft Ranch was in the farming business. Some mules were raised on the

by Coleman-Fulton Pasture Company with sketches of Gregory and Taft, the two towns it created, p. 20.

[18] Statement, Company Farms, 1913; Statement, Tenant Farms, 1913; both in CFPC.

[19] *San Patricio County News*, September 19, 1913.

[20] *Ibid.*

[21] Minutes of the Coleman-Fulton Pasture Company Heads of Departments Meeting (hereafter cited as Minutes of Departmental Meeting), June 18, 1913, CFPC.

ranch, but most were purchased from Missouri or from Joseph F. Green and Company, lessee of the Catarina Ranch in Webb, Dimmit, and La Salle Counties in Southwest Texas.[22] The Green Company imported high-grade jacks and bred them to large mares, producing a mule that made a good work animal. For cultivation purposes one team of mules pulling a one-row plow was considered sufficient for each fifty acres of land.[23] Large mule herds were maintained on each semi-autonomous farm with a *caporal,* or mule tender, on duty to feed the animals well and to keep them in condition to work.[24] Tenant farmers, of course, were on a more limited budget and did not have a mule pool to draw from. They followed the same ratio of one team of two animals for each fifty acres, but usually they had an extra team on hand to use in case of illness and to serve as buggy power.[25]

In keeping with its experimental nature the Taft Ranch in 1914 planted a portion of its crop the first week in February, from two to eight weeks earlier than the customary planting time for that region. With this method the stalks could mature sufficiently before the coming of the usual heavy spring rains, which frequently injured them. The editor of the *San Patricio County Press* summed up its coverage of the test by stating: "This experiment will likely be watched with interest by the farmers in the gulf coast country and may be means of 'early planting' in this vicinity."[26] As a result of this test, the ranch began planting the bulk of its crop early, and other farmers followed it in that practice, noting the advantage of selling lint before the price decreased when the majority of the nation's cotton hit the market.

The company's good fortune from the beginning of its cotton cultivation in 1904 to 1913 did not continue during the four-year period of 1914–1917. The price of cotton collapsed following the opening of World War I, and the weakness lingered into 1915, when Taft Ranch cotton sold for an average of 10.08 cents a pound, well under the 1912 and 1913 prices.[27] A prolonged drouth that started in the fall of 1915

[22] Interview with Edward N. Tutt, Taft, August 3, 1961.

[23] *Ibid.* Taft *Tribune,* February 7, 1924. *Senate Documents,* 64th Congress, First Session, Serial No. 6938, Doc. No. 415, p. 9215.

[24] Interview with Emmett Yglesias, Taft, July 28, 1961.

[25] Interview with Mr. and Mrs. J. D. Moore, Sinton, November 18, 1961.

[26] *San Patricio County Press* (Gregory and Taft, Texas), February 6, 1914.

[27] Fetick to Commissioner of Internal Revenue, CFPC. United States De-

prevented planting of the acreage allotted to cotton. Professor Alvord estimated the area in production as one-twentieth of capacity, and even that small crop was demolished on August 18, 1916, when a disastrous hurricane hit the Coastal Bend.[28]

After the turbulent weather subsided the department foremen surveyed the destruction and reported that windmills and silos were either blown down or badly impaired, glass windows were broken, several Latin American houses were blown down or tipped over, paper roofing was blown off the elevator seedhouse, the bathhouse and wharf at La Quinta were destroyed, and some damage was done to the La Quinta residence—altogether a loss of over $25,000.[29] Following the storm a long drouth set in that lasted for eighteen months, causing a partial loss of the 1917 crop when enough rain fell to make seed sprout, but insufficient to produce a good crop. The dryness lingered until the planting season of 1918.[30]

The 1918 crop was the best on record to that date when the net revenue per acre for the company farms was $41.30, and for the tenant farms, $15.46.[31] The following year another record harvest appeared to be in the making, with the excellent combination of adequate precipitation and of high prices, but the coastal prairies were again lashed by a West Indian hurricane. On September 14, 1919, the eye of the storm hit directly against Corpus Christi, causing extensive damage to property and taking many lives. Destruction of unpicked cotton remaining in the fields was estimated at one-third to one-half of the entire crop.[32]

partment of Agriculture, *Statistics on Cotton and Related Data*, Bulletin No. 99, pp. 130, 145.

[28] Fetick to Commissioner of Internal Revenue, CFPC. Charles H. Alvord, Gregory, Texas, to W. J. Morse, Washington, D.C., June 26, 1916, United States Department of Agriculture, Office of Forage Crop Investigations, Record Group 54.

[29] Minutes of Departmental Meeting, September [no day given], 1916, May 4, 1918, CFPC. *San Patricio County News*, August 25, 1916.

[30] Minutes of Departmental Meeting, May 4, 1918, CFPC. Fetick to Commissioner of Internal Revenue, CFPC. George Frederic Stratton, "Mr. Taft's Tenants: How They Earn Farms on His Big Texas Ranch," *Country Gentleman*, LXXXIV (March 1, 1919), 37.

[31] Statement of Tenant Farms and Company Farms, 1918, CFPC.

[32] *San Patricio County News*, September 19, 1919.

In 1920 the Taft Ranch harvested its largest yield in agricultural commodities. By that time only three company farms remained—Numbers 21, 23, and 24; but from the 3,350 acres they comprised, with approximately 20 per cent of that amount in feed, workers picked a total of 2,512 bales of cotton. Proceeds from all growing crops amounted to an average net revenue an acre of $66.53.[33] The twenty-six quarter-share tenants produced 3,473 bales from 4,300 acres, including the customary acreage in grain, for a total net revenue an acre of $22.84.[34] The following year the farmers' trait of optimism was needed, for the tenant farms did well to break even after deducting expenses, while the company farms suffered a sharp loss at an average of minus $11.58 an acre.[35] Here then is positive proof of the uncertainty of farming.

The Taft Ranch aroused a great deal of interest in its experimental agriculture and its large demonstration farms from agriculturally oriented people in the state and the nation. In 1915 the United States Senate Commission on Industrial Relations held public hearings in Dallas on the agricultural industry of the United States, looking specifically at the land and tenantry problem of Texas and Oklahoma. Superintendent and general manager Joseph F. Green and farm superintendent Charles H. Alvord, called to testify, discussed the purpose and the practice of the Taft Ranch, mentioning that the ranch was humane with its tenants to the point of encouraging them to buy land from the company and to become independent farmers.[36] As Alvord explained to the committee chairman, Senator Frank P. Walsh, the ranch treated the Latin American laborers well, allowed them to share in the coupon system of credit at the company stores, and provided a company physician for them when ill.[37] Undoubtedly, Senator Walsh marvelled at this arrangement, which represented a somewhat advanced agrarian social outlook for 1915.

At the time of the hearing the Taft Ranch had approximately 10,000 acres under cultivation and rented one-third of this amount on one-third and one-fourth shares to men who operated it as their own farms,

[33] Statement of Company Farms, 1920, CFPC.

[34] Statement of Tenant Farms, 1920, CFPC.

[35] Statements of Tenant and Company Farms, 1921, CFPC.

[36] *Senate Documents*, 64th Congress, First Session, Serial No. 6938, Doc. No. 415, pp. 9214–9228. Dallas *Morning News*, March 21, 1915.

[37] *Ibid.*

each working from 50 to 150 acres.[38] Joseph F. Green personally selected each of the tenants before a contract was signed. The Taft Ranch received a great deal of publicity about its fertile soil and its scientific method of farming; therefore, Green always had a waiting list of applicants. The contracts were reasonable, but required a person to show aggressiveness and hard work on his place or his contract would not be renewed.[39] Weeds on the fence rows and in the fields were to be chopped to the center of the road. One hears amusing stories concerning the farm inspections by Superintendent Green. The tenants knew that the boss always drove along the turnrows looking for weeds and that he never walked through the fields. They took advantage of him when rushed for time by hoeing only a "seeing distance" from the road rather than the entire patch.

Renters were furnished a four-room house with bath, a large barn for animals and feed storage, abundant fresh water, and, for Latin American laborers that might be hired, several small two-room cottages.[40] The company encouraged its sharecroppers to raise hogs for fresh meat during the wintertime. All had their own milk cows and sold the offspring to the Taft Packing House at a substantial profit.[41] Most of the tenants who came to the Taft Ranch were permanent, leaving only to purchase land in the community, many times from the company itself. Green estimated in 1915 at the Senate Industrial Relations Commission hearings that 75 per cent of those who had worked for the ranch since it started cotton farming in 1904 were still there, which was sufficient evidence that they were well treated.[42] The number of share farms varied from the original four in 1904 to twenty in 1912, twenty-five in 1915, thirty-seven in 1917, and down to eighteen in 1921 as the company concentrated its efforts on selling land.[43]

At the height of the big-business-type farming by the Taft Ranch,

[38] *Ibid.*

[39] Interview with Mr. and Mrs. J. D. Moore, Sinton, November 18, 1961.

[40] Stratton, "Mr. Taft's Tenants," *Country Gentleman*, LXXXIV, No. 9 (March 1, 1919), 37.

[41] *Senate Documents*, 64th Congress, First Session, Serial No. 6938, Doc. No. 415, pp. 9214–9228.

[42] *Ibid.*

[43] Statements, average revenue per acre from tenant farmers, 1912 and 1915; statements for Tenant Farms, 1917 and 1921; both in CFPC.

there were six units of approximately 1,000 acres each on the reservation along the railroad between Taft and Portland. Each farm had a large, well-built house for the foreman, with several rows of two-room cottages for Latin American laborers. Nearby were situated an extremely large barn with the number of the farm painted on the roof, and sheds for the animals and equipment, silos, and livestock corrals.[44] All houses and other buildings were painted white trimmed in green, presenting a pleasant sight to visitors and residents alike, while giving an air of prosperity. An average of twenty to twenty-five regular men on each farm received $1.00 a day, until austere times in 1914 forced the company to reduce wages to eighty cents.[45] By 1919 the rate for most regular workers was from $1.25 to $1.50 a day.[46]

Superintendent Green interviewed each regular worker prior to employment, attempting to hire only industrious persons. In the event the subordinate failed to live up to Green's expectations, or when a personality conflict occurred, the superintendent instructed the auditor to attach a pink slip to the individual's paycheck. The pink slip was commonly understood by all as a sign that the laborer had been dropped from the payroll. According to stories in circulation around Taft and Gregory today, the superintendent did not discuss the release with the victim beforehand, but did make it a point to be in another vicinity of the ranch until the employee's initial shock of being fired wore off. The pink slip became a symbol of falling from grace and made one alert and energetic about one's job to avoid the "axe."

During harvest season hundreds of extra laborers were hired, part of them just drifting in, but most of them coming from the Texas-Mexico border. At times the ranch contracted with persons in Laredo to hire the desired number of workers for a season and frequently sent ranch officials to the border to recruit laborers. Special trains chartered from Brownsville or Laredo brought workers in locked cattle cars to Taft, where foremen waited to take them to the farms.[47] Many times the

[44] Stratton, "Mr. Taft's Tenants," *Country Gentleman*, LXXXIV, No. 9 (March 1, 1919), 37.

[45] *Senate Documents*, 64th Congress, First Session, Serial No. 6938, Doc. No. 415, pp. 9214–9228.

[46] Coleman-Fulton Pasture Company Pay Roll Book, CFPC.

[47] Interviews with Edward N. Tutt, Taft, November 27, 1961; with E. I.

Latin Americans were so weak from malnutrition that they had to be fed for a time before they were strong enough to work.[48] When the ranch discovered that the laborers preferred goat meat to beef, it transported thousands of goats from the Catarina Ranch. Housing was scarce for seasonal workers, and many lived in tents or moved into two-room cottages with other families. The idea of a common messhall or chuck wagon was spurned, as the Mexicans wanted to cook food to their own liking. Anglo-American residents in Taft had a saying that the Latin Americans liked their beans dry and their goats alive so that they could prepare them in their own way.[49] Each year after the harvest the laborers returned to their point of origin at the ranch's expense.

These migrant workers were regarded with suspicion during the years when corporate farming was introduced, not because they posed a threat individually but because banded together they might raid Anglo-American homes. The Texas-Mexico border conflict, in progress at this time, did not directly affect the Taft Ranch, although some community residents feared that an armed uprising might occur. The ranch continued to hire Latin Americans, but corporation officials made it a point to hire only men with families, trusting that a man would be law-abiding for his family's sake. Precautions were taken, however, in the long chance that trouble might develop.

After the United States and the Texas governments sent armed men to the border in 1915, and after the town of Sinton formed a rifle club "For the purpose of true sport, social association, and the benefits to be derived from rifle practice,"[50] the Coleman-Fulton Pasture Company also organized a rifle club. Ranch officials purchased weapons, .30–30 rifles and .38 pistols, distributed them among ranch employees, and held target practice sessions. The firm requested members of the club, or the "home guard," as they were called, to be ready to go to any part of the ranch on call in time of emergency.[51] Superintendent

Crow, Taft, November 2, 1961; with Mr. and Mrs. D. Lard, Taft, October 28, 1961.

[48] Interview with E. I. Crow, Taft, November 2, 1961.

[49] Interview with Mr. and Mrs. D. Lard, Taft, October 28, 1961.

[50] *San Patricio County News,* April 24, 1914.

[51] Minutes of Departmental Meeting, June 7, 1916, CFPC. Interview with Edward N. Tutt, Taft, November 27, 1961.

Green appointed a committee to investigate the possibility of purchasing a rapid-fire gun in the summer of 1916, as a future precaution.

> . . . there is practically no danger of any disturbance now, but if we should get a cotton crop and have a thousand or two Mexican pickers here, then there might be some danger of some one trying to get them to make an uprising of some sort and . . . it would be good policy for this reason to have a gun of this kind and have some of the men trained so they understand using it.[52]

The weapon, kept in storage until needed, would be placed on the front of a truck with a mount specially designed for that purpose, then chauffeured quickly to any point on the ranch. No evidence exists in the company records, substantiated by conversations with persons who were there, that the corporation actually obtained a machine gun. The crisis soon passed, and the Pasture Company called in the rifles and pistols from its vigilance committee.[53]

These militaristic activities did not affect the harmonious relationship between the corporation and those Latin Americans who had been regular employees for several years. In fact the ranch was forced to work large numbers of them because of a labor shortage. This ethnic group was not hired because it would toil for less money, Green pointed out to the Senate Committee, but because not enough Anglo-Americans were available to fill all vacancies. Most of the Anglo-Americans were mechanics, artisans, or foremen.[54] The seasonal laborers harvested the cotton, feed, and various other crops with which Professor Alvord experimented from time to time.

In 1916 Alvord and Green encouraged the cultivation of peanuts among Coastal Bend farmers, but enthusiasm for the legume was short-lived because the black waxy soil of the Taft Ranch was unsuited for that purpose. Before peanut growing was abandoned, the Taft Oil and Gin Company made peanut meal, which it advertised as "the best hog feed there is. Also fine for cows and horses. Try a sack on your milk cow."[55]

[52] Minutes of Departmental Meeting, July 19, 1916, CFPC.

[53] Interview with Edward N. Tutt, Taft, November 27, 1961.

[54] *Senate Documents*, 64th Congress, First Session, Serial No. 6938, Doc. No. 415, pp. 9214–9228.

[55] *San Patricio County News*, September 29, 1916, January 5, 1917.

The drouth ruined the possibility of planting the acreage allotted for cotton in 1916; therefore, in order to achieve full benefit of the soil, Professor Alvord sought a product that could be planted in midsummer. Through the Office of Forage Crop Investigations of the Department of Agriculture he obtained soybeans for cultivation on approximately seventy-five acres of the Taft Ranch, but his experiment was unsuccessful, as the plants were badly affected by rust and did not produce.[56] Through actual practice it was proved that the soil and climate of the coastal plains were not suited to the growing of soybeans; but, if the experiment had succeeded, a new cash crop would have been introduced to the farmers of South Texas as a diversification from cotton and feed. The Taft Ranch deserves a great deal of credit for testing different plants in an attempt to determine those that would grow profitably in that region, a feat that no other farm, large or small, was doing at the time.

Charles H. Alvord left the employment of the Coleman-Fulton Pasture Company in 1917, after six years of commendable service to Texas agriculture, to accept the position of Southwestern Field Agent of Extension Service, United States Department of Agriculture, with headquarters in Washington, D.C.[57] His successor was R. O. Tackett, a Taft Ranch cotton-marketing official who had been connected with cotton production most of his life as a farmer and as an agent.[58]

Although the Coleman-Fulton Pasture Company did not discontinue its range-cattle program during the era of big-business agriculture, it did give priority to cotton production, with the result that the size of its herd diminished. Of the 9,661 head on hand in 1912, 789 of which were registered, the total number declined to 7,779 in 1914, 5,663 in 1917, and 4,897 in 1921.[59] During this decade the majority of livestock sales were made to the Taft Packing House, but several

[56] Charles H. Alvord, Gregory, to W. J. Morse, Washington, D.C., July 14, 1916, May 2, 1917; Morse to Alvord, July 15, 1916; all in United States Department of Agriculture Office of Forage Crops Investigations, Record Group 54.

[57] Taft *Tribune*, June 21, 1923, October 1, 1925. *San Patrico County News*, September 7, 1917.

[58] Interview with C. J. Meyer, Taft, March 2, 1961; with James Colon Russell, Sinton, August 8, 1961.

[59] Financial Statements of the Coleman-Fulton Pasture Company, 1912–1921, CFPC.

purebred and highly graded bulls were sold to neighboring farmers to upgrade their small herds.[60] The bovine division of the ranch was separated into departments as were the farming and industrial establishments. Foremen were in charge of range cattle, Shorthorns, Herefords, Jerseys, and Holsteins.[61]

The ranch raised large numbers of hogs, principally to supply the demand at the Taft Packing House, but also to utilize the waste of grain scattered by the mules and horses around the company's feed lots. Not all the swine were kept merely as an adjunct to the company farms, for a 3,000-acre Hog Ranch was established five miles north of Taft on Chiltipin Creek where the products of the Taft Oil and Gin Company were utilized.[62] When the packing house began its first big year of operation in 1912, the ranch owned 962 hogs on the ranch. Increasing to 3,333 in 1915, the number dropped because of the drouth of 1916–1918 and the subsequent shortage of feed.[63] For two years the Taft Packing House was closed for repairs, retaining just enough animals to provide winter meat for the ranch employees. By 1921 only 277 hogs were on hand.[64]

The population of mules and horses fluctuated during this period, but the decade ended with practically the same number. From a total of 370 mules in 1912, holdings increased to a high of 507 in 1915, and then dropped to 352 head in 1921.[65] The principal draft animal, for both plows and vehicles, was the mule. Although the herd was not raised for the market, occasionally the ranch hands culled it, leaving the largest and best stock for farm work. In 1916, when the European belligerents sent buyers to South Texas, the Coleman-Fulton Pasture Company sold many of its small mules at top prices.[66] Horses were used primarily for cattle work, though some served as buggy power and as horseback transportation. The number on the ranch

[60] Stratton, "Mr. Taft's Tenants," *Country Gentleman,* LXXXIV, No. 9 (March 1, 1919), 40.

[61] Interview with Edward N. Tutt, Taft, November 27, 1961.

[62] Interview with Mr. and Mrs. Henry Moore, Taft, November 24, 1961.

[63] Financial Statements of the Coleman-Fulton Pasture Company, 1912–1921, CFPC.

[64] *Ibid.*

[65] *Ibid.*

[66] Minutes of Departmental Meeting, May 3, 1916, CFPC.

varied from year to year: 200 in 1912, 306 in 1915, 153 in 1918, and 194 in 1921.[67]

During the second decade of the twentieth century the Taft Ranch became widely known for its scientifically operated demonstration farms and its industry. The ranch was one of few firms that owned the land, produced the commodities, and marketed the finished product, as it did with its meats, shortening, and prepared livestock feeds. Visitors representing agricultural colleges and experiment farms all over the United States came to study the techniques of farming; in addition, persons from countries throughout the world visited the ranch. In 1912 alone La Quinta entertained guests from Africa, Cuba, Brazil, Austria, Jamaica, Java, France, Mexico, and Germany who came to observe.[68] Superintendent Green, at a meeting of the department foremen in 1913, stated that Rothschild's, the large Frankfort, Germany, banking house, was sending a man to the Taft Ranch to study equipment and methods used in raising cotton, in order that he might obtain data for Rothschild's future agricultural reclamation of Palestine.[69] Green posed the question, "Why did these visitors come to the Taft Ranch?" and then gave the answer; ". . . we have done something out of the ordinary."[70]

During this period Joseph F. Green maintained control of the ranch, and with a competent staff he guided it to a responsible position of leadership in American agriculture. As Charles P. Taft became older, he relinquished his office as treasurer, which he had held since David Sinton gained administrative control of the corporation in 1894. Bert E. Kinder, cashier of the Taft Ranch Bank, was appointed to the vacated post on January 1, 1912, but in May of that year the offices of superintendent, secretary, and treasurer were combined into one and Joseph F. Green filled it.[71] As compensation for the extra work ex-

[67] Financial Statements of the Coleman-Fulton Pasture Company, 1912–1921, CFPC.

[68] Minutes of Departmental Meeting, January 14, 1913, CFPC. Unlabeled, July, 1913, newspaper clippings in possession of Mrs. May Mathis Green Watson, Corpus Christi.

[69] *Ibid.*

[70] Unlabeled, July, 1913, newspaper clippings in possession of Mrs. May Mathis Green Watson, Corpus Christi.

[71] Minutes of the Coleman-Fulton Pasture Company Board of Directors'

pected of him, Green's stipend was $9,000; and it remained at that figure until 1916, when it was reduced to $7,200.[72] In 1916 Joseph F. Green replaced John M. Green as vice president, turning over the duties of secretary to William Howard Taft II, of New York, who also shared the responsibility of assistant treasurer with Margaret Sheeran of Gregory, a long-time employee in the company office.[73]

William Howard Taft II, son of Horace Taft of Watertown, Connecticut, and nephew of the Coleman-Fulton Pasture Company president, owned and operated a farm near Gregory in 1915 and 1916. He resigned as an official of this ranch in 1917, when the New York National Guard unit in which he was a reserve officer was activated, and accompanied General John J. Pershing into Mexico to join the futile chase after Pancho Villa.[74] For a brief time Raymond Mullen, the young son of a community farming family, served as assistant secretary under Taft, until H. V. Fetick of Cincinnati assumed secretarial duties.[75]

Fetick, an employee of the Tafts in Cincinnati for several years, came to the ranch at a time when Joseph F. Green had increased the corporation's debt to approximately $800,000. The motive behind Fetick's transfer was for him to serve as a one-man watchdog committee over the superintendent and the company's expenditures.[76] The newcomer encroached on the sanctity of Green's position in the corporation by obtaining Anna Sinton Taft's proxy in 1918 and by voting her 76 per cent of the capital stock to make himself the treasurer with control over the superintendent's extraordinary expenses.[77]

For over a decade the Board of Directors had consisted of Charles P. Taft, Joseph F. Green, and John M. Green. A quorum of two had conducted most of the business because Taft visited the ranch infrequently, but the Ohioan had controlled the Board's policy making

Meeting (hereafter cited as Minutes of Directors' Meeting), January 1, 1912; Minutes of Stockholders' Meeting, May 6, 1912; both in CFPC.

[72] Minutes of Directors' Meeting, May 5, 1913, May 1, 1916, CFPC.

[73] *Ibid.,* May 1, 1961, August 8, 1917, CFPC. Watson and Lillico, *Taft Ranch*, p. 32.

[74] Watson and Lillico, *Taft Ranch*, p. 30.

[75] Minutes of Directors' Meeting, May 7, August 8, 1917, CFPC.

[76] Interview with Edward N. Tutt, Taft, November 27, 1961.

[77] Minutes of Stockholders' Meeting, May 6, 1918, CFPC.

because of his wife's majority stockholding. In 1918 Taft instructed that there should be five directors. This decision, coming at the time when Fetick's authority increased, leads one to believe that Taft's motive was to temper the influence of Green over company affairs. Accordingly, with an amendment of the By-Laws two new members were added to the Board: H. V. Fetick, and Walter P. Napier.[78] Napier, a member of the law firm of Templeton, Brooks, Napier, and Ogden of San Antonio, served for the following dozen years as the company's legal counselor.

Although the record is vacant on the subject, one can speculate that Green highly resented the purpose of Fetick's presence, and worked to remove the nuisance. The superintendent scored a victory the following year when the Board of Directors reverted to its original size of three members, composed of Taft, Joseph F. Green, and Napier. Fetick, relinquishing the positions of secretary, treasurer, and director, returned to Cincinnati, and John M. Green resigned to devote full time to ranching. In the reorganization that followed, Joseph F. Green gave up the office of vice president and took Fetick's place as secretary-treasurer, Napier became vice president, and Edward N. Tutt, Green's personal secretary, was elected assistant secretary of the corporation. Margaret Sheeran retained her position of assistant treasurer as did Taft in the presidency.[79]

Tutt, formerly of Liberty, Missouri, first visited the Taft Ranch in 1914, when his aunt, Miss Etta Ellifrit, was Green's personal secretary; then he returned in 1917 and remained associated with the corporation until it dissolved in 1930.[80] Four months after the big rearranging of company officers, C. J. Meyer, a clerk in the auditing department since 1916, replaced Sheeran as assistant treasurer. Meyer, recently of Waller, Texas, also was one of the few persons who remained as an employee until the charter expired.[81]

On March 1, 1920, H. V. Fetick returned to Taft and once again became a ranch official, this time as secretary and assistant superintend-

[78] *Ibid.*

[79] *Ibid.*, February 8, May 5, 1919, CFPC.

[80] Interview with Edward N. Tutt, Taft, November 27, 1961.

[81] Minutes of Directors' Meeting, June 7, 1919, CFPC. Interview with C. J. Meyer, Taft, March 2, 1961.

ent, with a stipend set at $6,000 a year. Green received $7,200 annually as superintendent and treasurer, and as vice president when Walter Napier resigned. Fetick replaced Napier on the Board of Directors. Green appointed Edward N. Tutt, C. J. Meyer, and Lee Mullen, of the Taft Ranch community, as assistant treasurers; Tutt and Meyer also doubled as assistant secretaries under Fetick.[82]

At the time the power play was going on between Green and Fetick the Pasture Company harvested two good cotton crops, which, together with the extensive land-sale program then in progress, eased its burden of indebtedness. All during the past decade the ranch had engaged in the sale of real estate, through Superintendent Green, who received a commission,[83] and through an agent. For the most part the Taft Ranch did not employ outside persons to assist in the disposition of its acreage, but it made one exception when it contracted with State Senator John G. Willacy of Portland on June 7, 1910, granting him the exclusive right to sell company property in Portland and the adjoining two sections fronting on Corpus Christi Bay.[84] On May 20, 1911, Willacy organized the Portland Development Company under a fifty-year charter from the Texas Secretary of State.[85] The incorporators were Willacy, J. M. Eskridge of San Antonio, and E. G. Wessendorff of Fort Bend County, Texas, who were authorized to issue capital stock of $60,000 divided into 600 shares of $100 each.[86]

The Coleman-Fulton Pasture Company had visions of making a port and town at Portland. A large area in Portland and near there was surveyed, platted, and placed on sale, by both the Portland Development Company and the Pasture Company. To handle shipping, the ranch built a large $28,000 wharf with railroad facilities, but the railroad never did reach it.[87] In 1911 the ranch expended $10,000 to

[82] Minutes of Stockholders' Meeting, May 3, 1920, CFPC.

[83] Minutes of Stockholders' Meeting, June 4, 1910, CFPC.

[84] Sales contract between the Coleman-Fulton Pasture Company and John G. Willacy, June 7, 1910, ratified and approved by the Coleman-Fulton Pasture Company Stockholders at a meeting in Gregory, May 1, 1911, as recorded on the Minutes of Stockholders' Meeting, May 1, 1911, CFPC.

[85] Portland Development Company, Charter No. 23182, May 20, 1911, Office of the Texas Secretary of State.

[86] *Ibid.*

[87] Interview with Edward N. Tutt, Taft, November 27, 1961. Minutes of Stockholders' Meeting, May 5, 1913, CFPC.

improve the Portland townsite by clearing land, by building roads, streets, and sidewalks, and by constructing a pleasure pavilion in connection with the wharf.[88] The 1916 hurricane destroyed the big recreation center and the wharf, as well as many other improvements in Portland, none of which were replaced. A large part of the land for the Portland townsite development was turned into acreage for farming; after that the ranch concentrated its promotion schemes on Taft.[89]

To raise money to meet indebtedness arising from erecting industrial plants and from putting land into cultivation, the corporation's stockholders voted in 1913 to sell 10,000 acres between Taft and Chiltipin Creek, a distance of approximately four miles, extending east and west for approximately five miles.[90] When this sale was approved, the Coleman-Fulton Pasture Company owned 8,305 acres in Aransas County and 78,668 acres in San Patricio County.[91] Later Joseph F. Green had authority to transact sales of company real estate that he deemed advisable for the welfare of the ranch, without first obtaining permission from the stockholders.[92]

Between 1913 and 1918 Green sold only 2,661 acres, owing to the discouragement of agricultural prices brought on by World War I and by drouth.[93] At the close of the excellent crop year of 1918 the company sold 3,512 acres at prices ranging from $30.00 to $125.00 an acre averaging $83.63 an acre.[94] One reason for the sale of so much land when prosperity returned was to pay off a large debt to Mrs. Anna Sinton Taft.[95] Before any sales were made that year, and at a time when it seemed that only the strictest economy practices would enable the corporation to pull through the several years of drouth, Charles P. Taft, the firm's controlling stockholder, directed that the 1908 de-

[88] Minutes of Stockholders' Meeting, May 1, 1911, CFPC.

[89] Interview with Edward N. Tutt, Taft, November 27, 1961.

[90] Minutes of Stockholders' Meeting, May 5, July 7, 1913, CFPC.

[91] Tax Statement for 1912, CFPC.

[92] Minutes of Stockholders' Meeting, May 1, 1916, CFPC.

[93] Anna Sinton Taft, Cincinnati, Ohio, to United States Internal Revenue Agent, Dallas, November 30, 1928, Income Tax Information Folder, CFPC.

[94] *Ibid.*

[95] Fetick to Commissioner of Internal Revenue, CFPC. Charles P. Taft, Cincinnati, to Joseph F. Green, Gregory, and H. V. Fetick, Gregory, a copy of the letter in the Minutes of Stockholders' Meeting, May 6, 1918, CFPC.

cision to give a commission on land sales to Joseph F. Green be rescinded.[96] The following year, however, Green was again allowed a reward for selling real estate, retroactive to 1918, but under less favorable conditions. He was to receive a 5-per-cent commission on lands he sold and a 2½-per-cent allowance on sales consummated by agents whom he contracted; nothing was to be paid the general manager until the ranch's entire indebtedness to Mrs. Taft was extinguished.[97]

The Pasture Company owed a great deal of money to Mrs. Taft. In addition to borrowing from her, at times heavily, the ranch received loans from regional banks, using real or personal property as collateral. Superintendent Green, under authority from the corporation's stockholders, had full authority to negotiate loans. By virtue of this provision he borrowed $200,000 from Mr. and Mrs. Charles P. Taft in 1911.[98] With this advancement, and with $500,000 more allotted by the Tafts and by various banks in 1912, the ranch completed the packing house, built and equipped farm buildings, machine shops, and blacksmith shops, grubbed additional land and put it into cultivation, constructed the waterworks system, erected an office, bank, and store building in Gregory, started a ranch hospital, and encouraged the development of Portland.[99] At the close of the 1913 fiscal year the actual indebtedness of the Coleman-Fulton Pasture Company was $830,786.43, of which $441,800.00 was due the Tafts.[100] With good crops in 1912 and 1913 the corporation was able to reduce its liability to $424,300.00, but it was not so fortunate during the next five years, as its farm earnings dropped considerably owing to low prices in 1914, to a hurricane in 1916, to the 1916–1918 drouth, and to continued development of the land. Nevertheless, Mr. and Mrs. Charles P. Taft retained their faith in the ranch and extended more financial support. Their confidence was justified, for the bumper crops of 1918 and 1920 coupled with the sales of land at elevated prices enabled the ranch to extinguish its entire indebtedness by January 1, 1921.[101]

[96] Minutes of Stockholders' Meeting, May 6, 1918, CFPC.

[97] Minutes of Directors' Meeting, September 6, 1919, CFPC.

[98] Minutes of Stockholders' Meeting, June 4, 1910, May 1, 1911, CFPC.

[99] *Ibid.*, May 1, 1911, May 6, 1912, CFPC.

[100] Fetick to Commissioner of Internal Revenue, CFPC.

[101] Minutes of Stockholders' Meeting, June 7, 1915, January 1, 1917, Febru-

During this age of bigness in South Texas agriculture the Taft Ranch mobilized its resources to make giant strides toward the development of its land. Through the introduction of new crops and extensive production of the standby commodity, cotton, the aim of diversification was achieved. The old emphasis on livestock raising diminished as row-crop farming became profitable. Owing largely to the forceful leadership of Joseph F. Green, and hard work by his subordinates, the Taft Ranch played an active role in the development of the South Texas Plains. Thousands of productive acres broken to the plow expanded the revenue potential of the Pasture Company, and also San Patricio County through increased tax assessments. Solvency, the long sought after goal since the days of Colonel Fulton, was at last achieved by the ranch.

ary 28, 1920; all in CFPC. Minutes of Directors' Meeting, May 2, 1921, CFPC. Interview with C. J. Meyer, Taft, March 2, 1961.

XI. THE FINAL YEARS

MUSIC AND GAIETY greeted visitors to Taft on the sunshiny morning of June 1, 1921. The air of festivity was conspicuously present as people gathered in groups to chat about the auction to be held that day. The Coleman-Fulton Pasture Company was selling lots in the town of Taft and farms nearby. The First Subdivision of Taft Farm Lands was planned by the corporation's stockholders earlier that year when they realized that the charter would expire in a relatively brief time, and that if the maximum value of the real and personal property were to be achieved they must inaugurate a program of selling the land and improvements.

The Pasture Company had organized under a single franchise in 1880 to deal in livestock, but since had branched out into many phases of manufacturing and farming; therefore, a single permit to do business would not cover its extensive enterprises. Also the majority stockholders were increasing in age, had used a great deal of their funds to develop the region, and now were ready to get financial returns from their investment. The good cotton year of 1920 was undoubtedly the impetus for the First Subdivision, because neighboring farmers and those from over the Southwest would have money to invest. In preparation for the beginning of its final years the ranch commissioned J. H. Kirkpatrick, a San Antonio realtor, to conduct the June 1 auction.

During the spring of 1921 the ranch surveyed and platted fifty-two acres into town lots, graded, paved, and curbed the streets, extended electric-power lines, installed sewerage, water, and natural-gas mains, and divided approximately three thousand acres of outlying land into family farm units.[1] After the date was set, Kirkpatrick publicized the affair by placing a half-page advertisement in a recently inaugurated local newspaper, the Taft *Tribune,* and distributed copies of that issue over the entire state. The land was declared to be quite suitable for farming as the notice indicates.

PUBLIC SALE AT TAFT JUNE 1
Town Lots — Stores — Farms
The Heart of the Famous Black Belt of Texas

The farm lands comprising the great Taft Ranch have for many years produced record crops. Rich black lands with splendid sub-soils and blessed with ideal climatic conditions have made this section the most productive and profitable for the successful raising of farm and live stock crops. Every industrious farmer who has settled in or around Taft has become prosperous beyond his hope.[2]

The article mentioned that the farms were divided into tracts of sixty to one hundred acres, that each was on a graded road leading to the main highway, and that the price ranged from $50 to $75 an acre with payments distributed over a ten-year period.

Kirkpatrick was quite specific in announcing the type of people he wished to attract.

During the past thirty years, the original owners and developers of the Taft properties have helped hundreds of industrious toilers towards farm and home ownership. To those who demonstrate an earnest desire to do their share in the further development of these rich properties every aid and co-operation will be offered by the owners. There are no idle fortunes in Taft for dreamers, schemers or promoters. We do not offer any encouragement to get-rich-quick prospectors. The man who is willing to invest a little money

[1] Minutes of the Coleman-Fulton Pasture Company Stockholders' Meeting (hereafter cited as Minutes of Stockholders' Meeting), February 4, May 2, 1921, Coleman-Fulton Pasture Company Records (hereafter cited as CFPC). Taft *Tribune,* May 5, 1921, July 31, 1941 (Twentieth Anniversary Edition). Interview with Edward N. Tutt, Taft, November 27, 1961; with C. J. Meyer, Taft, March 2, 1961.

[2] Taft *Tribune,* May 12, 1921.

and a great deal of honest toil will find the fullest reward in the various opportunities offered in this sale.[3]

On June 1 approximately five thousand persons were in Taft, many coming, no doubt, merely for the excitement and the free barbecued-beef dinner.[4] While the Taft Ranch Band and the Beeville High School Band performed, the ranch employees served dinner on the grounds. Several people inspected the real estate nearby, while others looked over the farm tracts, carried there by automobiles. After speeches by Kirkpatrick and Green, the auction began. An auditorium with a seating capacity of five hundred erected especially for the sale was too small to house the group, so the meeting moved across the street where a large canvas tent was assembled.[5] The day was sunny and warm, vegetation appeared fresh and green from a rain the day before, all of which put the guests in a cheerful mood. Competitive bidding brought some of the lots to a high figure; however, not all of the property was sold the first day. Finally, the ranch sold fifty business lots, sixty residential lots, and a number of farm tracts.[6]

Following the June 1, 1921, transactions, the ranch office in Gregory and Kirkpatrick's San Antonio realty company continued disposing of the property. With the influx of new persons to the area, the town of Taft expanded as merchants were attracted to the growing community, and within a short time businesses of every description had sprung up there.

The Pasture Company invested in a large two-story brick building in the main business district for the company's use and for renting to other firms. Authorized in the fall of 1921, the $50,000 structure was completed in 1923. Immediately space was leased to banks, a drug store, physicians, a fraternal lodge, and administrative departments of the Taft Ranch.[7] In 1922 Joseph F. Green transferred the company's

[3] *Ibid.*

[4] Diary of Mrs. May Mathis Green, entry dated June 1, 1921, in possession of Mrs. May Mathis Green Watson. Taft *Tribune*, June 2, 1921.

[5] Taft *Tribune*, June 2, 1921, July 5, 1924. Sales Day Program, Taft, Texas, June 1, 1921, in possession of Mr. and Mrs. Manton Williams.

[6] Taft *Tribune*, June 5, 1924, July 31, 1941. *San Patricio County News* (Sinton, Texas), June 3, 1921.

[7] Statement, Taft Office and Bank Building, 1923; Minutes of the Coleman-Fulton Pasture Company Board of Directors' Meeting (hereafter cited as

offices to Taft; the Green Hotel was also moved to Taft to serve ranch personnel and prospective buyers.[8]

When the real-estate and business concerns were placed on the market, the ranch gave even more attention to the community's future expansion by providing an additional financial institution. The First National Bank of Taft, organized on January 6, 1923, was not owned by the Coleman-Fulton Pasture Company, but the stockholders and officers were largely identical in both.[9] Two days later a group of businessmen and farmers of San Patricio County formed the First State Bank of Taft.[10] The existence of three money establishments in a town of five hundred prompted a newspaper reporter to write that the new banks were "a good barometer of the stability and growth as well as the push and energy of the people of the county."[11] To assist the First National Bank of Taft and to have its funds close at hand, the ranch made the new firm an official depository soon after it began.[12]

For the convenience of those who came to look at the farm land, and for the motoring public in general traveling on the King of Trails, the ranch erected a tourist camp on the outskirts of Taft with free gas, water, and lights.[13] As each sector was disposed of, another tract was surveyed and placed on the market. T. N. Blackwell, the sales manager, advertised in newspapers, placed large painted signs in neighboring cities, and issued a descriptive booklet with pictures of industrial plants, growing crops, and prosperous homes to emphasize that the Taft community was a good place to live.[14] Altogether, five consecutively numbered detachments of farm lands were sold, extending from Taft to Chiltipin Creek on the north and Puerto Bay on the east, a Rincon Subdivision, and two separate tracts known as the Gregory

Minutes of Directors' Meeting), October 22, 1921; both in CFPC. Taft *Tribune*, February 15, 1923.

[8] Corpus Christi *Caller-Times*, May 9, 1954, March 11, 1955.

[9] Taft *Tribune*, January 11, 1923.

[10] *Ibid.*

[11] *Ibid.*, January 18, 1923.

[12] Minutes of Stockholders' Meeting, June 11, 1923, CFPC.

[13] Taft *Tribune*, September 14, 1922.

[14] T. N. Blackwell (compiler), *Taft Ranch, San Patricio County, Texas: The Land of perpetual Sunshine, Sea Breezes, Fat Cattle, Hogs, Dairy Cows, Cotton, Feed, Prosperity and Happiness.*

Farm Blocks adjoining Gregory.[15] Individuals bought real estate with one-fourth down and paid the balance at 6-per-cent interest.[16]

The company installed roads and drainage ditches. It continued to give abstracts of title, and from the purchase price it deducted these expenses as well as the costs for commissions, surveying, advertising, and mapping. The company auditor figured the cost of selling during the period 1923–1926 at 18 per cent of the land's value, or $9.98 an acre average. During that time 62,685 acres were vended for a total consideration of $3,496,744, at prices ranging from $5, $10, $20, $35, $50, $75, to $125 an acre.[17]

On the remaining land the company and tenant farms continued in operation. Average yields were recorded in 1922, followed by a bumper crop in 1923 that gave a net return of $31.64 an acre on 5,010 acres tilled by the company, and $14.67 an acre on 2,646 acres worked by the one-fourth–share tenants.[18] A relatively good harvest in 1924 preceded a drouth the following year, when a substantial loss occurred in farming revenue with only 311 bales harvested from 3,118 acres.[19] The ranch had reserves to absorb the deficit, but farmers paying for land from expected profits were in a predicament. To the credit of the Taft Ranch, it came to the rescue of the would-be landowners by granting a moratorium and by inducing the Taft Bank, Unincorporated, the First National Bank of Taft, and the First National Bank of Gregory to grant financial aid to those cultivating former company lands until better times returned and payments could be made on the notes.[20]

During this period the large company farms were placed on the market, and gradually the total acreage under cultivation dwindled. Major purchasers and property obtained were: George Floerke, a community farmer, Farm 25; J. E. Garrett, president of the Texas State

[15] Coleman-Fulton Pasture Company Sales Map, 1925, compiled and drawn from surveys and records by Fred M. Percival, Fulton, Texas, CFPC. Taft *Tribune*, January 11, July 19, August 30, 1923; May 8, 1924; April 23, 1925; April 26, 1926.

[16] Interview with Edward N. Tutt, Taft, November 27, 1961.

[17] Statement, Selling Expenses, Cost of Roads, Ditches and Commission, January 1, 1923, to December 31, 1926, CFPC.

[18] Statements for Company and Tenant Farms, 1922 and 1923, CFPC.

[19] *Ibid.*, 1924 and 1925, CFPC.

[20] Minutes of Stockholders' Meeting, July 7, 1925, CFPC. Interview with Edward N. Tutt, Taft, November 27, 1961.

Bank and Trust Company of Corpus Christi, Farm 23, "Portland"; T. A. McKamey, Gregory farmer, "Mustanga" and Farm 22, "Terre Belle"; and J. H. Harvey and W. B. Ray, Corpus Christi promoters, the 16,000-acre Rincon Pasture.[21] By far the largest buyer was Joseph F. Green, the Pasture Company's general manager, who bought 4,892 acres between Gregory and Corpus Christi Bay, the area known as the La Quinta tract, including the house; 789 acres adjoining the industrial site northwest of Taft; all livestock, feed, and farming equipment on the ranch, except on those tracts that continued as company farms; the dairies; the animals on leased pastures at Catarina and in Colorado; and the packing house.[22]

After these sales the ranch's agricultural pursuits were limited to the 2,297-acre Puentez Ranch; Farm 20, 646 acres; and Farm 21, "Terre Bonne," 1,136 acres. These units continued in operation until 1928, when they in turn were sold to small, independent farmers.[23] The year 1926 was the last time the ranch employed share tenants.

During the last decade of its existence the Taft Ranch continued to encourage scientific and diversified farming on the Coastal Bend. Under the direction of C. H. McDowell, the new superintendent of farms after 1923, the company embarked on a program of plant selection, that is, of removing rogues, nontypical plants, from the fields, whereby the remaining crop would be pure seed of a true type with a uniform appearance in heads and stalks. McDowell, a graduate of the Agricultural and Mechanical College of Texas and the director of the Denton County State Experiment Farm before joining Joseph F. Green's staff,[24] installed a new cottonseed cleaning-and-culling ma-

[21] Taft *Tribune*, April 15, 22, September 30, 1926. May M. Green Watson and Alex Lillico, *Taft Ranch: A history of the Fifty Years of Development sponsored by Coleman-Fulton Pasture Company with sketches of Gregory and Taft, the two towns it created*, p. 34.

[22] Minutes of Stockholders' Meeting, December 14, 1925; Minutes of Directors' Meeting, December 14, 1925; both in CFPC. Deed Records, San Patricio County, January 2, 1926, Vol. 82, pp. 453–460. *San Patricio County News*, January 14, 1926. Joseph F. Green, Chicago, to Jennie Hunt, Gregory, January 6, 1926, unpublished manuscript in possession of Mrs. Fay Green Hunt. The La Quinta residence, sold to the Gulf Coast Shrine Club in 1928, burned to the ground in 1934.

[23] Statements, Company Farms, 1927 and 1928, CFPC.

[24] Taft *Tribune*, July 20, 1922.

chine at the company's seedhouse in Taft to delint and test the seed for fertility, not only for the company's use, but for that of the tenants and the community farmers as well.[25]

Special attention was given to selected fields of cotton, cane, and kafir in this new process to develop "certified seed." Not only did more of the seed germinate, but they sprouted more quickly after being placed in the soil and afforded a greater yield. Representatives from the State Board of Plant Breeder Examiners of the Agricultural Department of the State of Texas checked the produce, found them to be of a high degree of varietal purity and uniformity, and allowed the ranch to use the department's certificate for its future sales.[26]

In 1923 the ranch imported broomcorn seed from Illinois and conducted experiments on forty acres at three locations. As the season proved too dry for that commodity on the black waxy soil, the crop did not mature.[27] Even though future tests were discontinued in the Taft vicinity, broomcorn did become a staple crop near Beeville and other interior towns where the soil was a sandy loam rather than a heavy clay.

To advertise the grown or manufactured products of the ranch Green outfitted on the special train of the San Antonio and Aransas Pass an exhibit of articles to accompany those commodities produced elsewhere along the road. The schedule for a two-week tour in Texas provided for a stop at Taft on January 25 and at Gregory the following day, as well as for brief stays at each station along the line. Farm superintendent C. H. McDowell was in charge of the Taft Ranch car, one of fourteen, which featured fine livestock, packing-house and oil-mill goods, plus a sample of all the agricultural varieties cultivated on the farms.[28] The car exhibit, costing $489.55, was money well spent for advertising, because at this time most of the real estate was yet to be sold.[29]

In an effort to carry out his dream of diversification in agriculture,

[25] *Ibid.,* October 26, 1922.

[26] *Ibid.,* July 5, 1923, September 18, 1924.

[27] *Ibid.,* July 5, 1923. Minutes of the Coleman-Fulton Pasture Company Heads of Departments Meeting (hereafter cited as Minutes of Departmental Meeting), March 7, 1923, CFPC.

[28] Taft *Tribune,* December 28, 1922; January 11, 18, 26, 1923.

[29] Statement, "SAP" Car Exhibit, 1923, CFPC.

Green attempted in 1924 to grow oranges on the ranch. Since the boom days of the 1890's, citrus fruit had been grown in South Texas, on a limited scale at Rincon, Rockport, Coleman's Chiltipin Ranch, and elsewhere along the coast. When Sinton began its rapid growth following the activities of the George H. Paul Company in San Patricio County, horticulturists there developed orchards; but not until the early 1920's were measures taken to determine if fruit growing on a large scale would be successful. In late 1923 after the San Antonio and Aransas Pass Railway Company established an experiment farm at Rockport, acreage also went to the product in Bee, Jim Wells, Brooks, Nueces, and San Patricio Counties when imported trees arrived from Florida.[30] In January, 1924, Professor I. E. Cowart, former professor at the Agricultural and Mechanical College of Texas and currently superintendent of the Beeville State Experiment Station, came to Taft to assume command of the citrus-fruit department of the Coleman-Fulton Pasture Company.[31]

Always the showman, Green imposed only one condition on Cowart —to establish at least one orange grove along the highway so that it could be seen.[32] Otherwise he gave Cowart complete control of the industry. With $25,000 at his disposal the professor established large arbors and worked constantly at making the test successful, but did not accomplish his aim because of a dry year in 1925 and subsequent harsh winters.[33]

On the surface it appears strange that a concern would spend a large sum of money to develop a new industry for the region at the time it was selling its property. Who else could afford to do it? What agency in this area except the Taft Ranch would have done this in an attempt to leave a legacy to the community? But the scheme was not as altruistic as it may seem, because it is obvious that the farm subdivisions would have brought much more than the approximately $35-an-acre average actually received if it had been proved that San Patricio County was a citrus region.

[30] Taft *Tribune*, January 31, 1924.

[31] *Ibid.*, December 27, 1923.

[32] *Ibid.*

[33] Interview with Edward N. Tutt, Taft, November 27, 1961.

Green was noted for his selection of talent to head the company departments. Cowart and the other foremen, most of whom had extraordinary ability in their specialties, shared their knowledge by conducting a series of what might be termed "adult-education" lectures under the general chairmanship of Green. In conjunction with the ranch departmental meetings convocations were held where ranch employees, tenant farmers, and the public in general were invited to hear addresses on "How To Get Money To Raise a Crop," "How To Raise and What Crop To Raise," "How To Make Stock Raising Profitable on a Farm," "How To Beautify Home Yards," and other talks on some theme of improvement.[34] For some sessions Green asked delegations from the Agricultural and Mechanical College of Texas to be guest speakers. Eventually the gatherings turned into social affairs, with an invocation given by a minister, music selections by the Taft Ranch Band, vocal harmonizing by the locally renowned Taft Male Quartet, speeches to stimulate the agrarians toward better things, and informal conversation afterwards.[35]

Since Joseph F. Green believed that the region's future lay with young people, he therefore in 1922 encouraged boys and girls to organize agricultural clubs and, on behalf of the Coleman-Fulton Pasture Company, gave $400 in cash prizes to contest winners of pig, calf, poultry, and canning clubs in the Gregory, Taft, and Portland area. Through arrangements with the Taft Bank, Unincorporated, and the First National Bank of Gregory, Green assisted young people by helping them get loans to purchase livestock for their projects.[36] The following year school children from the West Portland district competed; then in 1924 Green expanded the competition to the entire county, increased the donation to $700, and opened participation to three additional clubs—cooking, sewing, and dairy animals.[37]

Under the Smith-Hughes Act of 1917 Green acquired for the Taft school district the services of a vocational agriculture teacher, beginning with the academic year 1924–1925, to assist children in their club-

[34] Taft *Tribune*, January 5, November 9, 1922.
[35] *Ibid.*, February 28, 1924.
[36] *Ibid.*, November 9, 16, 1922.
[37] *Ibid.*, June 21, 1923.

work and to share his knowledge with community farmers. The federal government paid one-half of the instructor's salary, the school district the remainder.[38]

Experimentation was not limited to row crops, but extended to livestock. The federal quarantine line, first established in 1889, excluded from Northern markets South Texas cattle that had not been treated with extensive sanitary measures, such as dipping in a chemical solution. For several years emphasis had been on feeding ensilage to cattle in order to fatten them for the packing-house market at a rate more rapid than that for similar quality animals eating nothing but grass.

Practically all the range cattle in the 1920's were Herefords, with some highly graded Shorthorns. Green sought a breed that could withstand the semitropical summers of South Texas and that perhaps would be immune to the fever tick. On a trip to East Texas in 1922 Green stopped at Pierce, approximately seventy miles southwest of Houston, and examined the Brahman cattle imported from India by the Abel Head "Shanghai" Pierce estate. Convinced that this breed could handle the Texas heat and the parasites, Green purchased ninety-two head of bulls for the Coleman-Fulton Pasture Company.[39] The Taft Ranch crossed the newly acquired Brahmans with Herefords and Shorthorns on the range, and put an animal known as the "Sacred Bull" with the registered Shorthorn cows with satisfactory results. However, the fine appearance in the hybrid offspring did not command the price expected because the Indian breed did not dress out as well as did the European types. The King Ranch also experimented with crossbreeding Brahmans and Shorthorns about this time and developed a separate breed, the Santa Gertrudis, which had the Brahman's resistance to heat and to diseases while retaining the Shorthorn's good beef qualities.[40]

The Taft Ranch kept its Shorthorn-Brahman combination females; by January, 1924, it had 125 good quality, mixed heifers slated for experimentation when they matured sufficiently. The ranch tried its hand raising a brood herd of the humpbacked cattle after its purchase

[38] *Ibid.*, May 22, July 3, 1924.

[39] *Ibid.*, May 4, 1922.

[40] *Ibid.*, June 21, 1923. Interview with Edward N. Tutt, Taft, November 27, 1961. Tom Lea, *The King Ranch*, II, 651.

in January, 1924, of forty-eight heifers and bulls from the Tom East Ranch at Hebbronville, Texas.[41] The foundation herd did well and supplied the ranch with top-quality Brahmans until all the Pasture Company's livestock were sold in 1926 to Joseph F. Green.

Through extensive use of dipping vats ranchers eradicated the tick from San Patricio County. When the quarantine line was removed from its part of South Texas, the Coleman-Fulton Pasture Company began to send livestock to the Fort Worth, Kansas City, and Saint Louis markets.[42] Large feeding pens were established near silos, where calves raised on the company range and also feeder animals purchased in San Antonio or other neighboring towns were fattened and sent to the Midwestern stockyards. In 1922 the ranch had only 4,683 head of cattle, and about the same number the following year; but when San Patricio County was removed from the restricted district the feeding program began in a big way. At the close of business in 1924 the ranch had 12,329 head on hand.[43]

Much of this increase can be accounted for by the fact that the Coleman-Fulton Pasture Company leased the Catarina Ranch in Dimmit and Webb Counties in 1924 and subsequently stocked the 228,091-acre tract. Charles Phelps Taft and Anna Sinton Taft had recently sold the land to S. W. Forrester, an oil-well driller and land promoter of Wichita, Kansas, who in turn granted annual grazing rights to the Coleman-Fulton Pasture Company for twenty-five cents an acre.[44]

Of the 4,683 head of cattle in 1923, 344 were registered. Each year the number climbed: 515 in 1924, and 727 in 1925.[45] For the most part these purebred animals were foundation herds for the beef and dairy breeds; also, some were members of the Shorthorn and Jersey exhibit groups. Green, who believed that demonstrating his best livestock at agricultural fairs was good advertising, followed the show ring faithfully for the quarter of a century he was the general manager. The Taft Ranch was a regular attender at the Dallas Fair, the Fort

[41] Taft *Tribune*, January 10, 1924.

[42] *Ibid.*, June 28, July 12, 1923; January 31, June 5, 1924; April 16, 1925.

[43] Statements, Coleman-Fulton Pasture Company, 1922 to 1927, CFPC.

[44] S. W. and Anna L. Forrester to Coleman-Fulton Pasture Company, a lease of the Catarina Ranch in Dimmit and Webb Counties, April 1, 1924; Minutes of Directors' Meeting, April 7, 1924; both in CFPC. Taft *Tribune*, May 8, 1924.

[45] Statements, Coleman-Fulton Pasture Company, 1922 to 1927, CFPC.

Worth Fat Stock Show, and the International Livestock Show in Chicago; in many of the exhibits it won prizes.[46]

It has been said of Superintendent Green that he could not tolerate defeats, and that he usually purchased the stock that topped his at the expositions.[47] The ranch did obtain a great number of the better individuals at the shows. For example, Green bought the grand champion Shorthorn bull and two of his heifers at the 1922 Dallas Fair, in addition to the first-prize two-year-old bull and a top winner in an older class at the 1922 International Livestock Show in Chicago; the last mentioned bull, a Scottish import, became the principal sire for the Taft Ranch Shorthorn department.[48]

Green favored Jerseys to all other strains of dairy animals and spent a great deal of money building up a powerful, pedigreed herd. Prize-winning Jersey bulls and cows were brought to Taft, among them the internationally acclaimed Masterman of Oaklands, imported from the Isle of Jersey after receiving honors as the best bull of all ages and classes on the Isle. Upon the bull's arrival in America, S. A. Guy of Crosbytown, Texas, bought him for $25,000, but the animal diminished in value when the new owner did not exhibit him. The Taft Ranch purchased Masterman for approximately $5,000 and again put him in the show circuit.[49]

The main reason for the existence of the dairy herd was milk production, not exhibition. In December, 1925, the Pasture Company owned 425 registered Jersey females, 15 purebred bulls, and 400 high-grade Jersey cows at seven locations: La Quinta, Gulf Coast, Number 3, Rincon, Taft, Farm 29, and Chiltipin dairies.[50] On January 2, 1926, Joseph F. Green purchased all the dairy equipment and livestock, added to his holdings by purchasing winners at fairs, and sent his dairy-farms manager, Ben H. Cummins, to Canada and the Northeast to buy the

[46] Statements, Rincon Ranch Cattle, 1923, CFPC. Taft *Tribune,* October 11, 1923; March 20, October 23, 1924.

[47] Interview with Ben H. Cummins, Taft, March 4, 1961.

[48] Taft *Tribune,* October 19, December 21, 1922; December 27, 1923; February 28, 1924.

[49] *Ibid.,* March 20, December 18, 1924; interview with Ben H. Cummins, Taft, March 4, 1961. Masterman of Oaklands became the prize sire in South Texas; Jersey cattle in that region today are reported to be his direct descendants.

[50] Taft *Tribune,* December 17, 1925.

best Jerseys available.[51] Approximately 7,000 head of beef cattle also were transferred to the company's general manager in 1926, including all the registered and range stock in San Patricio and Aransas Counties, at the Catarina Ranch, and on a leased pasture near Hayden, Colorado.[52]

Other kinds of animals owned by the ranch until the sale to Green on January 2, 1926, included goats kept on hand to provide a large quantity of meat to Latin American employees and sheep and hogs to supply the Taft Packing House.[53] During the 1920's eleven mammoth jacks were placed on a special tract known as the Green Ranch, six miles northwest of Taft, where valuable mares and stallions of the Percheron Norman and Morgan breeds were kept. Of the 502 head of horse stock on hand in 1923, over 300 were mares maintained for raising mules for the ranch and for selling.[54] At the time Green sold all ranch livestock, 545 mules and 666 horses were on hand. The contract read that only enough animals would be retained to cultivate the three remaining company farms, which amounted to 107 mules and 18 horses, according to the Coleman-Fulton Pasture Company's statement of assets for 1926.[55]

The bumper cotton production in 1920 caused the Taft community farmers to realize that storage facilities were drastically inadequate, as many bales were damaged by weather while awaiting shipment from the gin yards. Largely through the efforts of R. O. Tackett, Coleman-Fulton Pasture Company farm superintendent from 1917 to 1923, a campaign was started to erect a warehouse to care for local crops. His drive was joined by community farmers; the main impetus, however,

[51] Joseph F. Green, Chicago, to Jennie Hunt, Gregory, January 6, 1926, unpublished letter in possession of Mrs. Fay Green Hunt. Minutes of Directors' Meeting, December 14, 1925; Minutes of Stockholders' Meeting, December 14, 1925; both in CFPC. Watson and Lillico, *Taft Ranch,* p. 34. Interview with Ben H. Cummins, Taft, March 4, 1961; Mr. Cummins later purchased the Jersey herds and operated the dairies for himself.

[52] Minutes of Directors' Meeting, December 14, 1925; Coleman-Fulton Pasture Company Summary of General Trial Balance, January 2, 1926, before and after sale to Joseph F. Green; both in CFPC.

[53] Taft *Tribune,* July 12, 1923; Statements, Coleman-Fulton Pasture Company, 1922 to 1927, CFPC.

[54] Taft *Tribune,* July 12, 1923, February 7, 1924.

[55] Statements, Coleman-Fulton Pasture Company, 1922 to 1927, CFPC.

came when Joseph F. Green promised Taft Ranch financial support for the venture. Subsequently, an organizational meeting on April 4, 1923, formed a co-operative firm known as the Taft Compress and Warehouse Company, with capital stock of $66,000.[56] Farmers bought shares, or rather gave their notes pledging to take a certain number after the 1923 harvest. The firm bought eight acres near the Taft gins, erected buildings, installed adequate machinery, and placed the plant in operation.[57]

Other new industries begun at Taft in the 1920's to attract potential farm buyers were a chick hatchery and a creamery. A $4,000 investment, the hatchery was operated by C. O. Wantland of San Antonio, who moved to Taft in August, 1923, to operate the plant. The ranch advertised that a 40,000-egg hatchery would provide a market for farm eggs, a supplemental income heretofore unavailable, and would give persons wanting to start high-grade poultry flocks a place to purchase the initial stock at reasonable rates.[58] To lend an air of high importance to the enterprise, Wantland transferred the *Lone Star Poultry Journal,* a 16,000-subscriber magazine, to Taft.[59]

Community residents were afforded a market for surplus milk, provided they had Jersey cows, by the Taft Ranch Creamery, which began operating on June 1, 1924. White trucks traveled a route from farm to farm in the Taft vicinity and as far away as Tuleta, twelve miles north of Beeville or fifty-two miles from Taft, gathering cans of sweet cream. The $35,000 plant in Taft pasteurized the product and made it into butter and ice cream for sale in local stores and on regional markets.[60] A profitable operation continued until March, 1926, when the Mistletoe Creamery of San Antonio purchased the machinery and real estate,

[56] Taft *Tribune,* April 5, 1923, July 31, 1941 (Twentieth Anniversary Edition). Taft Compress and Warehouse Company, Charter No. 39,689, April 17, 1923, Office of the Texas Secretary of State.

[57] Minutes of Directors' Meeting, June 11, 1923, CFPC. Deed Records, San Patricio County, July 31, 1923, Vol. 71, pp. 541–542; March 15, 1924, Vol. 76, pp. 539–540. Interview with Edward N. Tutt, Taft, November 27, 1961.

[58] Taft *Tribune,* July 19, 1923; May 15, 1924. Blackwell, *Taft Ranch,* 11.

[59] Taft *Tribune,* July 19, 1923.

[60] *Ibid.,* August 2, 1923; May 1, 15, 1924; April 16, 1925. Minutes of Departmental Meeting, December 1, 1923, CFPC.

adding the Taft enterprise to their already growing creamery business in San Antonio, Corpus Christi, and Weslaco.[61]

Why would the Taft Ranch dispose of property that might be classed as "going concerns"? One must keep in mind that the corporation charter was to expire in 1930, and that the primary purposes for promoting industry were to aid development of the community and to increase the value of property possessed by the Pasture Company.

In 1925 ranch officials discussed what might be the most efficient manner of selling its industries before the firm dissolved, searching for a way to change ownership that would not interrupt the operations of the businesses. Subsequently, a study group was appointed by the stockholders to decide how the transfer should be conducted. In a report submitted on May 13, 1925, a plan was disclosed to organize the main industries into two corporations: a packing house and a public-service utility company.[62] At the close of the meeting a resolution was adopted stating that the Coleman-Fulton Pasture Company was in liquidation, and that the activities of the firm would henceforth be directed toward that end; only the necessary operation of the various enterprises would be conducted, awaiting their final disposition.[63]

Seven months after this declaration negotiations with James C. Kennedy of San Antonio, president of the Texas Central Power and Light Company, were consummated by the sale of the entire waterworks, natural-gas, and electric-light systems owned by the Taft Ranch, as well as the ice-manufacturing plant. The bill of sale stated that the Pasture Company received $200,000 for the equipment, the real estate, and franchises on December 15, 1925.[64] Kennedy added his Taft purchase to the Central Power and Light Company's numerous holdings over South Texas, including Corpus Christi, Kingsville, Robstown, and Sinton.

Two weeks after this transfer of property Joseph F. Green made his gigantic purchase of company livestock, farming equipment, and the

[61] Taft *Tribune,* March 25, 1926.

[62] Minutes of Stockholders' Meeting, May 13, 1925, CFPC.

[63] *Ibid.*

[64] Deed Records, San Patricio County, December 15, 1925, Vol. 82, pp. 330 ff. Minutes of Stockholders' Meeting, December 14, 1925; Minutes of Directors' Meeting, December 14, 1925; both in CFPC.

packing house. However, in 1927 Kennedy obtained the packing house, making his company's ownership of industries in Taft virtually complete.[65]

The local telephone system with exchanges in Taft and Gregory was deeded to T. A. Vernor, a former resident of Gonzales and manager of the ranch communications department since 1923. For $12,000 Vernor received the wires, poles, telephones, switchboards, and equipment on March 1, 1926.[66]

An improvement in transportation facilities in South Texas that came too late to benefit the Taft Ranch, but one of inestimable value to Coastal Bend residents, was the development of a deep-water port at Corpus Christi. After the Aransas Pass Harbor Company surrendered its franchise in 1899, the federal government allotted piecemeal appropriations during the first two decades of the twentieth century, but the channel through the inlet between the offshore islands was not improved significantly.[67] The Taft Ranch transported its cotton by railroad to Port Aransas on Mustang Island until the 1916 hurricane destroyed the compresses there, after which it built a pier at Portland for shipping cotton bales by barge to Galveston for dispersal to world markets.[68]

In March, 1921, Robert J. Kleberg of the King Ranch, called a meeting of large landowners, bankers, merchants, railroad executives, and professional men from over Texas to meet at Kingsville. The Deep Water Harbor Association was organized and a board of directors was appointed to investigate the possibility of inducing the government to begin serious work on a South Texas port via Aransas Pass.[69] The group was successful in getting the United States Army

[65] Taft *Tribune,* June 17, 1943.

[66] Bill of Sale Records, San Patricio County, March 1, 1926, Vol. 2, pp. 302–308.

[67] *House Documents,* 78th Congress, Second Session, Serial No. 10881, Doc. No. 544, pp. 13–14.

[68] George Frederic Stratton, "Mr. Taft's Tenants: How They Earn Farms on His Big Texas Ranch," *Country Gentleman,* LXXXIV, No. 9 (March 1, 1919), 40. Interview with Edward N. Tutt, Taft, November 27, 1961; with S. Frank Hunt, Sinton, August 8, 1961.

[69] Mary C. Riley, "The History of the Development of the Port of Corpus Christi" (M.A. thesis), p. 114. Joseph F. Green was a director in that organization (Taft *Tribune,* November 16, 1922).

Corps of Engineers to recommend to the congressional Rivers and Harbors Committee a plan for improving navigation on the Coastal Bend. On September 22, 1922, President Warren G. Harding signed into law a bill designating that work would begin immediately on a port of Corpus Christi.[70] Within four years a twenty-foot channel two hundred feet wide was dredged from the pass to the south side of Nueces Bay; it was officially opened on September 14, 1926.[71] With ocean-going vessels coming to their door, South Texas farmers and ranchers profited through expanded markets, higher prices, and reduced costs in transporting their commodities to a shipping warehouse.

During the years of liquidation the Taft Ranch, mindful of the community, donated property for future constructions. As a public service to those who purchased real estate, property for schools and churches was set aside. After deeding to the Taft school district an entire block in 1921, the Pasture Company awarded additional gifts of ground in 1923 for a Latin American school in the Hidalgo Addition of Taft, and four more acres adjoining the high school in 1925.[72] In 1928 the Gregory school district received for one dollar[73] a town lot as a site for a Latin American school.

Largely through the influence of Joseph F. Green and the philanthropy of the Coleman-Fulton Pasture Company, a school for Latin American girls was established in Taft in 1924. When the Presbyterian Church of Texas Synod began looking for a suitable location for an educational institution for girls similar to the Texas-Mexican Industrial Institute for boys at Kingsville, Green invited the church elders to visit Taft. The site selected for the Presbyterian School for Mexican Girls, popularly known as "Pres-Mex," was a two-hundred-acre tract southeast of Taft and adjoining it on the Corpus Christi highway. The ground was the gift of the ranch, which also donated

[70] *House Documents,* 67th Congress, Second Session, Serial No. 8006, Doc. No. 321, p. 2; 78th Congress, Second Session, Serial No. 10881, Doc. No. 544, pp. 13–14.

[71] Corpus Christi *Caller,* September 11, 1926.

[72] Minutes of Directors' Meeting, June 11, 1923; Minutes of Stockholders' Meeting, May 13, 1925; both in CFPC. Deed Records, San Patricio County, October 5, 1928, Vol. 90, pp. 248–250.

[73] Minutes of Directors' Meeting, July 14, 1928, CFPC. Deed Records, San Patricio County, September 24, 1928, Vol. 90, pp. 104–105.

$5,000. The local Presbyterian organization matched that sum, and the Presbyterian synods in Texas and in other states added to it until a total of $50,000 was raised.[74] Dormitories and classrooms were constructed in time for the opening of scholastic and vocational-training classes in October, 1924.

Church congregations received land in Taft from the Pasture Company, usually at reduced prices. In 1921 two lots were given as common property to the Presbyterian and Methodist groups for one dollar; the Methodists, however, chose to organize separately, and in 1924 purchased six lots in Taft for one thousand dollars.[75] Real estate went also to the First Baptist Church, the Rising Star Missionary Baptist Church of the Lincoln Southern Association, and the Presbyterian-Mexican Church for the minimum legal fee of one dollar.[76] The land offerings for religious institutions were rounded out in 1928 when a Church of Christ group obtained approximately one-third of an acre for eight hundred dollars.[77]

No change in the personnel of the corporation's officials occurred during the era of liquidation except for the addition of Robert Alphonso Taft, son of President William Howard Taft and nephew of the Coleman-Fulton Pasture Company president. Beginning in 1923 the young Cincinnati lawyer, a member of the Ohio Legislature, represented his uncle in the business of the Texas ranch. After the Board of Directors was again expanded to five members, this event occurring in 1924, Robert A. Taft was elected the following year to serve on it, along with Charles P. Taft, Joseph F. Green, Edward N. Tutt, and Walter P. Napier.[78] When the paper work involved with the farm subdivisions increased the administrative burdens on Green, he asked

[74] Minutes of Departmental Meeting, July 7, 1923, CFPC. *San Patricio County News,* November 18, 1926. Mrs. John William Albin (compiler), "History of the First Presbyterian Church US, Taft, Texas, Presbytery of Western Texas," unpublished manuscript in possession of Mrs. John William Albin.

[75] Deed Records, San Patricio County, November 21, 1921, Vol. 71, p. 239; December 31, 1924, Vol. 79, pp. 83–85.

[76] *Ibid.,* July 24, 1924, Vol. 78, pp. 38–39; October 18, 1928, Vol. 90, pp. 273–275. Minutes of Directors' Meeting, July 14, 1928, CFPC.

[77] Deed Records, San Patricio County, August 1, 1928, Vol. 89, pp. 511–514.

[78] Minutes of Stockholders' Meeting, May 13, 1925; Minutes of Departmental Meeting, July 20, 1923; both in CFPC.

the corporation's stockholders to authorize a second vice president to assist in land matters. The request was quickly granted, and Napier assumed that office in 1924.[79]

Because of advanced age and of limited activity for her husband and herself, Mrs. Anna Sinton Taft appointed the National Bank of Commerce in New York as trustee effective on March 31, 1924, for her multimillion-dollar investments in property and securities, including the Coleman-Fulton Pasture Company.[80] The trust was to extend only to the collection of income; Robert A. Taft continued to represent the family in conducting ranch policy.

When H. V. Fetick withdrew from the Taft Ranch in 1925, Edward N. Tutt replaced him as secretary.[81] The greatest change in a quarter of a century came on November 20, 1926, when the man who was superintendent and general manager for twenty-six and one-half years, Joseph French Green, unexpectedly died in a Temple hospital following a tonsillectomy.[82] His passing was mourned throughout South Texas, for he had become a prominent figure in agricultural and banking circles. Perhaps the most eloquent eulogy came from Robert A. Taft:

Mr. and Mrs. [Charles P.] Taft and myself fully realize that he [Joseph F. Green] was an extraordinary man to whom the Company and ourselves owe a debt of gratitude and appreciation. When he went to Texas the Taft Ranch was land and cattle, and only land and cattle. He saw what could be made of the country, and he turned it into a thriving community, typical of the best in American development. In creating a real existence for his vision, he never wavered and was seldom ever discouraged. It is sad that he should die when he had reached the point where he could enjoy what he had created: but he did see a real success crown his efforts.

In carrying out his plan he acted for the best interests of the Company, of its stockholders, and the community in which he lived. He showed an extraordinary ability in working out his plan, and in nothing more than in his judgment of other men. I was impressed in 1923 by the exceptional

[79] Minutes of Stockholders' Meeting, May 5, 1924; Minutes of Directors' Meeting, May 5, 1924; both in CFPC.

[80] Declaration of Trust, Anna Sinton Taft to National Bank of Commerce in New York, March 31, 1924, CFPC.

[81] Minutes of Directors' Meeting, May 13, 1925, CFPC.

[82] Taft *Tribune,* November 25, 1926.

character of the men whom he had gathered around him. All of them were able, reliable and admirably fitted to their position; all were inspired by Mr. Green with the most earnest desire to give the best in them for the service of the company.

Fortunately for us the greater part of the company's work is done, & could not have been better done than by Mr. Green.[83]

At the January 3, 1927, stockholders' meeting Edward N. Tutt, who for a decade had served as personal secretary to Green, and who therefore had become thoroughly acquainted with ranch policy, was elected to the vacated post of vice president, superintendent, and general manager. Green also had held the office of treasurer at the time of his death, but that position was consolidated with the secretaryship under C. J. Meyer, a member of the office staff since 1916 and for many years the corporation auditor. A. Crafton Tutt, a brother of Edward N. Tutt, became assistant secretary and replaced Green on the Board of Directors.[84] A. C. Tutt, formerly of Liberty, Missouri, who had joined the Taft Ranch as a permanent employee in the early 1920's, served as ranch surveyor, bank cashier, and sales manager of the Taft Packing House before he became an official of the corporation.

The stockholders authorized the new superintendent to continue the sale of land and granted him the right to enter into contracts with agencies. Edward N. Tutt operated under the same provisions that Green followed, that is, he could not expend more than 20 per cent of the value of the land in preparing it for disposal. That figure included making roads, abstracts, maps, surveys, advertisements, and a 5-per-cent commission to the general manager for his services in the matter.[85]

Before Green's death and following the May 13, 1925, resolution that the Coleman-Fulton Pasture Company was in a state of liquidation, the Tafts and Green joined forces on an 84.5-per-cent and 15.5-per-cent basis, respectively, to purchase $978,097.51 in vendor's lien

[83] Robert A. Taft, Cincinnati, Ohio, to Mrs. Joseph F. Green, Gregory, January 13, 1927, unpublished letter in possession of Mrs. May Mathis Green Watson.

[84] Minutes of Directors' Meeting, January 3, 1927; Minutes of Stockholders' Meeting, January 3, 1927; both in CFPC.

[85] Minutes of Stockholders' Meeting, January 3, 1927, CFPC.

notes received by the ranch in payment of farms. The sale was consummated on November 16, 1925.[86] For years prior to this time any capital profits the company gained had been reinvested in new industry, additional farming equipment, public welfare, or numerous other development schemes; now these improvements were no longer necessary. Therefore, on December 14, 1925, the stockholders agreed to declare a liquidating dividend of 118 per cent, payable on the last day of the year.[87]

As the sale of land continued, the vendor's lien notes were transferred to various financial institutions, such as the Dallas Joint Stock Land Bank of Dallas, the Martindale Mortgage Company of San Antonio, and the National Bank of Commerce in New York; proceeds gained from these sales were divided and distributed to the stockholders of the Pasture Company.[88] In November, 1928, following final disposal of real and personal property to the so-called Taft Property Syndicate, the final liquidating dividend was declared, altogether making 393 per cent distributed to holders of the 8,255 shares in only four years.[89] Surely this must be considered positive proof that the large outlay of capital by the Tafts and by Green over a score of years had enabled them to achieve their objective—to increase the value of the land as they developed the region!

Although the charter did not expire until 1930, and the company had two years after it dissolved to complete the liquidation, the officials wanted to dispose of the remaining real estate as quickly as possible. Since the year 1927 was unprofitable for farmers, the remnants of farming land would be difficult to sell in the current agrarian economic austerity. These realizations convinced the Board of Directors that they should accept the offer of five prominent Texas financiers to purchase the remaining assets of the Coleman-Fulton Pasture

[86] *Ibid.*, July 7, 1925; Minutes of Directors' Meeting, December 14, 1925; both in CFPC.

[87] Minutes of Stockholders' Meeting, December 14, 1925, CFPC.

[88] Interview with Edward N. Tutt, Taft, November 27, 1961. Deed Records, Aransas County, November 24, 1926, Vol. L–2, pp. 320–321; August 19, 1927, Vol. L–2, p. 612. Deed Records, San Patricio County, May 12, 1928, Vol. 89, p. 143.

[89] Minutes of Directors' Meeting, March 2, 1926; January 3, October 21, 1927; July 14, November 6, 1928; all in CFPC.

Company. Subsequently, on November 1, 1928, Robert Driscoll of Corpus Christi, D. C. Reed of Austin, J. Locke and H. Josey of San Antonio, and Will C. Hogg of Houston banded together in a partnership known as Taft Property Syndicate and concluded the transfer.[90]

Included in the conveyance were the townsites of Taft and Gregory, with a large number of town lots and approximately one hundred houses; the Taft Lumber Yard; two modern brick buildings, one each in Taft and Gregory; over 8,000 acres of farming land scattered in twenty-four different tracts; all livestock, feed, and farming equipment; all motor vehicles except one tractor and one automobile; and all improvements on the real estate released.[91] The only other possession of the Coleman-Fulton Pasture Company that did not go to the syndicate was the hospital, which was deeded to the Taft Cotton Oil Company, successor of the Taft Oil and Gin Company, with the same financial support.[92] Although the oil mill was not owned by the ranch, the relationship between the two was so close that under the tutelage of the mill the traditionally fine medical service to the community would be sustained; corporation officials had no assurance that the syndicate would have the same humanitarian concern.

With the November 1, 1928, transaction the Taft Ranch, which once spread over the southern half of San Patricio County and the western portion of Aransas County, sold its last acre. Since 1913, when the ranch became renowned as an agricultural and industrial show place, approximately 90,000 acres had been sold for a total of well over $4,000,000.[93]

The population of the Taft Ranch vicinity enlarged rapidly during the decade of the great subdivisions. Before the town-lot sale in 1921, there were 500 persons in Taft, 400 in Gregory, and 300 in Portland.[94]

[90] Taft *Tribune,* November 1, 1928.

[91] Deed Records, San Patricio County, November 1, 1928, Vol. 90, pp. 361–371. Deed Records, Aransas County, November 1, 1928, Vol. M–2, pp. 472–484. Bill of Sale Records, San Patricio County, November 1, 1928, Vol. 3, pp. 10–11. Minutes of Directors' Meeting, July 14, 1928, CFPC. Taft *Tribune,* August 16, November 1, 1928.

[92] Taft *Tribune,* November 9, 1939.

[93] Anna Sinton Taft, Cincinnati, Ohio, to United States Internal Revenue Agent, Dallas, November 30, 1928, Income Tax Information Folder, CFPC.

[94] *Texas Almanac and State Industrial Guide, 1926,* pp. 77 ff.

After the Coleman-Fulton Pasture Company disposed of its assets, Taft had 1,792 citizens, though the population of Portland and Gregory had not changed.[95] These numbers, however, do not include the many rural families near those towns. The census for all of San Patricio County gives a more accurate impression of the population gain, as the number of inhabitants climbed from 11,386 to 23,836 during the ten-year period.[96] The greater part of that increase came in the southern portion as a result of the sale of Coleman-Fulton Pasture Company real estate.

The expansion of fringe cities indicated that the Coastal Bend in general was becoming more densely settled. Sinton gained during the period from 1,058 to 1,852, while Corpus Christi grew from 10,522 to 27,741, as it became the chief regional market.[97] That coastal city's phenomenal growth came later when the full importance of the deep-water port was realized.

The people of Taft were saddened to learn that on December 31, 1929, the Coleman-Fulton Pasture Company president, Charles Phelps Taft, had died at Cincinnati.[98] This man, the chief executive of the ranch for thirty-six years, lived until three weeks before the company passed from existence. The final stockholders' meeting on January 8, 1930, arranged for the firm's dissolution by selling the remaining cash assets on an 85–15 ratio to Mrs. Anna Sinton Taft and to the Joseph F. Green estate.[99] The Board of Directors, on searching through the property books, discovered that the Pasture Company retained the title to Bellevue Cemetery at Taft and agreed to turn the property over to a cemetery association as soon as one could be formed.[100]

By a motion at the January 8, 1930, Board of Directors' meeting the Coleman-Fulton Pasture Company was declared dissolved effective January 15, 1930, and the officers were directed to deposit evidence to that effect with the Texas Secretary of State.[101] On January 20 the document was filed in the Austin state office to mark the passing of an

[95] *Texas Almanac and State Industrial Guide, 1933,* pp. 54 ff.
[96] *Texas Almanac, 1961–1962,* p. 203.
[97] *Texas Almanac, 1926,* pp. 77 ff; *Texas Almanac, 1933,* pp. 54 ff.
[98] "Charles Phelps Taft," *Who Was Who in America,* Vol. 1, p. 1213.
[99] Minutes of Stockholders' Meeting, January 8, 1930, CFPC.
[100] Minutes of Directors' Meeting, January 8, 1930, CFPC.
[101] *Ibid.*

enterprise which had led its section of the nation in scientific and diversified agriculture, improved stock breeding, farm industries, and which had set a national example of community planning through its keen regard for the public welfare.[102]

[102] Coleman-Fulton Pasture Company, Charter No. 1206, Certificate of Dissolution, January 20, 1930, Office of the Texas Secretary of State.

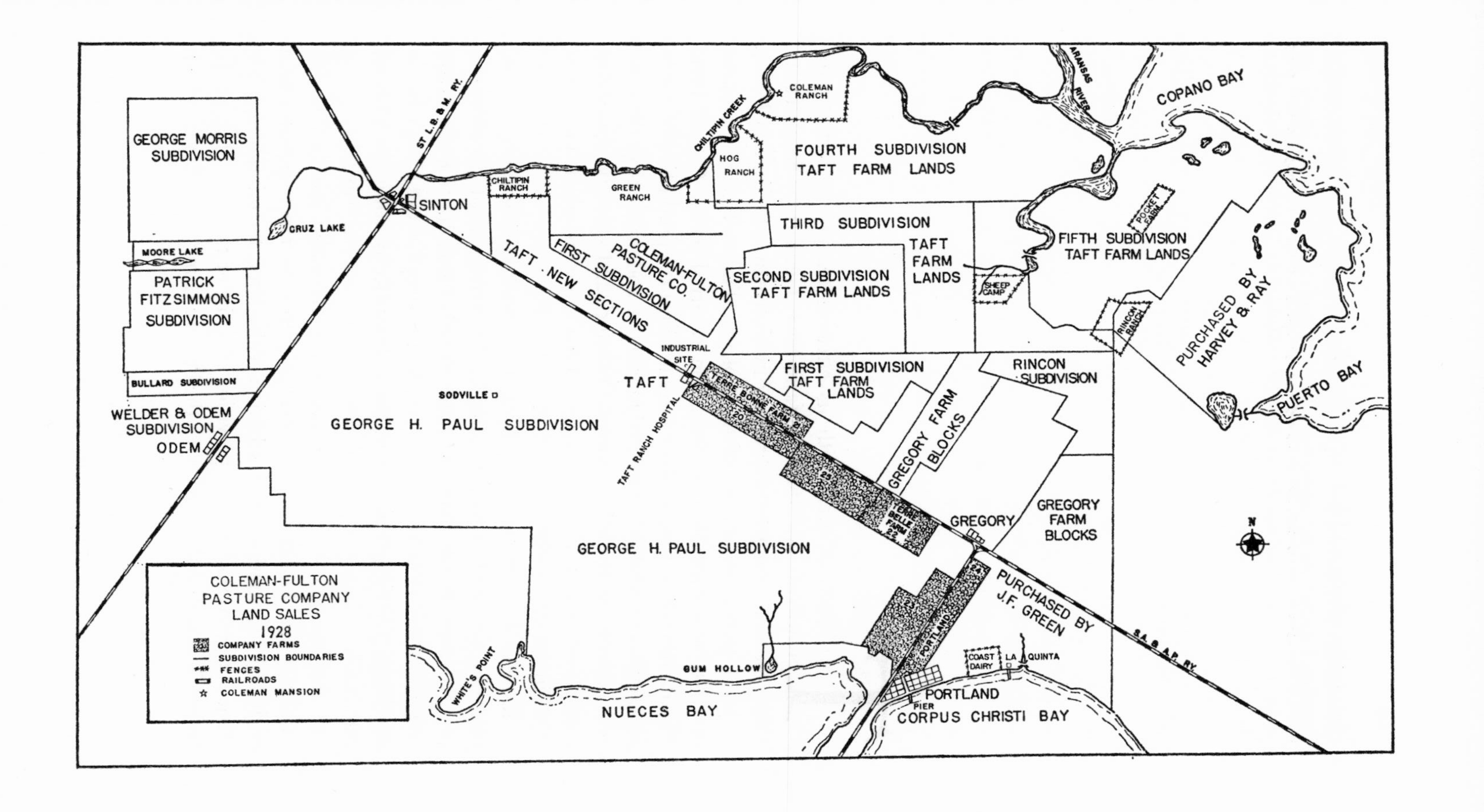
COLEMAN-FULTON PASTURE COMPANY LAND SALES 1928
COMPANY FARMS
SUBDIVISION BOUNDARIES
FENCES
RAILROADS
COLEMAN MANSION
GEORGE MORRIS SUBDIVISION
MOORE LAKE
PATRICK FITZSIMMONS SUBDIVISION
BULLARD SUBDIVISION
WELDER & ODEM SUBDIVISION
ODEM
CRUZ LAKE
SINTON
ST. L. B. & M. RY.
CHILTIPIN RANCH
GREEN RANCH
CHILTIPIN CREEK
HOG RANCH
COLEMAN RANCH
FOURTH SUBDIVISION TAFT FARM LANDS
ARANSAS RIVER
COPANO BAY
THIRD SUBDIVISION
TAFT FARM LANDS
SECOND SUBDIVISION TAFT FARM LANDS
COLEMAN-FULTON PASTURE CO.
FIRST SUBDIVISION
TAFT NEW SECTIONS
SHEEP CAMP
POCKET FARM
FIFTH SUBDIVISION TAFT FARM LANDS
RINCON RANCH
PURCHASED BY HARVEY & RAY
PUERTO BAY
INDUSTRIAL SITE
TAFT
TERRE BONNE FARM 2
20
FIRST SUBDIVISION TAFT FARM LANDS
RINCON SUBDIVISION
GREGORY FARM BLOCKS
SODVILLE
GEORGE H. PAUL SUBDIVISION
TAFT RANCH HOSPITAL
23
TERRE BELLE FARM 22
GREGORY
GREGORY FARM BLOCKS
N
GEORGE H. PAUL SUBDIVISION
24
21
PORTLAND
PURCHASED BY J.F. GREEN
S.A. & A.P. RY.
COAST DAIRY
LA QUINTA
GUM HOLLOW
WHITE'S POINT
NUECES BAY
PORTLAND
PIER
CORPUS CHRISTI BAY

EPILOGUE

THE TAFT RANCH with its effective leadership fostered the growth of agriculture and farm-related industry in South Texas. From the first purchase of property by Coleman, Mathis, and Fulton in 1871 to the dissolution of the Coleman-Fulton Pasture Company in 1930, a remarkable transformation occurred in the Coastal Bend region; instead of thousands of acres used for the production of scrubby Longhorn cattle that produced more bone and gristle than meat, the area became one featuring purebred livestock and scientific, diversified agriculture. The Taft Ranch alone did not cause this great change, but it led in the movement.

Impetus for the transition from a livestock-raising concern to an intensive agricultural venture came in the early years of the twentieth century when the San Patricio County Board of Equalization threatened to raise taxes on the land if the Coleman-Fulton Pasture Company did not begin farming. Green reluctantly began converting the pastures into fields, but soon he became enthusiastic over the capability of the soil and its potential for increasing the economic standard of the Coastal Bend. On large demonstration farms the ranch experimented with soil preparation, seed selection, cultivation techniques, and varieties of crops under the supervision of some of the best talent in the South. Through years of research the Pasture Company discovered both valuable and impractical agricultural methods and, without cost, passed this information to land purchasers, who stepped into a full-fledged community after the pioneering was over. The Taft Ranch area with its fertile soil would have developed into a productive region without the Taft-Green leadership, but in all probability not nearly as rapidly.

The introduction of industry made the Coastal Bend more appealing to agrarians, as it supplied ready markets for surplus commodities at greater profits because of the decreased transportation expense. The business enterprises were established in the 1909–1913 period to develop the agricultural possibilities of the real estate of the Coleman-Fulton Pasture Company, and not explicitly to found permanent institutions. Occasionally the factories suffered from operating losses, but since their existence was to increase the value of the firm's main asset, land, they served their purpose well! Property that was carried on the ledger in 1880 at $2.34 an acre sold in the 1920's for $80 to $100 an acre for proved farms, and $35 an acre for undeveloped pastures.

By 1930 improved transportation facilities opened new and distant markets heretofore unavailable, and local farmers no longer relied on the Taft industries. Climate and productivity of the soil were perhaps more practical reasons for the enterprises of the ranch to be short-lived. San Patricio County weather was not conducive to extensive citrus orchards. Although the fruit grew well, it had no protection from winter freezes. The packing house became unprofitable when the region shifted from cattle raising to cotton production with greater profits.

Dairy and poultry farming could not be justified since no large cities were near to consume these commodities, and since the land, which these industries occupied, was expensive. Also grain crops, necessary to support this stock, dominated land that was more suitable for cotton. Farmers could sell enough eggs from a small barnyard flock to meet demands of the market and also could keep cows for home consumption of milk and butter. Without an abundant supply of milk, the creamery soon closed its doors.

By and large the only industry introduced by the Taft Ranch or by its personnel that succeeded was the oil mill. One must keep in mind that the Coastal Bend was a cotton country with only the bare minimum of land devoted to products for mule or cow feed. In 1927 the partnership between Charles Phelps Taft, Anna Sinton Taft, and the Joseph French Green estate was incorporated as the Taft Cotton Oil Company.[1] A tremendous market for cottonseed existed in San Patricio and surrounding counties; with prudent management and fairness to the customers the oil mill prospered until it too was disposed of in 1952, the last of the Taft interests in Texas to go.[2] Times change and institutions are altered by them. A consolidation of oil mills over the state into the hands of a few large corporations rendered impractical the continued operation of a small, independent cottonseed-oil refinery; hence the plant was sold while it was still profitable.

In 1928 the Coleman-Fulton Pasture Company transferred its ranch hospital to the Taft Cotton Oil Company, which operated the institution until 1932, when it was leased to the head nurse, Mrs. Alice Wolf. In 1936 Mrs. Wolf purchased the property, maintained the clinic, but closed it permanently in 1939 when such an enterprise was no longer practical. Good roads and high-powered vehicles streamlined communications for Taft community residents to large cities with improved health-care facilities and medical specialists, thus ending the existence of an institution founded on humanitarian principles by a large landowner with a concern for the public welfare.

In addition to the heritage of advanced agricultural techniques left by the Taft Ranch, purchasers of ranch property were further rewarded in 1935 when the Plymouth Oil Company brought in the region's discovery petroleum well.[3] By mid-century oil and gas fields were in abundance on the Coastal Bend, supplementing the already lucrative income from the fertile cotton-producing soil.

In succeeding years the Taft Ranch Syndicate sold most of the property it had purchased in 1928. T. N. Blackwell, the land agent of the Pasture Company in the 1920's, continued in that capacity for the syndicate. In the early 1950's, when he learned that the five Texas financiers wanted to dissolve their partnership, he assessed all the re-

[1] Taft Cotton Oil Company, Charter No. 48864, June 28, 1927, Office of the Texas Secretary of State.

[2] Corpus Christi *Times,* July 31, 1953. Interview with W. Leroy Weber, Taft, November 17, 1961; with C. J. Meyer, Taft, November 26, 1961; with Edward N. Tutt, Taft, November 27, 1961.

[3] Louis B. Engelke, "Our Texas Towns: Taft," San Antonio *Express Magazine,* April 15, 1951, p. 18.

maining holdings, lumped together five groups of property of equal value, and allowed the five to draw, in lottery fashion, for their share.[4] With the disposal of this last vestige the Coleman-Fulton Pasture Company passed into history.

[4] Interview with C. J. Meyer, Taft, November 26, 1961.

APPENDIX: *Extent of the Coleman-Fulton Pasture Company Range in 1894*

IN 1894 the Coleman-Fulton Pasture Company owned 183,805 acres in South Texas. The limits of the range, as recognized by the state of Texas, were drawn along boundaries of bounty land grants patented to individuals and later acquired by the Coleman-Fulton Pasture Company. The names of the recipients are given on subsequent maps issued by the Texas General Land Office; from these maps one may define the exact 1894 range by using the following information that was recorded on January 10, 1894, in the San Patricio County Deed Records, Volume C, pages 179–187.

Commencing at a point on Corpus Christi Bay at the SE corner of Survey No .... for Thomas L. Williamson near the southern end of the fence dividing this tract from the pasture owned by the heirs of John W. Vineyard, thence North to the South West corner of a 160 acre tract in the name of J. W. Page, thence with the forementioned fence to the East line of said survey—thence North with the fence between the lands hereby conveyed and heretofore sold to T. P. McCampbell, to the fence inclosing the Pasture known as the "Rincon" thence with the line of said last mentioned fence, to its junction with the "Puerto Bay"—thence with the meanders of the shore of Puerto & Copano Bays, to the mouth of the Aransas River thence with the said River with its meanders to the mouth of the Chiltipin Creek, thence with the meanders of the said Chiltipin Creek, to the NW corner of 1280 acres in name of Julian Damion, thence south with the West line of said tract to a point due East from the South boundary of a Survey in the name of a tract in the name of Catharine Dougan, thence due west to a SW corner of the said Dougan survey, Thence North with the West boundary of the said survey to the Chiltipin Creek. Thence with the meanders of said creek to the NE corner of 160 acres now owned by John H. Wood around said tract to the Chiltipin Creek, thence with said creek & its boundaries heretofore established between the lands of John Welder deceased, and the late firm of Coleman, Mathis & Fulton to the North boundary line of the

John Pollan, aforesaid, and the George Morris League, to the NW corner thereof, which is the NW corner of the body of land hereby conveyed—Thence South with the Western boundary of the said Morris and the Fitzsimmons league and the west line of the Burgess, Preston & Hornsby tracts, to a point due west from the SW corner of a 660 acre tract in the name of Morehead Wright, thence due East to the West boundary of a third of a league in name of Harrison Williams, thence South with said boundary line to a fence division of the lands of Darius C. Rachal and this Company—thence East with said fence to a west line of what is known as the "Big Pasture" of this Company thence South to the shore of Nueces Bay at the corner of a 640 acre tract in the name of Geo. W. Fulton thence with the meanders of Nueces Bay to the extreme end of the point of land between the said Bay and Corpus Christi Bay, thence with the meanders of the Corpus Christi Bay to the point of beginning, including all the tracts of land lying with said boundaries, Also all that certain tract and parcel of land situated on the peninsula known as Live Oak Point, in Aransas County, Known as the "Little or Shipping Pasture," of the said Coleman-Fulton Pasture Company, to-wit: 1344.8 acres of land of the Joseph Fessenden tract, 275 acres of the Anselmo Bergara tract, & 640 acres patented to H. Hill, assee, of Fitzpatrick and 600 acres off of the west end of Joseph Hollis tract in all aggregating 3666 acres more or less, save & except from within the metes & bounds of the two tracts above, all those lands which have been heretofore sold by the Coleman-Fulton Pasture Company & also 2214 acres undivided out of the George Morris league.

BIBLIOGRAPHY

Primary

Manuscript Materials

Personal Archival Collections

Brown (John Henry) Collection. Archives, University of Texas Library, Austin.

Fulton Collection, 1836–1911 (cited as FC). Archives, University of Texas Library, Austin.

Contains 3,855 documents with a total of 19,919 pages: Of most importance to this study was the correspondence received by George Ware Fulton, Sr.; George Ware Fulton, Jr.; James C. Fulton; Coleman, Mathis, and Fulton; Coleman and Fulton; and the Coleman-Fulton Pasture Company between 1836–1911, a total of 4,250 pages; and fifteen letter-press books of correspondence from the Fultons and the Coleman-Fulton Pasture Company between 1886–1907, a total of 4,544 pages; also helpful were the approximately 10,000-page remainder, which includes a diary, bills, account sheets, receipts, patents, deeds, tax receipts, land papers, field notes, newspaper clippings, pamphlets, booklets, daybooks, a time book, a minute book, a bill book, a stock book, a receipt book, journals, ledgers, invoice books, a trial-balance book, cashbooks, and a voucher file.

Sinton (David) Collection, 1869–1900. Archives, Historical and Philosophical Society of Ohio, Cincinnati.

Taft (Charles Phelps and Anna Sinton) Collection, 1893–1930. Archives, Historical and Philosophical Society of Ohio, Cincinnati.

Contains documents, land-sale books, ledgers, and journals pertaining to the Taft Ranch, altogether comprising approximately fifty volumes on this subject.

Organizational Collections

Cattle Raisers' Association of North Western Texas. Proceedings. First through sixteenth annual meetings, 1877–1892. Copied from the original minutes belonging to Texas and Southwestern Cattle Raisers' Association. Archives, University of Texas Library, Austin.

Coleman-Fulton Pasture Company Records, 1876–1930 (cited as CFPC), Taft.

Contains approximately 2,500 documents with a total of approximately 50,000 pages. The main sources of information for this study are twenty-four letter press books, 1876–1905, with 12,582 pages; minutes of stockholders' meetings and minutes of directors' meetings, 1881–1930, 476 pages altogether; and minutes of departmental heads' meetings, 169 pages. Essential supplementary facts were gained from office blotters, bills-payable books, cashbooks, cattle registers, checkbook stubs, collection registers, daybooks, financial-statement records, farm contracts, journals, ledgers, land-sales books, pasturage books, payroll books, receipt books, shipping registers, maps, bound volumes of certificates of capital stock, surveys and land grants, tax receipts, income-tax reports, and trial-balance books. A hospital register and minutes of hospital committee meetings were helpful in piecing together the story of the ranch's humanitarian role.

Lodge Records, Gregory Lodge No. 998, Ancient Free and Accepted Masons, 1910–1930, Taft.

Government Records

Texas (state) County Records

(References are to Texas counties; materials cited are in the courthouses of the respective counties.)

ARANSAS COUNTY:

Bill of Sale Records, 1872–1930, Vol. A;
Commissioners' Court Minutes, 1872–1930, Vols. 1–7;
County Court Minutes, 1876–1930, Vols. 1–3;
Deed of Trust Records, 1872–1930, Vols. A, G, H, 1–4;
Deed Records, 1871–1930, Vols. B–Z, A2–N2;
District Court Judgments in Civil Cases, 1871–1930, Case Nos. 1–1865;
District Court Minutes, 1866–1930, Vols. 1–4;
Map Records, 1890–1930, Vol. 1;
Record of Animals Slaughtered, 1895–1898, Vol. 1;
Record of Hides Inspected for Butchers, 1889–1894, Vol. 1;
Record of Inspection of Animals by the Inspector of Aransas County, Texas. As sold, or as leaving or going out of this County, for sale or shipment, and of all Animals driven or sold to Packeries or Butcheries, 1885–1893, Vol. 1;
Transcribed Deed of Trust Records, 1867–1871;
Transcribed Deed Records, 1867–1871, Vols. A, B.

SAN PATRICIO COUNTY:

Bill of Sale Records, 1896–1930, Vols. 2–3;

Commissioners' Court Minutes, 1867–1930, Vols. 1–7;

Deed of Trust Records, 1875–1930, Vols. A–Z, 27–32;

Deed Records, 1867–1930, Vols. 3–95;

District Court Judgments in Civil Cases, 1867–1930, Case Nos. 41–3624;

District Court Minutes, 1867–1930, Vols. 2–3, 1–3, 3, A (total of seven volumes);

Map Records, 1891–1930, Vols. 1–3;

Marks and Brands Book, 1854–1930, Vols. "A–B–C," 1;

Stock Sales, 1867–1894, Vols. A, 2;

Surveyor's Records, 1858–1930, Vols. 1, 2.

Texas (republic)

General Land Office. Field Notes, Refugio County Bounty, File 17. Survey Made October 21, 1839, by John R. Tally, Deputy Surveyor, Refugio County; 1280 acres, two surveys, 640 acres each, for George Ware Fulton's Republic of Texas Land Certificate No. 666. General Land Office, Austin.

———. Land Certificate No. 666, issued to George Ware Fulton, Houston, Texas, December 2, 1837; signed by Barnard E. Bee, Secretary of War; approved September 15, 1845, signed by Ben F. Hill, acting Secretary of War and Marine. General Land Office, Austin.

Treasury Department. Fulton, George Ware, File. Audited Military Claims. Texas State Archives, Austin.

United States

Department of Agriculture. Office of Forage Crops Investigations. Letters Received: Correspondence of W. J. Morse and Charles H. Alvord; Record Group 54. National Archives, Washington, D.C.

Department of Commerce. Bureau of the Census. Manuscript Census Returns. *Tenth Census*, 1880, Aransas County, Texas; *Tenth Census*, 1880, San Patricio County, Texas. Microfilm copies at the E. C. Barker Texas History Center, University of Texas Library, Austin, Texas; and at the Texas State Archives, Austin, Texas.

Department of Commerce and Labor. Bureau of Corporations. Report No. 172: T. A. Carroll to Commissioner of Corporations; File 666, Part 8. National Archives, Washington D.C.

Office of the Adjutant General. Mexican War Army of Occupation. Letters Received: Correspondence of Captain William Wallace S. Bliss, Lieutenant Colonel T. F. Hunt, and Brevet Brigadier General Zachary Taylor; Record Group 94. National Archives, Washington, D.C.

Post Office Department Records. Map of parts of San Patricio and Refugio (later Aransas) Counties, February, 1872, Record Group 28. National Archives, Washington, D.C.

Taft, William Howard, Papers. Presidential Series, Letter Books, 1909–1913, Manuscript Division, Library of Congress.

Articles and Booklets

Albin, Mrs. John William. "A Brief Outline of Schools in Taft, 1904–1930," compiled by Mrs. John William Albin, Taft, and in her possession.

———. "History of the First Presbyterian Church US, Taft, Texas, Presbytery of Western Texas," compiled by Mrs. John William Albin, Taft, and in her possession.

Moore, Lamar. "Texas Cattle Brands with Historical Sketches," unpublished typescript. Copied from original by Archives Division, University of Texas Library; loaned by Lamar Moore, Winslow, Arizona, March, 1943.

Watson, Mrs. May Mathis Green. "Josiah Mathis and His Descendants: A Genealogical Record of the Mathis Family in the United States," mimeographed booklet compiled by Mrs. May Mathis Green Watson, Corpus Christi, and in her possession.

Letters and Diaries

Bart, Joseph L., Jr., Public Relations Manager, Southern Pacific Company, Houston, Texas, to author, February 6, 1962.

Coleman, Thomas Atlee, San Antonio, Texas, to Anna Margaretta Coleman, Rockport, Texas [?], undated, in possession of Mrs. Maurice W. Cochran, Fulton, Texas.

Green, Joseph French, Chicago, Illinois, to Miss Jennie Hunt, Gregory, Texas, January 6, 1926, in possession of Mrs. Fay Green Hunt, Gregory, Texas.

Green, Mrs. May Mathis, unpublished diaries, 1910–1928, in possession of Mrs. May Mathis Green Watson, Corpus Christi, Texas.

Haisley, Mrs. Waldo E., Sinton, Texas, to Mrs. Luella Mendenhall, Marshalltown, Iowa, September 17, 1909; August 27, 1911; August, 1913; in possession of Mrs. Lyra Haisley Sparks, Taft, Texas.

Miller, Effie, Kelowna, British Columbia, to author, February 23, 1962.

Paul, George H., Omaha, Nebraska, to author, October 6, 16, 31, November 11, 1961.

———, to Mrs. Lyra Haisley Sparks, Taft, Texas, August 9, 12, October 8, 18, 21, 26, 27, 1961; January 3, 31, 1962; in possession of Mrs. Lyra Haisley Sparks, Taft, Texas.

Sparks, Mrs. Lyra Haisley, Taft, Texas, to author, a continuing correspondence since 1961 on the Taft Ranch and on South Texas history.

Taft, Robert Alphonso, Cincinnati, Ohio, to Mrs. Joseph F. Green, Gregory, Texas, January 13, 1927, in possession of Mrs. May Mathis Green Watson, Corpus Christi, Texas.

Traylor, Harry, Rockport, Texas, to W. R. Woolrich, Austin, Texas, August 8, 1945, in possession of W. R. Woolrich, Austin, Texas.

Woolrich, W. R., Austin, Texas, to Mrs. Ann Armstrong, New Orleans, Louisiana, September 12, 1945, in possession of W. R. Woolrich, Austin, Texas.

United States Government Records (published)

House Documents

55th Congress, Third Session. Serial No. 3746, Doc. No. 2, Part 1, p. 289.

———. Serial No. 3747, Doc. No. 2, Part 2, pp. 1527–1570.

56th Congress, Second Session. Serial No. 4089, Doc. No. 2, Part 1, pp. 392–393.

———. Serial No. 4092, Doc. No. 2, Part 4, pp. 2336–2340.

57th Congress, Second Session. Serial No. 4532, Doc. No. 439, Vol. I, pp. 40–42.

58th Congress, Third Session. Serial No. 4833, Doc. No. 382, pp. 1–315.

67th Congress, Second Session. Serial No. 8006, Doc. No. 321, Vol. 18, pp. 1–76.

78th Congress, Second Session. Serial No. 10881, Doc. No. 544, Vol. II, pp. 1–35.

House Executive Documents

42nd Congress, Second Session. Serial No. 1504, Doc. No. 1, Part 2, Vol. II, pp. 526–531.

46th Congress, Second Session. Serial No. 1904, Doc. No. 1, Part 2, Vol. II, Part 1, pp. 928–937.

46th Congress, Third Session. Serial No. 1953, Doc. No. 1, Part 2, Vol. II, Part 1, p. 149.

———. Serial No. 1954, Doc. No. 1, Part 2, Vol. II, Part 2, pp. 1245–1256.

47th Congress, First Session. Serial No. 2011, Doc. No. 1, Part 2, Vol. II, Part 1, pp. 202–203.

———. Serial No. 2012, Doc. No. 1, Part 2, Vol. II, Part 2, pp. 1358–1365.

47th Congress, Second Session. Serial No. 2092, Doc. No. 1, Part 2, Vol. II, Part 1, pp. 199–200.

———. Serial No. 2093, Doc. No. 1, Part 2, Vol. II, Part 2, pp. 1469–1475.

48th Congress, First Session. Serial No. 2183, Doc. No. 1, Part 2, Vol. II, Part 1, pp. 204–205.

———. Serial No. 2184, Doc. No. 1, Part 2, Vol. II, Part 2, pp. 1091–1904.

48th Congress, Second Session. Serial No. 2278, Doc. No. 1, Part 2, Vol. II, Part 1, pp. 219–220.

———. Serial No. 2279, Doc. No. 1, Part 2, Vol. II, Part 2, pp. 1312–1316.

———. Serial No. 2304, Doc. No. 267. SEE United States Government Publications, Nimmo, Joseph, Jr.

49th Congress, First Session. Serial No. 2370, Doc. No. 1, Part 2, Vol. II, Part 1, pp. 229–230.

———. Serial No. 2371, Doc. No. 1, Part 2, Vol. II, Part 2, pp. 1464–1467.

49th Congress, Second Session. Serial No. 2462, Doc. No. 1, Part 2, Vol. II, Part 1, p. 226.

———. Serial No. 2463, Doc. No. 1, Part 2, Vol. II, Part 2, pp. 1330–1334.

50th Congress, First Session. Serial No. 2534, Doc. No. 1, Part 2, Vol. II, Part 1, pp. 191–192.

———. Serial No. 2535, Doc. No. 1, Part 2, Vol. II, Part 2, pp. 1431–1433.

50th Congress, Second Session. Serial No. 2629, Doc. No. 1, Part 2, Vol. II, Part 1, pp. 175–176.

———. Serial No. 2630, Doc. No. 1, Part 2, Vol. II, Part 2, pp. 1307–1320.

51st Congress, First Session. Serial No. 2716, Doc. No. 1, Part 2, Vol. II, Part 1, pp. 205–206.

———. Serial No. 2718, Doc. No. 1, Part 2, Vol. II, Part 3, pp. 1564–1568.

51st Congress, Second Session. Serial No. 2832, Doc. No. 1, Part 2, Vol. II, Part 1, p. 185.

———. Serial No. 2833, Doc. No. 1, Part 2, Vol. II, Part 2, pp. 1810–1812.

52nd Congress, First Session, Serial No. 2922, Doc. No. 1, Part 2, Vol. II, Part 1, p. 235.

———. Serial No. 2924, Doc. No. 1, Part 2, Vol. II, Part 3, pp. 1942–1943.

House Journal

45th Congress, Second Session. Serial No. 1792. H. R. 4743, H. R. 4744, p. 1020.

House Miscellaneous Documents. SEE United States Government Publications, Department of Interior.

Senate Documents

64th Congress, First Session. Serial No. 6938, Vol. 28, Doc. No. 415, Vol. X, pp. 9214–9228.

Senate Executive Documents

52nd Congress, First Session. Serial No. 2900, Doc. No. 45, Vol. 5, pp. 1–59.

Senate Miscellaneous Documents

45th Congress, Third Session. Serial No. 1833, Doc. No. 69, Vol. 1, p. 1.

47th Congress, First Session. Serial No. 2002, Doc. No. 124, Vol. 10, Part 6, Sect. V, Vol. II, p. 498.

United States Statutes at Large

51st Congress, First Session, XXVI, Chap. 201, 105–106.

United States Government Publications

Cole, T. W., and William M. MacKellar. "Cattle Tick Fever," *Animal Diseases* (*Yearbook of Agriculture*, 1956). Washington, D.C.: Government Printing Office, 1956.

Bureau of Census. *Census for 1910: Supplement for Texas; Population, Agriculture, Manufactures, Mines and Quarries.* Washington, D.C.: Government Printing Office, 1911.

Department of Agriculture. Animal Disease Eradication Division. Agricultural Research Service, *The Fight Against Cattle Fever Tick, PA–475.* Washington, D.C.: Government Printing Office, 1961.

Department of Agriculture. "Tick Fever," Farmers' Bulletin No. 1625. Washington, D.C.: Government Printing Office, 1930 (revised 1949).

Department of Agriculture. Bureau of Agricultural Economics. *Statistics on Cotton and Related Data.* Statistical Bulletin No. 99. Washington, D.C.: n.p., June, 1951.

Department of Interior. Bureau of the Census. *Report on the Productions of Agriculture as Returned at the Tenth Census, 1880.* Volume III. Washington, D.C.: Government Printing Office, 1883. (*House Miscellaneous Documents.* 47th Congress, Second Session. Serial No. 2131, Vol. 13, Part 3, Doc. No. 42, Part 3, Vol. 3: *Agriculture.*)

Nimmo, Joseph, Jr. (Bureau of Statistics, Treasury Department). "A report from the Chief of the Bureau of Statistics, in response to a resolution of the House calling for information in regard to the range and ranch cattle traffic in the Western States and Territories," February 28, 1885, *House Executive Documents*, 48th Congress, Second Session, Serial No. 2304, Doc. No. 267, Vol. 29, pp. 1–200.

Newspapers

(All newspapers listed are in Texas unless otherwise indicated.)

Advertiser (Corpus Christi). August 21, 1869.

Advocate (Victoria). September 28, 1924 (Eighty-eighth Anniversary Edition).

Caller (Corpus Christi). December 23, 1883; March 15, June [?], December 6, 1885; February 7, 1886; November 10, 1893; December 8, 1905; March 16, October 26, 1906; January 14, 17, 31, March 6, 27, May 1, June 12, 19, July 17, 24, August 28, September 4, November 6, 1908; January 20, February 24, 1911; July 6, 1919; September 11, 1926; February 16, 1936; May 9–29, 1937; January 27, 1938; October 22, 1939; January 18, 1959.

Caller-Times (Corpus Christi). September 29, 1940; November 30, 1947; March 11, 1950; May 6, 9, September 26, 1954; March 11, 1955; January 15, 1956; January 18, 1959; August 6, 1961.

Caller-Times Library (Corpus Christi). Files of clippings on Taft Ranch and neighboring towns.

Chronicle (Houston). April 3, 1955.

Daily Herald (San Antonio). July 4, November 9, 1866; June 14, 28, 1867.

Daily News (Galveston). December 12, 1873.

Express (San Antonio). December 6, 1953.

Flake's Bulletin (Galveston). July 6, 1869; September 28, December 10, 1870.

Herald (Aransas Harbor). Partial file for 1891 and 1892.

Morning News (Dallas). March 21, 1915.

News (Fairmount, Indiana). February 5, 1909.

Picayune (New Orleans, Louisiana). July 13, 1869.

Pilot (Rockport). July 13, 1923; August 31, 1939 (Seventieth Anniversary Edition); August 14, 1958; March 26, 1959.

Progress (Aransas Pass). April 9, 1909, to 1921.

San Patricio County News (Sinton). February 4, 1909, to 1963.

San Patricio County Press (Gregory and Taft). May 29, 1913; February 6, 1914.

The Standard (Clarksville). March 25, 1881.
Times (Corpus Christi). September 13, 1956; December 17, 1958.
Tribune (Taft). May 5, 1921, to 1963.
Tri-Weekly State Gazette (Austin). November 14, 1870.

Almanacs

Burke's Texas Almanac and Immigrant's Handbook With Which Is Incorporated Hanford's Texas State Register Containing an Almanac for Texas; Farm and Garden Hints; Descriptions of Various Counties; Lists of Postoffices; Court Calendars; Lists of Newspapers; Information for Immigrants on all points; and much other matter relative to Texas. Houston: James Burke, Jr., Publisher, 1875–1885.

Texas Almanac and State Industrial Guide (1857–1962). Galveston and Dallas: A. H. Belo and Company, 1856–1961. No numbers were issued for 1874–1903, 1905–1909, 1913[?], 1915–1924. Subtitle varies: 1857–1868, *The Texas Almanac . . . with federal and state statistics; historical, descriptive, and biographical sketches, etc., relating to Texas;* 1869–1873, *The Texas Almanac . . . and Emigrant's Guide to Texas*; 1904–1962, *The Texas Almanac and State Industrial Guide*. 1857–1873 were published by Richardson and Company, Galveston, Texas.

Interviews

(All towns cited are in Texas unless otherwise stated.)

Mr. and Mrs. John William Albin, Taft, November 26, 1961.
Mr. and Mrs. Claud Boykin, Taft, frequent conversations on the Taft Ranch during the summer and autumn of 1961.
Mr. Conn Brown, Aransas Pass, November 4, 1961.
Mrs. Maurice W. Cochran, Fulton, July 28, 1961.
Mrs. Elinor Fulton Conger, Corpus Christi, March 2, 1961.
Mr. Alvin Crow, Taft, November 3, 1961.
Mr. E. I. Crow, Taft, November 2, 3, 1961.
Mr. Ben H. Cummins, Taft, March 4, 1961.
Mr. Jack E. Dodson, Sinton, August 8, 1961.
Mr. and Mrs. Dalton Green, Taft, November 22, 1961.
Mr. Ernest Guedin, Taft, November 17, 1961.
Mrs. May Fulton Hoopes, Ingleside, March 2, 1961.
Mrs. Fay Green Hunt, Gregory, August 7, 1961.
Sheriff S. Frank Hunt, Sinton, August 8, 1961.
Mr. and Mrs. Ben Ivey, Taft, October 31, 1961.

Mr. and Mrs. D. Lard, Taft, October 28, 1961.

Mr. C. J. Meyer, Taft, frequent conversations during the summer and autumn of 1961.

Mr. and Mrs. Henry R. Moore, Taft, November 24, 1961.

Mr. and Mrs. J. D. Moore, Sinton, November 18, 1961.

Mr. George H. Paul, Omaha, Nebraska, May 3, 1963.

Mr. Walter Roberts, Taft, November 22, 1961.

Judge James Colon Russell, Sinton, August 8, 1961.

Mr. and Mrs. E. W. Sandars, Taft, August 9, November 5, 1961.

Mr. Henry Schmidt, Rockport, July 27, 1961.

Mr. and Mrs. Walter C. Sparks, Jr., Taft, frequent conversations during the summer and autumn of 1961.

Mr. Edward N. Tutt, Taft, frequent conversations during the summer and autumn of 1961.

Mrs. May Mathis Green Watson, Corpus Christi, March 2, 1961.

Mr. and Mrs. John Weber, Fulton, March 1, 1961.

Mr. and Mrs. W. Leroy Weber, Taft, November 16, 17, 1961.

Mrs. Alice Wolf, Taft, November 3, 1961.

Mr. Emmett Yglesias, Taft, July 28, 1961.

Booklets and Brochures

Blackwell, T. N. (comp.). *Taft Ranch, San Patricio County, Texas: The Land of perpetual Sunshine, Sea Breezes, Fat Cattle, Hogs, Dairy Cows, Cotton, Feed, Prosperity and Happiness.* San Antonio: Alamo Printing Company [1923]; published for the Coleman-Fulton Pasture Company.

[Fulton, George Ware], *Organization, Charter and By-Laws of the Coleman-Fulton Pasture Company, Rockport, Texas.* Cincinnati: Wrightson and Company, Printers, 1881. Copies may be found in the Coleman-Fulton Pasture Company Records, Taft, Texas, and in the Fulton Collection, Archives, University of Texas Library.

Green, Joseph F. *Farm Experience on Taft Ranch.* A speech given before the Convention of the Bankers of the Second District, Texas Bankers Association, Corpus Christi, Texas, February 15, 1913. Houston: Cumming & Son, Art Printers, 1913 (published in booklet form for the Union National Bank, Houston, Texas).

Homes in Texas! 160,000 Acres of the Best Land in Texas Are Now Ready for Occupancy, brochure issued by the Coleman-Fulton Pasture Company, date unknown [ca. 1891]. Copy may be found in the Coleman-Fulton Pasture Company Records, Taft, Texas.

Taft Farms, San Patricio County, Texas . . . Where Permanent Prosperity

Rewards Honest Effort, brochure issued by the J. H. Kirkpatrick Company, 1921.

Rockport, Fulton, Laredo, and Mexican Pacific Railroad, Charter of, November 11, 1871, brochure originally in the Fulton Collection, Archives, University of Texas Library, but presently located in the Eugene C. Barker Texas History Center, University of Texas Library.

Wentz, C. C., and F. Z. Bishop (comps.). *Bishop, Texas*, and *Surrounding Country*. Bishop, Texas: Bishop Printing Company, 1911[?].

Broadsides

Sales Day Program, Taft, Texas, June 1, 1921. Broadside in possession of Mr. and Mrs. Manton Williams, Sinton, Texas.

Menu [1916?], Taft Hotel, Taft, Texas. Broadside in possession of Mrs. May Mathis Green Watson, Corpus Christi, Texas.

Scrapbook Materials

Hunt, Mrs. Fay Green. Newspaper clippings in her possession, Gregory, Texas.

Sparks, Mrs. Lyra Haisley. Newspaper clippings in her possession, Taft, Texas.

Watson, Mrs. May Mathis Green. Scrapbooks of newspaper clippings on the Taft Ranch, Corpus Christi, and the Coastal Bend in general; also a large number of photographs relating to the same subjects. In her possession, Corpus Christi, Texas.

Woolrich, W. R. Unlabeled, undated newspaper clippings in his possession, Austin, Texas.

SECONDARY

Books

Acheson, Sam. *35,000 Days in Texas: A History of the Dallas News and Its Forbears*. New York: Macmillan Company, 1938.

Allhands, James Lewellyn. *Gringo Builders*. N.p.: Privately printed, 1931.

———. *Uriah Lott*. San Antonio: Naylor Company, 1949.

Brown, John Henry. *Life and Times of Henry Smith, the first American Governor of Texas*. Dallas: A. D. Aldridge and Company, 1887 (reprinted by the Steck Company, Austin, 1935).

Burrell, Howard A. "George H. Paul," *History of Washington County, Iowa: Also Biographical Sketches of Some Prominent Citizens of the County*. Volume II. Chicago: S. J. Clarke Publishing Company, 1909.

Butt, Archibald Willingham. *Taft and Roosevelt: The Intimate Letters of Archie Butt, Military Aide.* Two vols. New York: Doubleday, Doran and Company, Incorporated, 1930.

"Charles Phelps Taft," *Who Was Who in America.* First Edition. Chicago: A. N. Marquis Company, 1942.

Clark, Joseph L., and Elton M. Scott. *The Texas Gulf Coast: Its History and Development.* Four vols. New York: Lewis Historical Publishing Company, Incorporated, 1955.

Cox, James. *Historical and Biographical Record of the Cattle Industry and the Cattlemen of Texas and Adjacent Territory.* Saint Louis: Woodward and Tiernan Printing Company, 1895.

Dale, Edward Everett. *The Range Cattle Industry: Ranching on the Great Plains from 1865 to 1925.* Norman: University of Oklahoma Press, 1930 (New Edition, 1960).

Daniell, Lewis E. *Personnel of the Texas State Government with Sketches of Representative Men of Texas.* San Antonio: Maverick Printing House, 1892.

Dobie, J. Frank. *A Vaquero of the Brush Country.* Dallas: Southwest Press, 1929.

Dunn, John Beamond. *Perilous Trails of Texas.* Dallas: Southwest Press, 1932.

Eaves, Charles Dudley, and C. A. Hutchinson. *Post City, Texas: C. W. Post's Colonizing Activities in West Texas.* Austin: Texas State Historical Association, 1952.

Fite, Gilbert C., and Jim E. Reese. *An Economic History of the United States.* Cambridge: Houghton Mifflin Company, The Riverside Press, 1959.

Gilbert, J. C. *A History of Investment Trusts in Dundee, 1873–1938.* London: P. S. King & Son, Limited, 1939.

Hafen, LeRoy R., and Carl Coke Rister. *Western America: The Exploration, Settlement, and Development of the Region beyond the Mississippi.* Englewood Cliffs, New Jersey: Prentice-Hall, 1941 (Second Edition, 1950).

Haley, J. Evetts. *The XIT Ranch of Texas and the Early Days of the Llano Estacado.* Norman: University of Oklahoma Press, 1953.

Huson, Hobart. *Refugio, A Comprehensive History of Refugio County from Aboriginal Time to 1955.* Two vols. Woodsboro: The Rooke Foundation, Incorporated, 1955.

Johnson, Elmer H. *The Natural Regions of Texas.* University of Texas

Bulletin No. 3113; Bureau of Business Research, Research Monograph No. 8. Austin: University of Texas, 1931.

Johnson, Frank W. *A History of Texas and Texans.* Edited by Eugene C. Barker and Ernest William Winkler. Two vols. Chicago and New York: The American Historical Society, 1914.

Lea, Tom. *The King Ranch.* Two vols. Boston: Little, Brown and Company, 1957.

McCampbell, Coleman. *Texas Seaport: The Story of the Growth of Corpus Christi and the Coastal Bend Area.* New York: Exposition Press, 1952.

McCoy, Joseph G. *Historic Sketches of the Cattle Trade of the West and Southwest.* Reprint, Washington, D.C.: The Rare Book Shop, 1932 (First edition, 1874).

Miller, Mrs. S. G. *Sixty Years in the Nueces Valley, 1870 to 1930.* San Antonio: Naylor Printing Company, 1930.

Oberste, William H. *Texas Irish Empresarios and Their Colonies: Power and Hewetson. McMullen and McGloin; Refugio—San Patricio.* Austin: Von Boeckmann-Jones Company, 1953.

Osgood, Ernest Staples. *The Day of the Cattleman.* Chicago: University of Chicago Press, 1929.

Paxson, Frederic Logan. *History of the American Frontier, 1763–1893.* Cambridge: Houghton Mifflin Company, Riverside Press, 1924.

Potts, Charles S. *Railroad Transportation in Texas.* University of Texas Bulletin No. 119; Humanities Series, No. 7. Austin: University of Texas, 1909.

Pringle, Henry F. *The Life and Times of William Howard Taft: A Biography.* Two vols. New York: Farrar and Rinehart, Incorporated, 1939.

Reed, Saint Clair Griffin. *A History of the Texas Railroads and of Transportation Conditions under Spain and Mexico and the Republic and the State.* Houston: The Saint Clair Publishing Company, 1941.

Riegel, Robert E. *America Moves West.* Third Edition. New York: Holt, Rinehart, and Winston, 1956.

Sampson, Arthur W. *Livestock Husbandry on Range and Pasture.* New York: John Wiley and Sons, Incorporated, 1928.

Sterling, William Warren. *Trails and Trials of a Texas Ranger.* n.p.: n.p., 1959.

Stoddard, Henry L. *As I Knew Them: Presidents and Politics from Grant to Coolidge.* New York: Harper and Brothers, 1927.

Towne, Charles Wayland, and Edward Norris Wentworth. *Cattle and Men.* Norman: University of Oklahoma Press, 1955.

Webb, Walter Prescott. *The Great Plains.* Boston: Ginn and Company, 1931.

———. *The Texas Rangers, A Century of Frontier Defense.* Boston: Houghton Mifflin Company, The Riverside Press, 1935.

Wilson, Neill C., and Frank J. Taylor. *Southern Pacific: The Roaring Story of a Fighting Railroad.* New York: McGraw-Hill Book Company, Incorporated, 1952.

Winter, Nevin O. *Texas the Marvellous: The State of Six Flags. Including accounts . . . of this marvellous state.* Boston: The Page Company, 1916.

Booklets

Simmon, John T., Jr. "A Search of the Records of the General Land Office," *Report of the Fifth Texas Surveyors Short Course,* February, 1952. [Austin]: Texas Surveyors Association, 1952.

Watson, May M. Green, and Alex Lillico. *Taft Ranch: A history of the Fifty Years of Development sponsored by Coleman-Fulton Pasture Company with sketches of Gregory and Taft, the two towns it created.* [Taft: Taft *Tribune*, 1936; reprinted 1962].

Periodicals

Anonymous. "Developer of Bishop Opened 80,000 Acres," Corpus Christi *Caller-Times*, January 18, 1959.

Baldwin, H. B., "The Development of Agriculture in San Patricio and Nueces counties," Taft *Tribune*, May 15, 1924.

Burrell, Howard A. "George H. Paul," *History of Washington County, Iowa.* SEE Books, Secondary.

"Charles Phelps Taft," *Who Was Who in America.* SEE Books, Secondary.

Clark, Wallace R. "Portland's Bay View College Destroyed by 1916 Hurricane," Taft *Tribune*, October 18, 1956.

Cole, T. W., and William M. MacKellar. "Cattle Tick Fever." SEE United States Government Publications, Primary.

Currie, Barton W. "100,000 Acres of Business Farming; the Taft Ranch Has Revolutionized the Cattle Industry," *Country Gentleman*, LXXX, No. 24 (June 12, 1915), 1010–1011.

Engelke, Louis B. "Our Texas Towns: Taft," San Antonio *Express* Magazine, April 15, 1951, pp. 18–19.

Fulton, George Ware. "Big Pastures, but a Necessary Step in the Progress from the Evils of Free Grass to Agricultural Prosperity," *The Texas Stockman*, July 6, 1886.

[Gibson, Mrs. Gladys]. "Authentic History of Fulton Mansion Told by Descendant," Rockport *Pilot*, March 26, 1959.

Harwood, Sue. "Ropes' Premature Dream: To Create Texas' First Deep Port," Corpus Christi *Caller-Times*, January 18, 1959 (Seventy-fifth Anniversary Edition).

Haupt, Lewis M. "Harbor Bar Improvements," *Journal of the Franklin Institute*, CXXVIII, No. 1 (July, 1889), pp. 23–33. Reprint in Fulton Collection, Archives, University of Texas Library.

Herring, Mrs. Clark, and Miss Grace Smith. "Hide and Tallow Played Import Role in Early Days," Rockport *Pilot*, August 31, 1939 (Seventieth Anniversary Edition).

Hornaday, W. D. "Where the President Will Rest," *Technical World*, October, 1909.

"Joseph French Green," *Journal of the Texas Historical and Biographical Record*, October, 1940.

La Roche, Clarence. "Mansion by the Sea," San Antonio *Express* Magazine, February 24, 1952.

Love, Clara M. "History of the Cattle Industry in the Southwest," *Southwestern Historical Quarterly*, XIX, No. 4 (April, 1916), 370–399; XX, No. 1 (July, 1916), 1–18.

McCampbell, Coleman. "Green Sea Turtles," Corpus Christi *Caller-Times*, January 18, 1959.

Moses, Tad. "Early Day Cattlemen," *The Cattleman*, XXXIV, No. 6 (November, 1947), 25 ff.; XXXIV, No. 7 (December, 1947), 27 ff.; XXXIV, No. 8 (January, 1948), 39 ff.; XXXIV, No. 9 (February, 1948), 23 ff. The reprint of this article, entitled "Some Texas Cattlemen and Their Operations," may be found in the University of Texas Library.

Nalley, Donna. "Mrs. [Adele] Fisher Recalls Portland's Early Days," Corpus Christi *Caller-Times*, August 6, 1961.

Payne, O. C. "Corporation Farming in Texas," *Farm and Ranch*, Vol. 33, No. 22 (May 30, 1914), pp. 2 ff.

Price, Theodore H. "A 100,000-Acre Business," *World's Work*, XXV, No. 3 (January, 1913), 271–275.

Schreiner, George A. "The Taft Ranch," *The Texas Magazine*, I, No. 2 (December, 1909), 35–38.

Stratton, George Frederic. "Mr. Taft's Tenants: How They Earn Farms on His Big Texas Ranch," *Country Gentleman*, LXXXIV, No. 9 (March 1, 1919), 5 ff.

"The Tafts of Cincinnati," *Life*, May 26, 1952.

Texas Land News (Rockport and San Antonio), April, 1892.

Texas Stockman and Farmer (San Antonio), XXVIII, No. 28 (June 30, 1909).

Ward, Hortense Warner. "Hide and Tallow Factories," *The Cattleman,* XXXIV, No. 9 (February, 1948), 21 ff.

Woolrich, W. R. "Mechanical Refrigeration—Its American Birthright," *Refrigerating Engineering*, Vol. 53, No. 3 (March, 1947), pp. 196 ff.; and Vol. 53, No. 4 (April, 1947), pp. 304 ff.

Theses (unpublished)

Cummins, Agnes Brown. "The Physical and Cultural Geography of Parts of San Patricio and Aransas Counties, Texas." M.A. thesis, University of Texas, 1953.

Ford, Elton D. "The Development and Economic Contributions of the Taft Ranch in Southwest Texas." M.A. thesis, Texas College of Arts and Industries, 1951.

Nims, Dorothy Louise. "A History of the Village of Rockport." M.A. thesis, Southwest Texas State Teachers College, 1939.

North, Gene. "A Historical Survey of the Taft Ranch." M.A. thesis, University of Houston, 1956.

Pearce, William Martin. "A History of the Matador Land and Cattle Company, Limited, from 1882 to 1915." Ph.D. thesis, University of Texas, 1952.

Riley, Mary C. "The History of the Development of the Port of Corpus Christi." M.A. thesis, University of Texas, 1951.

Warburton, Sister Margaret Rose, "A History of the O'Connor Ranch, 1834–1939," M.A. thesis, Catholic University of America, 1939.

INDEX